MarketMD™ Your Manufacturing Business

MarketMD™ Your Manufacturing Business

Chip Burnham
Brian Kent

Cover design by Samantha Salvaggio and Jessica C. Harding
Internal graphic design by Tristen Click and Jessica C. Harding

ISBN-13: 978-0692985359 (Fairmont Concepts)
ISBN-10: 0692985352

ACKNOWLEDGMENTS

Jessica C. Harding
Tom Condardo
Tristen Click
Samantha Salvaggio
Elisa G. Roberts
Brad Kent

Table of Contents

Introduction

Over the past decade, the explosion of digital technology has dramatically changed our expectations in the way products and services are marketed and sold. The rate of change shows no signs of slowing down, so businesses must adapt.

Thanks to the power of the internet, mobile devices, and social media, over two thirds of a buyer's research is conducted online before they ever contact you. To respond to this rapid technological growth, many marketing and sales leaders focus on pursuing the latest shiny object – the newest CRM, Marketing Automation software, chat bot, or mobile app. They write endless blog posts and get active on social media.

The result? Marketing and sales leaders are getting lost trying to keep up. Their yearly goals are stuffed full of technology implementations. IT departments have grown to twice the size of the marketing department in many mid-sized manufacturing businesses I visit.

Technology is important, but it can't take the place of sound business principles, the "blocking and tackling." If the marketing and sales team fails to identify their best target end markets, uncover and prioritize customer needs, or create compelling messaging, all the technology in the world isn't going to help them.

Before you can effectively leverage any technology, you need a solid foundation on which to build your *commercial engine* - the company's system for obtaining leads, selling, and serving the customer. The MarketMD™ business health checkup and solutions are designed to help you build or improve that critical base.

The MarketMD business health checkup is a self-service tool that takes a step back and identifies the strengths and weaknesses of your commercial engine. After all, no one knows your business like you do. The checkup highlights the areas of your commercial engine that will provide the best ROI from your efforts (www.fairmontconcepts.com/businss-health-checkup).

After you've identified the weaknesses bogging down your commercial engine, move to the corrective action part of the MarketMD system. This section provides a playbook of proven solutions you can implement and doesn't require massive investment in expensive new technology.

The solutions described in this book are proven techniques that are simple to execute. These *"How To"* recommendations can be carried out by marketing and sales staff in a near to medium-term timeframe. Although the concepts in this book can be adapted for any company, it is specifically addressed to manufacturing companies that sell high dollar items of over $10,000 each, and generate $20MM to $200MM in revenue per year.

The bottom line? The MarketMD System identifies and provides simple, executable solutions designed to improve the weakest areas of your commercial engine - identified by you - and gets you moving toward peak performance right away.

This book is all about self-diagnosing your marketing and sales commercial engine, obtaining cross-department agreement on the issues, and then fixing them. Brian Kent and I founded Fairmont Concepts to employ the MarketMD system and ensure you work on the specific issues that will deliver the highest return on investment – and do so with full buy-in from leaders, peers, and staff.

MarketMD is a unique system that addresses 10 key topics selected with three criteria in mind:

1. **Vital**: Each has proven to be critical to the performance of a marketing and sales commercial engine.
2. **Executable**: Each can be changed and improved as a direct result of the actions of the marketing and sales organization.
3. **Immediate:** Each can be addressed in near to medium-term.

Note: The business health checkup system's 10 key topics for business success:
➢ *Finding your best end markets*
➢ *Uncovering the voice of the customer*
➢ *Creating great messaging*
➢ *Generating more leads*
➢ *Nurturing your existing leads*
➢ *Building a great sales team*
➢ *Creating customer loyalty*
➢ *Rightsizing the marketing budget*
➢ *Making your current offerings more attractive*
➢ *Hitting your profit goals*

MarketMD checkup results reveal your strengths and weaknesses in 10 topics, enabling you to create a plan for addressing key issues.

The power of the business health checkup system:

- *Delivers an ROI driven versus a reactive approach*
  Too often manufacturing companies address issues that gain attention from recent incidents. "Fix this problem right away," is heard from the president's office. When you and your team take a step back and assess your entire commercial engine before jumping into solutions, you give your company the chance to work on the problems that will deliver the best ROI, rather than work on problems that became the most visible to senior management.
- *Provides accurate self-assessments*
  Analyzing your commercial engine through self-diagnosis is more accurate than outside consultant assessments. No one knows your business like you do.
- *Leverages multiple sources of input*
  Including a cross section of peers and leaders in the business health assessment provides wisdom through many perspectives. All of us are smarter than one of us.
- *Energizes the company through alignment*
  Including a cross section of peers and leaders builds alignment and focuses organizational energy.

The second part of the MarketMD system provides solutions and tools to strengthen your performance on the 10 key topics. The solutions are designed to let you handle issues internally with your own staff. If you don't have sufficient time or staff, it will provide enough insight into the solution that you can confidently bring in outside resources to help you execute.

The power of the 10 solutions:

- *Builds on proven best practices in a step by step approach*
  Breaks down complex problems into easy to execute solution steps. Fundamentally sound best practices and tools are at the heart of each solution.
- *Elevates your team*
  Trains your team on problem solving techniques and tools they can use repeatedly to address future issues.
- *Executable in the near to midterm*
  Delivers results quickly. When your commercial engine falters there is not time to waste – careers and jobs are on the line.
- *Drives results*
  Drives your commercial engine toward peak performance to deliver a robust sales pipeline, high revenue, and loyal customers.

MarketMD solutions are developed from decades of marketing high - dollars, B2B products in small to mid-sized companies. My approach is especially applicable to manufacturing companies with annual revenue from $20 million to $200 million and where products sell for $10,000 to over $1 million each. These solutions are not designed for commodity sales to consumers, though many of the principles apply.

Part One

The MarketMD Approach

An indication of a healthy marketing and sales commercial engine is a full sales pipeline containing quality leads, swift movement of projects through the funnel, closing business that consistently meets revenue and profit targets, and having an exceptionally loyal customer base. The MarketMD system focuses on ways to reach these goals. The self-diagnosis spans many aspects of the commercial engine: marketing, sales management, and business management.

Marketing

1. Finding Your Best End Markets

Many manufacturing companies target end markets based entirely on those that bring in the most sales dollars, even though top revenue does not always equal most valuable. I'll show you how to conduct objective market evaluations and identify the end markets that deliver the most bottom-line profit. Focusing on the right end market is key to peak performance.

2. Uncovering the Voice of the Customer

Every company has some idea of their customer needs, but I'll show you a proven, effective method for uncovering primary needs of your customers in their own words, and how to get your customers to prioritize those needs. The result is a clear picture of the marketplace, vital for creating messaging, generating leads, winning business and obtaining customer loyalty.

3. Creating Great Messaging

Many manufacturing companies don't have clearly defined messaging used throughout the company, making it difficult to build brand recognition, establish credibility, convey benefits, generate leads, and win orders. I'll help you create a simple hierarchy to organize your messaging, and provide you with a message creation tool that allows your team to create persuasive messaging that resonates with the marketplace.

4. Generating More Leads

Consistently rated as a top problem facing sales and marketing organizations, lead generation fills your sales pipeline. I will provide you with an effective lead qualification and funnel system, along with a set of tools and methods to help you analyze your current lead generation sources, identify your top ROI activities, and get more leads.

Sales Management

5. Nurturing Your Existing Leads

Once you've invested time and money to generate your leads, make sure you devote the proper resources to promote lower-quality leads into sales-ready leads. Approximately one third of all leads are never followed up and you can't let that happen in your organization. I'll help you create a lead nurturing program that gets the potential customer the information they want at the right time, delivered the way they want it, to help them move along the buyer journey. Close more business from the leads you already have.

6. Building a Great Sales Team

Generating leads alone isn't sufficient. I'll help you maximize the win rate of your sales team through proven sales training techniques that include selling strategies, overview pitches, and sales skills development. Improve win-rate with an efficient and trained sales team.

7. Creating Customer Loyalty

Loyal customers generate greater profits and consume fewer resources, yet most manufacturing companies don't focus enough on cultivating loyalty. I'll show you techniques for obtaining and tracking transactional satisfaction and overall customer loyalty. Improve revenue and profit while you create a culture that retains your best customers and your best employees.

Business Management

8. Rightsizing the Marketing Budget

There are often heated debates about the amount of money spent on marketing. Is the money being used efficiently? Would a greater investment in marketing deliver more revenue and profit? I'll show you how you can use benchmarks to establish how you should be spending, and how to justify to leadership a healthy and reasonable marketing budget that fuels your commercial engine. Right size your marketing budget to maximize company profit and reach growth potential.

9. Making Your Current Offerings More Attractive

You aren't always able to develop new products to grow sales. I'll provide you with tools and techniques to dig deeper and uncover the hidden advantages in your *existing* offerings to improve perceived value. Increase revenue by breathing new life into old products.

10. Hitting Your Profit Goals

The marketing and sales teams are responsible for delivering revenue and profit. I'll show you the levers your commercial team can pull to help consistently hit your profitability targets.

These 10 topics covered in the MarketMD approach drive the performance of your commercial engine. Taking the marketing and sales health checkup will provide you with clear insight into how your commercial engine is performing and will identify opportunities for improvement.

The Checkup

The MarketMD journey starts here. The business health checkup is a free, simple, online questionnaire and takes only three minutes to complete. You don't need to be an expert in every facet of your company's inner workings. In fact, you don't need any preparation at all. If you don't have enough information to answer a specific question, you can respond "I don't know." Typically, we see an individual response to over 80 percent of the questions.

All responses follow the Likert scale, where you choose one of six answers:

Strongly disagree
Disagree
Neutral
Agree
Strongly agree
I don't know

Though you may get valuable results from taking the checkup on your own, you will gain much more comprehensive insight by having three to 10 people from your company answer the questions (most common is three to four, but can be dozens). Data can be pooled if anonymity is important. For the best results, have staff from sales, marketing, and service who are knowledgeable in the ways of your customers and your company's inner workings take the checkup. If you have people from engineering, product management, project management, production, or finance who are familiar with your customers and markets, include them as well. Have at least one senior leader, preferably the top executive (perhaps your CEO, or president), complete the checkup to help you get complete buy-in. The more informed respondents you get to participate, the more accurate the results.

Your answers are subjective. Getting actual hard numbers to determine your performance on the 10 topics would be impossible – and frankly unnecessary. Your responses provide a relative rating of your commercial engine on 10 key topics, which is all you need to determine which ones present the best opportunity for improvement. The test results will highlight where to invest staff, time, and money to get the highest ROI. You will avoid wasting resources on things you are already good at and help you focus your team on the right opportunities for improvement.

Fairmont Concepts will email you your results. If more than one person from your organization takes the checkup, we will provide you with aggregate results. If you provide demographic data, we can send benchmark data. Although results from other companies are interesting, the real value is the relative rating your team gives your company performance in the 10 areas.

Note: **To take the survey**

To take the 3-minute MarketMD Business Health Checkup online, follow this URL: https://fairmontconcepts.com/business-health-checkup

---

Test Results

The first item listed on your results page is an aggregate of all 10 scores represented as a percentage – the Commercial Engine Rating. A 100 percent commercial engine rating means every person from your organization who took the health checkup selected "strongly agree" for every question. That's not going to happen. Most commercial engine scores fall between 50 and 70 percent, with the average coming in around 65 percent.

You will likely find, as most companies do, that you will rate at least three topics below "Neutral." Hundreds of companies have taken our health checkup, and based on the overall average here is a listing of the issues beginning with the most frequent weakness listed first:

Average Results in Priority
All Companies, All Industries

Most Frequent Weakness		
	1.	Generating more leads
	2.	Creating great messaging
	3.	Rightsizing the marketing budget
	4.	Uncovering the voice of the customer
	5.	Nurturing your existing leads
	6.	Hitting your profit goals
	7.	Building a great sales team
	8.	Making your current offerings more attractive
	9.	Creating customer loyalty
Least Frequent Weakness	10.	Finding your best end markets

The average results show the top four weaknesses as lead generation, consistent messaging, adequate budget, and knowing customer needs. Don't be concerned if your priority order is different. When we convert the answers to numerical values there is only a 25 percent difference between the first (leads) and last (end markets) issue. Different companies score high and low on any given topic with no single issue always coming out as the biggest weakness for all companies. What is important is your company's relative rating. You want your own weaknesses and strengths in priority so you can use that information to create an improvement plan that has the best ROI.

The 10 topics are related. A commercial engine is no different than any mechanical or biological engine – all the parts work as a system, each impacting the performance of the others. For example, if you don't clearly understand the needs of the market, you are not likely to create the right messaging that enables you to acquire enough leads to fill your pipeline. And if your sales team is not efficient, then the poor win rate will drive profits down and the need for leads up.

To help you interpret your results, here are two examples - one from a manufacturer and one from a service provider.

Manufacturer, Revenue of $180MM/year

A company who manufactures commercial printing equipment forecasts a shortfall in revenue and profit. The director of marketing asks a few people from his company to join him in taking the checkup to determine where they should focus their improvement efforts. The CEO, vice president of sales, service manager, a product manager, and an experienced sales professional join the director of marketing in taking the checkup.

Although there were a few topics that had disparate responses, there was enough consistency that when the team (including the CEO) reviewed the results, they felt the data was a fair representation of company status. This alignment is key to ensuring that the go-forward plan gets is executed quickly and effectively.

Here is an aggregate of all responses for the manufacturer:

Manufacturer Example
Health Checkup Prioritized Results

Nurturing your existing leads
Generating more leads
Uncovering the voice of the customer
Creating great messaging
Creating customer loyalty
Hitting your profit goals
Making your current offerings more attractive
Rightsizing the marketing budget
Finding your best end markets
Building a great sales team

The commercial engine rating of this particular manufacturer is 62 percent – near our historical average. Their top two areas of weakness involve nurturing leads and generating leads. The next two are uncovering the voice of the customer and creating great messaging.

Although their initial inclination is to focus on their top two priorities – lead nurturing and lead generation - they really must address two other problem areas first: uncovering the voice of the customer and creating messaging. As they discuss the results, they come to realize that they should not pursue new lead generation or create new lead nurturing programs while they show weakness in uncovering the voice of the customer and messaging. They see how they must start by conducting voice of the customer research to uncover customer needs, then use that information when creating great messaging if they hope to be effective in generating and nurturing leads. The solutions in Part 2 of this book provide the tools and methods for executing such a plan.

Service Provider, Revenue of $22MM/year

In this example, a company that provides services is looking to improve its commercial engine. The Sales Manager and the Marketing Manager take the health checkup, and the results are not consistent. Here are the two individual responses from the service provider company:

Service Provider Example
Health Checkup Prioritized Results

Sales Manager Results:	Marketing Manager Results:
Generating more leads	Building a great sales team
Uncovering the voice of the customer	Rightsizing the marketing budget
Finding your best end markets	Hitting your profit goals
Creating great messaging	Creating customer loyalty
Nurturing your existing leads	Making your current offerings more attractive
Hitting your profit goals	Nurturing your existing leads
Making your current offerings more attractive	Creating great messaging
Creating customer loyalty	Finding your best end markets
Rightsizing the marketing budget	Uncovering the voice of the customer
Building a great sales team	Generating more leads

The checkup results for the two managers are shown separately rather than averaged together because the ratings are so different. In fact, their opinions are nearly opposite.

When the results were sent back to the managers, the email included a concern that the results are inconclusive because of the wide disparity. It appears each manager feels the problems lie outside their department. In this case, the health checkup sparked a discussion between the two managers to better understand viewpoints, which lead to a deeper understanding of each team's struggles.

After talking through the issues, the managers retook the checkup and ended up with more consistent and usable results. If they had not resolved the disparity, they could choose to recruit additional knowledgeable people from the company to take the checkup, or bring in outside consultants to conduct an independent evaluation.

Moving on to the Next Step: Solutions

You have identified your areas of weakness, but that is only half the equation. Your results will help you determine which areas of your commercial engine to focus on first.

Part Two of the book provides proven solutions and a variety of usable tools for each of the 10 topics. You can read Part Two of the book straight through, looking for skills to learn in any of the solutions provided, or you can concentrate on just those sections where your results show you have gaps.

My goal in Part Two is to help your team learn new skills and execute effective solutions. The ideas are presented in a simple-to-follow format that your staff can easily handle. The solutions are not the only way to tackle each of the 10 topics, but they are the best ways that I have found to get effective results in the near to medium-term. The MarketMD approach is designed to be executable by your team, but if you lack internal resources you can bring in outside help.

Incorporating the ideas and tools in Part 2 will help you improve your commercial engine quickly, raise the skill level of your team for the long term, and get the results your business needs.

Part Two

Solutions for your Commercial Engine

In the first part of this book you take the MarketMD Business Health Checkup to self-diagnose your company's performance regarding 10 key areas of your commercial engine. Now, in Part Two, a solution chapter is provided for each of the ten areas.

Ten key areas vital to the performance of your commercial engine are:

1. *Finding your best end markets*
2. *Uncovering the voice of the customer*
3. *Creating great messaging*
4. *Generating more leads*
5. *Nurturing your existing leads*
6. *Building a great sales team*
7. *Creating customer loyalty*
8. *Rightsizing the marketing budget*
9. *Making your current offerings more attractive*
10. *Hitting your profit goals*

Solution 1: Finding Your Best End Markets

Many manufacturing companies employ the "Alice in Wonderland" method of marketing, as in the oft-quoted line, "if you don't know where you're going, any road will take you there."

In business, before you embark on your marketing journey, you'd better know where you are going. Reaching your business destination starts with finding your best end markets.

Doing that effectively means analyzing your existing customer base. You must determine your best customers – not just your largest revenue generators or those with the highest gross margin – but the ones who are driving the greatest bottom line profit.

Once you've identified these best customers, analyze the markets in which they reside and find clones of your best customers. This is where you should focus your efforts. However, you might not be able to classify an end market as "best" just because it includes one customer who is driving high profit. There also needs to be a viable number of available potential customers to justify mining that market.

In the end, that's the challenge: finding identifiable markets where not only best customer clones reside, but also those markets that are big enough to justify pursuit.

Many companies "sell to anyone interested." That's not a strategy, that's a reaction. Building a strong commercial engine – the company's system for obtaining leads, selling, and serving customers - requires starting at the beginning: identifying your best end markets.

Path to a Strong Commercial Engine

◎ Figure 1.1 A strong commercial engine builds from the selection of the best target end markets.

It takes a great deal of resources to uncover needs, create messaging, generate leads and win business. Therefore, it makes sense to carefully select your target end markets, and build your commercial engine from there.

The Importance of Segmentation

Buyers today expect you to understand their business and their needs and are instantly turned off when you communicate in a way that suggests you don't. Segment your markets into buckets of similar type and treat the ones you wish to pursue in a personal and compelling way. You have limited resources, so focus on understanding and serving the markets that give you growth and profit.

That's not to say you can't decide to pursue a completely novel end market. A company's technology portfolio often includes long shots – potentially lucrative investments in R&D and engineering. The same is true in marketing. Pursuing new end markets with high return opportunities is acceptable as long as you limit your risks and maintain enough focus on your core target markets.

This solution explains how to maximize company performance in the markets you already address - where the sure-fire profits reside.

The Two Steps in Selecting the Best Market Segments

Selecting your target end markets is a vital first step in creating an efficient commercial engine - a step that should not be taken lightly. Two main attributes define your best market segments:

1. **Pocket income potential**
   Your best market segments contain clones of your best customers. Your best customers are those who deliver your greatest bottom line income after cost-to-serve is taken into account. I call this "pocket income."

2. **Market viability**
   Your best market segments contain enough potential clones to provide your company a sufficient return on the marketing investment.

Pocket Income Potential

Pocket income is a way to look at the overall value a customer brings to your company. It compares a customer's specific bottom line profitability against that of the average customer after accounting for the cost-to-serve. Pocket income is different from the more commonly used pocket price and pocket margin.

Pocket price and pocket margin[1] are terms derived from a *transactional* analysis of price and margin erosion once you factor in extra rebates, volume based discounts, payment term discounts, or freight charges you cover. The terms are useful when looking at the bottom line profitability of a transaction. However, they are not sufficient to tell you which customers truly make you the most money overall since they do not include all purchases covered over a reasonable time, and they do not include resource drain (cost-to-serve). To understand which customers truly generate the most profit, you need to look at pocket income.

Note: **The 80/20 rule highlights the importance of segmentation**
Our minds are designed to find patterns. The familiar 80/20 rule or *Pareto Principle*, is a pattern often referenced in business discussions. In the early 20th Century, economist Vilfredo Pareto created a mathematical formula demonstrating that 20 percent of invested input is responsible for 80 percent of the results obtained. The rule has been repeatedly proven true throughout history.

The Pareto Principle applies to sales and marketing. For many businesses, 80 percent of the profit comes from 20 percent of the customers. However, identifying and cloning that critical 20 percent is where most businesses struggle. Careful segmentation and analysis are required.

Since pocket income compares specific customers against your average customer, you must first establish the cost structure and income for your average customer. Table 1.2 shows the format for calculating and reporting pocket income. It is a layout similar to a simplified income statement.

Pocket Income Analysis

		Average Customer	
1	Revenue		$100,000
2	Cost of goods	60%	$60,000
3	Expenses: Cost-To-Serve Related		
4	Marketing	2%	$2,000
5	Sales	5%	$5,000
6	Engineering	5%	$5,000
7	Service/Support	5%	$5,000
8	Warranty	2%	$2,000
9	Manager/Executive	1%	$1,000
10		20%	$20,000
11	Expenses: everything else	10%	$10,000
12	Total Expenses	30%	$30,000
13	Pocket Income	10%	$10,000

◎ Table 1.2 A sample pocket income statement.

Table 1.2 shows the average pocket income for all customers. The shaded areas represent the average cost to acquire and service the customer. The percentages in this area have been estimated on a departmental basis. Line 13 shows the aggregated pocket income for the entire customer base. Go to https://fairmontconcepts.com/tools-templates to download blank templates for calculating pocket income for your business.

Follow these steps to create a pocket income table.

1. *Get financial data*

   Have finance create a spreadsheet for all customers combined that contains Revenue, COGS, Expenses, and Income (lines 1, 2, 12, and 13 of Table 1.2) averaged over the past two years. This information is a general summary of the Income Statement. You will also need a breakdown of the expense categories shown in the shaded area (lines 4 through 9) – these items are cost to acquire and serve related. You are not looking for perfection. You are simply creating an average against which all other customers will be compared. Edit the rows of the shaded area as your business structure requires. For example, if you are a reseller then you might not have an Engineering category.

   The "everything else" category includes fixed costs and other expenses not related to acquiring or serving your customers.

2. *Sort by revenue*

   Sort all customers by revenue, highest to lowest.

3. *Select potential "best customers"*

   Select the customers you wish to analyze as potential best customers. Pick those who show revenue per year in the top 20 to 30 percent of all customers. Choose customers that represent a big enough market to move the needle. In addition, choose those with cost of goods percent (line 2) near or below average.

   Don't look at groups of customers or end markets yet. Analyze individual customers only. You will determine the end market of top candidates later.

   Include other customers you want to analyze who may have missed the cut. For example, you may include companies you have always considered outstanding customers, but that didn't meet the revenue per year criteria. They may deliver a positive result because of a low cost to serve. Or, they might be relatively new customers, but have great potential.

   Depending on your business diversity and size, you should end up with somewhere between 10 to 30 customers worth analyzing as potential "best."

4. *Estimate pocket income*

   Add a column for each selected customer and have finance insert their revenue and COGS data (see Table 1.3 below). Meet with a cross functional team representing the departments in the shaded area of Table 1.3 who are familiar with the customers you have selected. Based on the team's input, adjust the cost-to-serve _percentages_ in lines 4 through 9. It is significantly easier for your department managers to estimate and adjust the percentages for each customer as opposed to calculate dollar amounts. The dollar amounts will change automatically (if you're using our template download, or if you set up your own table accordingly).

Pocket income percent and dollars of row 13 are estimates, not firm numbers.

5. _Select top pocket income finalists_
   Once you have adjusted the expense percentages for each selected customer, choose four or five customers who rated highest in both pocket income percent and pocket income dollars. These are the ones that you will now carry forward to the next step of analyzing market viability.

Resource Drain Estimation Example

Here is an example of how the service manager – one of the members of your evaluation team - would adjust percentages based on the customer's drain on the service department.

Beta Corporation is considered a good customer, and they are added to the list of companies to analyze for pocket income. They bring in approximately twice the revenue as the average customer. The service manager asks the question, "Since Beta Corporation brings in twice the revenue of the average customer, do they drain resources from my department more or less than two-times the average customer?" The service manager knows Beta Corporation well because they are extremely demanding. Based on the revenue they provide, she estimates that Beta requires twice the support than they should, even when considering their high revenue contribution. Therefore, she plugs in 10 percent (twice the average of five percent) on the expense line for her department. Each manager goes through the same process until all the target customers' expense percentages are adjusted.

Pocket Income Comparison Table Example

Table 1.3 shows a comparison of two hypothetical customers against an average customer. The low maintenance customer tends to drain very little resources from the company while the high maintenance customer represents a significant drag on profitability.

Note: **How perfect does my data need to be?**
Should your version of Table 1.3 be a perfect reflection of the cost to serve your selected customers? No, it should not. You could spend months figuring out the cost to serve percentages for the average customer, and then a week analyzing each select customer, but that will result in a lot of unnecessary effort. Obtain your cost to serve estimates for the average customer from finance, and then meet with department experts to estimate deviations for each selected customer.

Spend only a few minutes on each selected customer. You are obtaining educated guesses, and that is OK because pocket income numbers don't need to be factual, they only need to be compared.

Pocket Income Comparison Table

	Average Customer	Low Maintenance Customer	High Maintenance Customer
Revenue	$100,000	$85,000	$125,000
Cost of goods	60% $60,000	60% $51,000	60% $75,000
Expenses: Cost-To-Serve Related			
Marketing	2% $2,000	2% $1,700	1% $ 1,250
Sales	5% $5,000	6% $5,100	5% $ 6,250
Engineering	5% $5,000	2% $1,700	7% $ 8,750
Service/Support	5% $5,000	3% $2,550	8% $10,000
Warranty	2% $2,000	2% $1,700	4% $ 5,000
Manager/Executive	1% $1,000	1% $ 850	3% $ 3,000
	20% $20,000	16% $13,600	28% $35,000
Expenses: everything else	10% $10,000	10% $ 8,500	10% $12,500
Total Expenses	30% $30,000	26% $22,100	38% $47,500
Pocket Income	10% $10,000	14% $11,900	2% $ 2,500

Table 1.3 shows two very different pocket income results for two customers when compared to the average customer.

Low Maintenance Customer: Low Maintenance Customer brings you near the average revenue compared to the average customer ($85,000), but because their expense drain is low they contribute a higher than average pocket income of 14 percent. They were added to the list for pocket income analysis because your team felt they would score well – even though their revenue is slightly below average. This is a highly satisfied customer that demands few engineering resources. They have trained their own staff to service and maintain your equipment and only come to you under unusual circumstances. Sales staff spends slightly more time with them than with the average customer, but there is no increase in management or marketing expenses versus an average customer. The analysis shows excellent pocket income percent and good pocket income dollars. This is a valuable customer who might make the cut to move to the next step – market viability analysis. Make note of their end market segment.

High Maintenance Customer: High Maintenance Customer looks favorable at a quick glance. Their slightly above average revenue and typical COGs percentage suggest they generate high gross profit dollars, but the pocket income analysis tells another story. High Maintenance Customer is demanding and unreasonable. They drain significant resources from your technical support team, managers, and executives, costing significantly more in time and money than the Average Customer. The constant barrage of service demands, product changes, and executive interaction drive up your cost to serve this difficult customer. Their pocket income percent and dollars are so low they will not make the cut to move to the next step.

While both customers look attractive in terms of revenue and gross profit margin, High Maintenance Customer provides little pocket income. Low Maintenance Customer, on the other hand, has low resource and warranty drain, so their pocket income is higher than average (especially their percent). Chasing clones of High Maintenance Customer will likely drain resources and profits.

Pocket income analysis will identify the types of customers that are best for your business and help you avoid the ones that aren't.

Market Viability

Pocket income is only one of the two primary factors to consider when selecting your target end markets. You also need to look at the viability of the market. Before you align your commercial engine to pursue an end market, you must make sure the end market contains enough worthwhile potential customers to sustain and grow your business.

Examine Similar Customers from your CRM

Make sure the select customers that showed high pocket income are not surrounded by other customers in your CRM with poor pocket income. Otherwise, you might pursue an end market based on one profitable customer that is essentially an outlier.

For example, if six other customers reside in the same end market as Low Maintenance Customer shown in Table 1.3, perform the pocket income analysis on each of them. If they provide below average pocket profit, then Low Maintenance Customer might be a diamond among the rocks. This further analysis can save your company from pursuing a poor end market.

Viable Market Size

Hot markets can burn out fast. Make sure to identify the size of your potential target market before committing to it.

The typical way of looking at the universe of your addressable market is illustrated in the familiar circle graph shown in Figure 1.4.

Market Potential Definitions

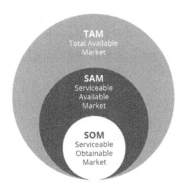

© Figure 1.4 A common depiction of the market universe.

Total Available Market (TAM) is the entire prospect universe for all your products and those of your competitors now and in the future.

• If you sell custom commercial vehicles in New Jersey, then your TAM is all global buyers of all types of commercial vehicles.

Serviceable Available Market (SAM) represents available markets which realistically can be reached by your organization and those of your competitors.

- If you sell custom commercial vehicles in New Jersey, then your SAM is all commercial vehicle buyers within your covered geography, whether the end market subsets are served by you or a competitor.

Serviceable Obtainable Market (SOM) is the subset of SAM you believe you can reasonably capture with your business structure and products.

- If you sell custom commercial vehicles in New Jersey, then your SOM is all commercial vehicle buyers within your covered geography, and in end markets you currently serve.

Some marketers then add a fourth even smaller circle called Penetrated Market, to reflect your customer base. It's easy for a marketing team to get wrapped around the axle about market size definitions. While there are many ways of sizing target markets, the choice of how broad to make your criteria really comes down to this: if you have no intention of modifying what you do (marketing, sales, product, support, geographic reach), you should look at the SOM. If you are willing to make changes and additions to your commercial reach, then you can consider the SAM.

Only a portion of your SAM – your SOM – can be mined for business today. Anyone can hockey stick an opportunity line graph and jack up future sales predictions by simply using the TAM. Most TAMs are huge. But, if you are banking your business on the results - not just the outcome of a presentation - then be realistic. Too many companies make bad business decisions based on a PowerPoint deck showing a massive –but unreachable – TAM opportunity. Small to mid-sized manufacturing companies need to look at the SOM for near-term market size and the SAM for long-term market potential.

How do you identify your SAM or SOM size? Conduct primary and secondary research.

Primary and Secondary Market Research

At this point you likely have more than one end market on your list. To get the best results, you need to narrow your focus to the right targets. Before launching into uncovering needs, creating messaging, and pursuing leads, conduct primary and secondary market research. *Primary research* is talking directly to experts or individuals in the market and drawing conclusions from your own data. *Secondary research* is analyzing published material.

The goal of your research is to create a comparison table to clearly describe your attractive end markets so you can select a subset to be your *target* end markets. Typical analysis covers evaluation of the market size, competitors in the space, and the predicted growth of the market. Companies usually start with secondary research, as it is less expensive and easier to gather. The market knowledge you gain conducting secondary research always proves useful when conducting primary research.

Secondary research

Conducting secondary research on target markets, especially those where there is little publicly available information, can be difficult. Search online to learn the language and business nuances, and to seek relevant information.

Secondary resources include:

- *Third party reports*
  Use the internet to find market research reports, blogs, and whitepapers on the target markets.
- *Industry codes*
  Use the NAICS code (service offered by D&BHoovers - www.hoovers.com), Manta, or other services to identify the classification of your best customer candidates. Use this code to find other companies with similar characteristics to your customers.
- *Review SEC filings.*
  Public companies in your target end market provide valuable information about typical business structures, industries they serve, investment tendencies, and financial strength.
- *Trade associations*
  Read industry related articles from trade publications and trade organizations.
- *Competitors*
  Review all other companies that directly compete in the space with similar products and services. Review all competitors in the space that offer alternatives to your offerings. Perform a SWOT analysis of each potential competitor.

Primary research

Conducting primary research takes time and energy – you are creating the data yourself through your own research effort. Many interviews will be short – likely 15 minutes or less – so focus on a few key questions. Treat your interview like a discussion, not an inquisition. Use open ended questions designed to start a dialogue and follow the thread of the conversation to keep your contact talking.

Primary sources include:

- Your own customers and potential customers
- Industry experts
- Competitors, if possible
- Competitor's customers
- Channel partners, such as agents and distributors. Channel partners often have valuable insight and might look at the market in a slightly different way than an original equipment manufacturer (OEM).

Beyond helping you choose which end markets to pursue, the primary and secondary research you conduct will also help you execute your commercial marketing and sales plans. Make note of the language your contacts use, the customer needs they bring up, the go-to market channels they prefer, the benefits and features they mention, and relevant buyer journey information. It is all valuable data you can use if you select that end market.

Tying your Research Together with an End Market Selection Table

Once you have completed your pocket income, market viability analysis, primary, and secondary research you can create an End Market Selection Table to help you make your final decisions. Market analysis for all but the biggest industries is not an exact science. It may be more helpful in your decision-making to compare the potential of the various end markets you are considering against each other. Putting together a table like the one shown in Table 1.5 below enables you to review your target end market finalists at a glance. The table is a catalyst for informed debate.

Comparing and Selecting End Markets – an example

Although your final selection table may look simple, the data behind it can be complex. Let's use an example of a small custom vehicle manufacturer.

ABC Custom Truck Works is a company based in New Jersey covering the NJ, NY and CT areas. They customize mid-sized vehicles (class 3 through class 6) and trailers built off pickup trucks, vans, and cube vans. There are 400,000 to 500,000 new vehicles sold per year in the U.S. by all competitors combined. Just over 15,000 vehicles are sold within ABC's geographic coverage area each year.

The company was founded to manufacture landscaper vehicles and trailers 15 years ago. They now sell 400 trucks annually, and offer aftermarket accessories and services. Although landscapers remain their largest revenue generator, they have also sold vehicles to plumbers, electricians, emergency response teams, town road crews, private snow plow operators, farmers, shipping companies, and a host of other small markets.

ABC has conducted a pocket income analysis of their customer base, and put their best candidates through a market viability analysis. After conducting primary and secondary research on each target market, they have filtered their final list to four markets: landscapers, electricians, carpenters and emergency response teams. They would like to further cull this number down to two or three target end markets.

ABC develops the table below to help them make informed decisions on selecting the best target markets.

Target Market Selection Table

Target Market	1. Landscaper Custom Vehicles	2. Electrician Custom Vehicles	3. Carpenter Custom Vehicles	4. Ambulance Custom Vehicles
Best Customer	Easton Property Maintenance	Orting Electric, LLC	Champaign Remodeling, Inc.	Brooklyn EMT Service, Inc.
Pocket Income % of best customer	15%	17%	13%	5%
Does best customer represent market?	Yes	Yes	Yes	Yes
SOM size/yr. & today's share	$95 million Share today = 3%	$85 million Share = 2%	$45 million Share = 0.1%	$45 million Share = 0.009%
TAM size/yr. nationwide	$2 billion	$1.7 billion	$1 billion	$4 billion
Match to core competencies	Yes, strong match, many patents	Yes, strong match, many patents	Yes, strong match, many patents	Poor: few relevant patents, need know-how
Competitive position	Strong	Strong	Strong	Weak
Key market considerations	Many competitors. We have a great local reputation	We have a good local reputation	Many customize standard vehicles on own. We are unknown	Big competitors. We are unknown. Average selling price = 6x higher than our other markets
Products and services purchased	Series 5000 flatbed trucks, Model 50 trailer Vehicle plus customization = $53,000, trailer $3,500. 3 year service package	Series 2000 vans Spool and tool accessories Vehicle plus customization = $58,000. 3 year service package	Series 5000 flatbed trucks Price vehicle plus customization $51,000 3 year service package	Model 1560 Ambulance w/ medical inserts Price vehicle plus customization $348,000 3 year service package

◎ Table 1.5 An example of the Target Market Selection Table for ABC Custom Truck Works.

Based on the results in Table 1.5, ABC Custom Truck Works' marketing and leadership team make the following observations and decisions:

1. Landscaper market - their largest market currently - remains attractive. They will continue to target this end market.
2. Electrician market represents their best opportunity for profitable growth. The market has strong pocket income, a solid market share base from which to build, and good local (SOM) and national (SAM) market potential. It will be a target market in the coming year.
3. The carpenter market is also attractive. ABC leadership selects this end market as a target as well because of good pocket income, and overlap of products and services with two other end markets. They understand

that the market research revealed that many carpenters purchase standard trucks and personally customize them, suggesting that the serviceable market might not be large, so they will proceed with caution.

4. They decide not to pursue the ambulance/emergency response vehicle market even though it is a large market with high Average Selling Prices (ASP). The TAM, which includes fire trucks, tow trucks, ambulances and all other types of emergency response vehicles is very large ($4 billion), though ABC's SOM of locally supplied ambulances is not larger than the other potential target markets ($45 million). They believe the low pocket income will persist, and they don't believe they can afford to overcome the high number of entrenched competitors. They also note that they have no Intellectual Property (IP), and limited knowledge and skills regarding customer needs and medical equipment.

The final results of ABC Custom Truck Works end market analysis have narrowed potentially dozens of serviceable markets to three: landscapers, electricians and carpenters. They are now ready to continue refining their commercial engine by uncovering market needs of these three target end markets.

Summary

Once you have established your best end markets, you have the information you need to focus your business on the best ROI.

Going through this crucial process may seem daunting, but it is imperative if you are to leverage your resources appropriately. Spending time, money, and human capital in pursuit of randomly selected markets will not deliver the results you need, regardless of how hard you work. When it comes to marketing and sales, it's not about working harder, but working smarter. Establishing the right markets on which to focus your attention is the first critical step in the process. Everything else discussed in this book follows from that.

Solution 1 References

1. McKinsey & Co., New York, NY. 2003 are attributed with coining the phrase Pocket Price Waterfall and creating a chart to describe the erosion of profit after invoice.

Solution 2: Uncovering the Voice of the Customer

Motivating someone to buy something inexpensive from you is hard. It's even more difficult when you are selling high-dollar items. Buyers have a lot on the line – money, reputation, a problem to solve – and so are often hesitant to make the purchase.

You shouldn't create your marketing and sales pitch based on what you *think* will motivate someone to want your offering. You can't rely on guesswork, legacy information, comments from sales, or luck. To sell effectively, you must have detailed information on what potential buyers need so you can provide it.

Where can you get that information? From your prospects and customers. They're out there – ask them.

Uncovering the voice of the customer (VOC) is the only way to truly determine what your prospects and customers need. VOC research is needs research.

Although, knowing the needs of your customers within your target markets is a fundamental and obvious requirement for selling, many manufacturing companies don't pay nearly enough attention to uncovering what their customers truly want. Some companies chase competitors, simply trying to match products and services at a lower price. They assume their competitor knows the customers' needs and fail to do any of their own research. Some companies develop products and services based on the few needs they do know. They assume uncovering more needs won't make a significant difference, so they stop short of full discovery. Other companies base their business on customer needs they uncovered years ago. They assume the customer needs haven't changed - a flawed and dangerous assumption.

Think about how much of your business is tied to customer needs: company structure, staffing, product development, local or global footprint, facilities and income. Everything involving your company and the reason for its existence is tied to customer needs. Find out what your customers need and then figure out how to be successful in business fulfilling those needs. Spend the time to uncover, understand, and leverage their needs. It's fundamental to building a strong commercial engine (see Figure 1.1).

Path to a Strong Commercial Engine

◎ Figure 1.1 A strong commercial engine builds from the selection of the best target end markets and knowing customer needs (Image repeated from Solution 1).

Emphasize the focus of your needs research on your best end markets. If your needs research is too generic – covering too many markets at one time – you can't obtain specific, detailed needs, and you won't be able to connect with potential customers on a meaningful level.

Note: **Marketers and sales people uncover needs for different reasons**
There are two distinct forms of needs analysis performed in marketing and sales organizations. Early in the selling process, a salesperson must uncover specific customer needs (Solution 6 *Building a Great Sales Team*) before attempting to provide solutions. Uncovering market needs is not about a single customer, but is instead about identifying the needs of all customers in an end market.

Uncovering market needs means finding out – directly from prospects and customers - the things your target end market customers truly value. Input from your own team is helpful, often accurate, and can set the direction of the research, but it can be subjective and is always incomplete. You must confirm the team's opinions and add insight through objective research. Use proven Voice of the Customer (VOC) and Voice of the Market (VOM) research techniques to ensure your results are comprehensive, free of bias, and accurately represent true customer needs.

Objective research not only provides believable results, but also credibility to the marketing department. Too many times I have heard managers, executives, service managers, product managers, and product development engineers doubt the words of the marketing staff when it comes to customer needs. They delay acting or ignore requirements because they don't believe the market data. They feel the stated customer requirements are "just guesses." Conducting and presenting *objective* VOC results will help gain the confidence of your peers from other departments, and get your company moving together in the same direction.

Note: Marketing is about brand promotion (shotgun) and end market focus (rifle)

Throughout this book, I speak of the need to emphasize marketing efforts on the target end markets. But, don't take this too far. Complement your focused, "rifle shot" marketing aimed at your target end markets with "shotgun" marketing pointed at the general TAM or SAM. Consider a 50/50 split (rifle/shotgun) from a budgeting and staff resource perspective. The rifle shot grows your business profitably today, while the shotgun blast helps you identify future opportunity and maintain end market diversity – yielding a more resilient business.

When you have completed your VOC research, you will have a comprehensive set of needs for your target end market. Many of those needs will also prove relevant to other end markets. Modify your messaging to be broad when promoting brand and general capabilities, and focused when selling into your target end market.

Adjacent Markets have Overlapping Needs

Voice of the Customer Research

VOC research is a subset of the broader Voice of the Market (VOM) research. Where VOM takes a wide view of the target market - competitive landscape, market size, end market annual projected growth, preferred channels, and customer needs - VOC focuses only on the last component - identifying and organizing customer needs.

Customers don't always articulate needs in the form of specific requests. When you talk to customers, you're looking for inspiration, not a specification. Your customers don't necessarily know the best solution.

Who Uses the VOC Results?

Your goal is to uncover a complete set of needs described in the customers' own words, and organized and prioritized the way customers think about them. Then leverage those needs to improve products, marketing activities, services, and sales tools.

◎ Figure 2.1 Illustrates the many departments benefiting from a clear understanding of target market needs.

VOC information is valuable for many departments within the company:

- *Marketing*
  Create compelling messaging to generate and nurture leads.
- *Sales*
  Create powerful sales tools and sales training to increase win rate.
- *Service*
  Provide programs that meet or exceed customer expectations, increase revenue per customer and customer loyalty.
- *Engineering*
  Develop and continuously improve winning products.
- *Production*
  Understand where to focus continuous improvement and cost/performance (value) efforts.
- *Leadership team*
  Provide essential input for developing company strategies, staffing, programs and budgets to maximize profitability and growth.

A Proven VOC Process

I have had great success using a VOC research approach developed by Applied Marketing Science (AMS).[1,2] Gerry Katz, now the vice chairman, trained me and my team of marketing, product management, and service managers when I worked as the marketing leader of a global machine tool company.

The results of the AMS process provide an objective set of needs as the customers describe them. If you already have a complete list of well-researched needs, you might only need to reach out to customers to refine what you have. However, if you rated yourself low on this topic during the business health checkup, you should invest the time to execute this technique.

Stephen Covey's second habit (of seven) of highly effective people says to "begin with the end in mind." The "end" of the AMS needs research process delivers a primary needs table and a market opportunity map - two powerful tools that provide a solid foundation for your sales and marketing efforts.

The primary needs table organizes the things your customers have told you they need and the market opportunity map tells you where you should devote your resources to best meet those needs. Examples from our fictitious company ABC Custom Truck Works follow.

Primary Needs Table

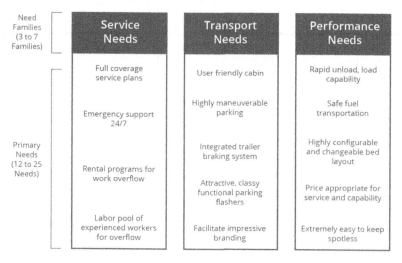

○ Figure 2.2 shows an example of a Primary Needs table for ABC Custom Truck Works - specifically their landscaper end market

Example Market Opportunity Map

Weaknesses	Strengths
• Price appropriate for service and capability • Labor pool of experienced workers for overflow • Highly maneuverable parking	• Full coverage service plans • Integrated trailer braking system • Rapid unload, load capability • Highly configurable and changeable bed layout
Monitor	**Over Emphasized**
• Rental programs for work overflow • Extremely easy to keep spotless • User friendly cabin	• Emergency support 24/7 • Attractive, classy, functional parking flashers • Safe fuel transportation • Facilitate impressive branding

Importance ——▶
(customer rating of importance regarding that need)

Performance ——▶
(customer rating of satisfaction regarding that need)

◎ Figure 2.3 The Market Opportunity Map for ABC Custom Truck Works, landscaper end market.

Primary needs tables, such as Figure 2.2, are the result of comprehensive research that uncovers and groups hundreds of individual needs. You will objectively identify customer needs, represented in the customers' own words.

Market opportunity maps, such as Figure 2.3, are created by having many users rate the needs found in the primary needs table based on importance to them and how the product they are currently using is performing in relation to those needs.

These two powerful charts present a clear, concise, prioritized summary of the things your target end market customers want. Learning this VOC approach can be invaluable as you develop and execute your marketing and sales plan.

Conducting the VOC Research

The AMS approach delivers comprehensive results that are free of researcher bias and prioritized by the customer.

The basic concept involves interviewing a small number of customers (20 to 40) carefully selected from a cross section of your target market. You use open-ended questioning techniques designed to uncover as many customer needs as possible described in the customers' own words. Research has shown that 20 to 30 interviews will usually identify 90+ percent of all the needs. The needs are then grouped by a few knowledgeable customers into 12 to 25 primary needs to create your primary needs table.

These needs are then sent in an email survey to as many users as you can reach in your target market. You ask the users to rate the primary needs on two factors: importance to them and your performance in meeting them. The survey results create the market opportunity map. In the end, you have a full set of primary needs in your customer's own words prioritized by the marketplace.

VOC Research Steps

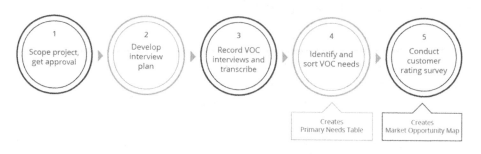

Figure 2.4 The steps for conducting the VOC research via the AMS approach.

The AMS VOC research process, shown in Figure 2.4, is conducted as follows:

1. **Establish project scope and obtain approval**
   Create scope document to plan your project and get leadership buy in.
2. **Develop the VOC interview plan**
   Determine the number of each type of customers and job titles you will

need and the questions you will use to start the conversation threads in search of needs.

3. **Conduct the VOC interviews**

   Record and transcribe the interviews.

4. **Identify and sort the VOC needs**

   Extract and group the needs into primary needs and families and create your primary needs table (your version of Figure 2.2).

5. **Conduct the broad customer rating email survey**

   Ask a large customer audience to rate the needs from 1 to 10 on importance to them and your performance in delivering on them. Normalize the data and create the market opportunity map (your version of Figure 2.3).

Conducted without outside resource assistance, this research typically takes approximately 10 to 14 weeks. You can expect two people to work 20 to 30 percent of their time on the project with other key stakeholders providing occasional support. Scheduling and conducting the interviews and culling the needs from transcriptions are the two activities that will take the most time.

Note: **Buyer Personas**

Buyer personas, sometimes called customer profiles or customer avatars, are helpful ways of communicating the key traits of your best customers to your entire organization.

A buyer persona is a composite sketch of a typical customer within a target market segment. At minimum, it is important for you to create a draft buyer persona to help focus your needs research plan. You will adjust the persona once your needs research is complete.

Suggested elements of your customer profiles include:
- A representative photo of the customers or their facility.
- Company annual revenue, private or publicly held.
- Buying team: job functions of buyers, interests, education or certifications
- Fears and pressures, motivations, values and goals
- What they want and need out of your offering
- Your key marketing message and the elevator overview pitch

Example buyer persona for ABC's Landscaper market follows.

Landscapers

Their Primary Needs:

Service Needs	Transport Needs	Performance Needs
Full coverage service plans	User friendly cabin	Rapid unload, load capability
Emergency support 24/7	Highly maneuverable parking	Safe fuel transportation
Rental programs for work overflow	Integrated trailer braking system	Highly configurable and changeable bed layout
Labor pool of experienced workers for overflow	Attractive, classy functional parking flashers	Price appropriate for service and capability
	Facilitate impressive branding	Extremely easy to keep spotless

How We Sell

ABC Custom Truck Works – Trucks that work.
Complete jobs faster. Keeping 'em safe, keeping 'em efficient.

Technology and convenience born from our 30 years of experience.
Custom configurations, all pre-engineered and proven out. We sweat the details.

You can trust ABC for service, expertise – your local business partner.

Demographics

Revenue: $1 to $5MM/yr

Buyers: Owner or general manager

Interests: Outdoor activities, sports, beer

Education: 75% no college degree

Characteristics

Values: Hard work, reliability

Fears and Pressures: Time pressure, labor issues, equipment reliability, customer satisfaction, finding more work, seasonal slowdowns

Goals: Sustainable profitability, market share in their region, very high WOM referrals, no injuries, no law suits

What They Want From Us: A vehicle they can depend on every day to get them to the job site and help them complete the job faster.

Once finalized, place small customer profile posters in conference rooms where service, sales, marketing, and product development staff meet to help remind everyone of who they are working to serve and satisfy.

Here are AMS's five steps explained in detail.

1. Establish Project Scope and Obtain Approval

Scope the project and get leadership buy-in. Your goal is to clearly describe the project to gain the confidence and approval of senior leadership.

Your scope details should include:

- *Purpose*
  Why do you need to conduct this research? What will the project encompass? How will the results be used and who will use them?
- *Background and assumptions*
  What end markets are targeted? What are the buyer personas?
- *Objectives and deliverables*
  The primary needs table and market opportunity map are the main deliverables, but you will also gather hundreds of individual needs in the customers' own words.
- *Internal and external resource demand*
  How long will it take? What will be accomplished with internal staff versus external?
- *Budget and ROI*
  What is the cost and what is the expected return on investment?
- *Approach*
  What is the VOC process from a high level?
- *Timeline with milestones*
  Project Gantt chart.
- *Reporting*
  Who will the project manager report to?
- *Signatures*
  Sign off of the scope by the appropriate leaders.

2. Develop the VOC Interview Plan

How many interviews are needed to obtain most of the needs? Surprisingly, research has shown that when proper interview techniques are used, 20 to 30 interviews are sufficient to gather more than 90 percent of customer needs. When researching one end market I recommend starting with a target of 20.

Note: Individual interviews or focus groups?
I have found one-on-one phone or face-to-face interviews at the customer site are usually more effective than using focus groups. Focus groups take a great deal of effort to set up, and require certain skills to avoid the loudest voice from dominating.

The best approach: combine the face-to-face interview at the customer's site with ethnographic research – seeing the product or service in action and watching for needs, issues, problems, and opportunities. With ethnography, you can observe what the customer does, as opposed to what they say they do – sometimes two very different things. Take photos and videos where allowed by the customer. These photos will reinforce the importance of needs when it comes time to use the information.

Design an interview plan that includes customers from a broad cross section of the market. Consider geographic location, title, industry, or other categories that make sense for your business.

In the example with ABC Custom Truck Works' investigation into the landscaper end market shown in Figure 2.5, they chose one axis to be States - the company is headquartered in New Jersey and covers New Jersey, New York and Connecticut. Currently, they obtain 51 percent of their revenue from NJ, 36 percent from NY, and 13 percent from CT, so they have elected to roughly follow those percentages as they populate their interview sampling plan. For the other axis, they selected the titles or roles of customers they wish to interview – operator, manager and owner. All three types of individuals might be part of the buying team and be able to add valuable thoughts and perspectives on product needs and vendor performance.

Interview Sampling Plan

	NJ (50%)	NY (35%)	CT (15%)	TOTAL
Operator (30%)	3	2	1	6
Manager (40%)	4	3	1	8
Owner (30%)	3	2	1	6
TOTAL	10	7	3	20

◎ Table 2.5 An example of an interviewing sampling plan.

The next step is to add contact names to each of the cells. As much as possible, use random sampling to select your target companies with one exception: try to include several early adopters or highly innovative customers. These interviews are often important sources of needs because the customer typically has a strong desire to maximize the performance of your offering. You will likely have some cells in Table 2.5 that will be hard to fill. If you need 20 interviews, start with a list of 80 to 100 names.

If you are addressing a wide range of markets or products, but feel they can be combined into a common interview pool, include 10 to 20 interviews per market or product segment. Track the responses from each segment separately so you can highlight significant differences.

Keep in mind additional interviews will add time to the project and increase the complexity of your research. Try to keep the scope of your project focused on as few segments as needed so you don't exceed 30 interviews. Anything more than that and project can get out of hand. Table 2.6 provides an example interview sampling plan covering two target end markets in one VOC research project.

Interview Sampling Plan
(example: expanded to 3 end markets)

	Landscapers			Carpenters			
	NJ (50%)	NY (35%)	CT (15%)	NJ (50%)	NY (35%)	CT (15%)	TOTAL
Operator (30%)	2	1	1	2	2	1	9
Manager (40%)	3	2	1	3	2	1	12
Owner (30%)	2	2	1	2	1	1	9
TOTAL	7	5	3	7	5	3	30

◎ Table 2.6 An Interview Sampling Plan with two related market segments - landscapers and carpenters - included in the same research project. The target in this sample is to conduct 15 interviews per segment.

You can expand your sampling plan further by including a percentage of competitive users. Once set, don't give in to the temptation to change your sampling plan by pursuing the easy interview. For example, avoid shifting to interviewing managers rather than owners simply because they may be easier to access. You developed your plan for a reason. Stick to it.

Conduct your interviews face-to-face when possible, but you can do them via phone if necessary. Schedule your interviews for 40 minutes each. However, once you engage you will find people are usually happy to talk so you will likely be able to extend that to an hour. Offer gift cards, if appropriate and legal, or other incentives if you are finding it difficult to get customers to agree to talk. An effective alternative to gift cards is offering to donate to a favorite charity.

3. Conduct the VOC Interviews

When scheduling the interview, explain to the customer the purpose of the project, why they were chosen, how long the interview will take, and set the time and location. Emphasize that the discussion is not a sales or service call, but instead a way to gather information and feedback. Follow up with an email meeting invite so the customer will have it on his or her calendar.

It's best not to ask the customer to sign a media release form during these interviews. You want the discussions to be as casual as possible. If they provide a quote you'd like to include in one of your marketing or social media campaigns, you can always circle back to ask for written approval later.

Setting up customer interviews in-person or phone can drag on for weeks if you are not diligent and focused. Be persistent – don't let the interview phase overly extend your project timeframe.

Recording the Interview

Before beginning the interview, ask for permission to record the conversation. Explain that this frees the interviewers from having to take notes and ensures that they will accurately capture the customers' thoughts and statements. In the very rare cases when the customer decides they don't want to be recorded, graciously accept their decision and end the interview.

Recording retains the answers and needs in the subject's own voice, removing interviewer bias and allowing you to transcribe them word-for-word later. You can jot down a thought you wish to come back to later, but don't try to write down needs - stay focused on the discussion thread.

Conduct the interviews in a quiet room - whether on the phone or face to face - where you and your contact can concentrate without distraction. You'll usually have two people from your company involved with each interview. One person is the main interviewer and the other is there to ask occasional follow-up questions to ensure a need thread is fully explored.

You will uncover qualitative comments, such as feelings, benefits, motivations, and problems as well as quantitative comments, such as who, how many, and how much. You will obtain many more qualitative than quantitative comments, which is good – these are the needs you are after. The quantitative comments are valuable for others to improve the product (valuable for sustaining engineering or service managers), so be sure to forward those quantitative comments to the appropriate managers.

Setting the stage for the interview

- Before you place the call or sit down for the face-to-face meeting, record the name of the company and the person being interviewed, date, and project name. Recording the appropriate setup information at the start of each interview makes it easier to categorize the interview later.

- Begin the interview by explaining to the customer what you are about to do.
- Identify who from your company is taking part in the interview.
- Tell the respondent why he or she was selected.
- Ask for permission to record the interview and explain why it is important to do so.
- Explain that you will be probing for details, so they should expect several follow up questions. Point out that some questions will feel redundant, but that is by design so that you can deeply explore all possible needs along certain important conversation threads and not because you are second guessing their initial response.
- Stress that you are not intentionally asking anything that would be considered confidential.
- Offer a sincere thank you to the respondent for helping you.

Interviewing Techniques

The interview is a guided conversation, not a question and answer interrogation. Prepare both "closed-ended" and "open-ended" questions. Closed-ended questions elicit specific answers to which, who, how many, or how much. For example, "Do you prefer A or B?" "How much should it weigh?" "How long must it last?" Closed-ended questions are used for surveys seeking numerical data or straight yes or no answers. They are not effective for uncovering new information. Closed-ended questions should be used sparingly in VOC customer interviews. I usually only ask them when setting up a new topic. For example, "Are you aware or involved at all with the maintenance of the product?" If the answer is yes, follow-up with open-ended questions. If no, then move onto the next topic.

Your interview should consist mainly of open-ended questions. Open-ended questions require a free-form answer. For example, "Why do you think that?" "What problems does that cause?" "In what way does that help your business?" "How do you decide when to upgrade your system?" These types of questions will best capture interviewee thoughts and provide opportunities to follow a thread to uncover root explanations. Whenever you feel you have identified an important need, paraphrase back to the person being interviewed and ask for clarification. This is the best way to verify that you understand the issue.

Examples of open-ended and closed-ended questions.

"Which do you prefer, A or B?"
Closed – might be a valuable answer to have, but is not uncovering any new needs.

"Why do you prefer that one?"
Open – might uncover a new need, or simply identify the reasoning for selecting one product over another.

"You mentioned you prefer B because it is faster. Can you explain your need for speed?"
Open - following a thread of the conversation to dig deeper to try to uncover the true need.

"So, speed is key because you currently have a bottleneck at this step. Is there any other reason for the bottleneck?"
Open – you have asked three questions on the same thread of exploring option B, and you have followed a thread about speed with two probing questions. Follow the "speed" thread to gain deeper understanding until you're sure there are no new needs to be uncovered by further exploration.

Note: **Things to avoid during interviews**
Here are some things to avoid.
- As you uncover problems guard against the interview becoming a troubleshooting call. Take note of issues, and pass them to the right people for follow up, but don't try to solve anything during the interview.
- Don't try to sell anything during this call. This is not a sales or service call.
- Avoid leading questions like, "You need something to keep your work area organized, don't you?" Or, "Like others I have spoken to, you want deliveries next day AM delivery, correct?

Interview Guide

Prepare 10 to 20 general questions, with in depth follow up questions for each in the event the customer doesn't understand or gives a quick reply – especially if you are speaking to someone who is in a position to provide more information. Use the same template for all customers, but the questions you actually use will depend on how the interview plays out.

When the customer expresses a need, dig in to explore it fully. Stay flexible and omit questions or take them out of order if necessary. Remember, you are going after needs, not trying to get through a list of questions. The interview guide is meant to be an aid, not a constraint. It's perfectly okay to ask questions that occur to you during the conversation, even if they are not in the guide.

Use simple questions to begin. Loosely follow chronologically, starting with the customer's first use of the product and moving to the present state. Start by asking about extremes such as "best" and "worst."

Look for key indicator words such as fast, economical, harsh, reliable, communication, service, difficult, easy, timely, or expensive. When they come up, probe for deeper explanations. Don't be afraid of going on tangents. Remember, the approach is to begin a topic and then hunt for needs, following the natural flow of the conversation. You will complete some interviews only having asked a few questions, and some you will exhaust all your primary and deeper dive questions.

4. Identify and Sort the VOC Needs

After conducting your interviews, we move to step 4 and create your primary needs table. Cull through the typed transcript to find needs and put them into a usable format. The following sequence will help complete the process.

Pull out needs, targets, and solutions: First, transcribe the recorded interviews. Many transcription services are available if you don't have administrative help to type up the recorded interviews for you.

Review the document to highlight needs and paste them verbatim into a spreadsheet. Look for needs that are characteristics or solutions, such as, "Quick load and unload of equipment," and target values, such as, "Unload equipment in 30 seconds." Look for personal comments, such as, "It takes too long to get the equipment unloaded" and for clearly articulated wants and needs, such as, "I want to increase productivity and not waste time loading and unloading my equipment."

Remove duplicates, target values, solutions, and opinions: Review the phrases on your spreadsheet. If a customer's words perfectly describe the need, leave the phrase in quotes and do not change it. This will be helpful when it comes time to use the needs information for content copy. If the answers are not concise, paraphrase the comment and remove the quotation marks. Sort to remove duplicates. The number of times a need is listed isn't relevant.

If you conducted 20 interviews you will likely end up with a list of between 400 and 1000 needs. Removing duplicates will reduce this number to 75 to 300 unique customer need statements.

Remove target values, solutions, and opinions. Your goal is to develop a list of "pure" qualitative needs, devoid of duplicates, target values ("I need 10 of each"), solutions ("If you could just redesign the widget to be thumb operated..."), and opinions ("Blue is cool"). Target values like should be put to the side. This information is valuable to product development and service.

Sort the needs and create the Primary Needs Table: You are now ready to create the all-important primary needs table - a list of 12 to 25 primary needs in three to seven needs families, as illustrated in Figure 2.2. Reduce the needs down to a manageable set to make it simpler for the various departments to work with the data. You want to retain individual needs because they are important when it comes time to use a single primary need.

To create the primary needs table, print each need clearly on a slip of paper so it can be easily handled. Bring in a review team of two or three well-informed customers per end market and conduct a workshop in which they place the needs into related groups. If you are unable to recruit customers, use knowledgeable individuals from within your company, but only as a last resort. Using customers instead of your own staff removes biases and keeps results truly customer driven. This step takes about an hour.

Have the reviewers sort the needs individually, compare results, and then finalize together. Instruct them to look for needs that "go together." Divide large groups into smaller groups. Some may have only one or two needs, and that is acceptable at this point. Later, help the reviewers place these outliers with another needs group when the exercise is completed, or leave them separate if they truly represent a unique customer need. Have the review team create a label that summarizes each needs group. The reviewers keep at it until they have 12 to 25 primary needs grouped in three to seven families. It is important that the reviewers doing the sorting create the label or header so that terms reflect the customer, not the supplier, perspective.

If you end up outside the 12 to 25 groups, coach the reviewers to help them get within that range. In our ABC Custom Truck Works example, you will find three families of primary needs related to service, transportation and performance. These three families contain a total of 14 primary needs (See Figure 2.2).

Before you have customers perform this sorting exercise, I recommend you show them a finished example. Use the example from this book if this is your first attempt.

When finished with these steps you will have created your primary needs table. You and your team should be thrilled for you now have a comprehensive list of primary needs grouped into families. It was created by a careful interview process followed by groupings of needs by your own customers – truly objective results. You now have a clear picture of your target end market, immediately available for use. You will obtain many needs you expected, but others will likely be a surprise.

As a reminder, it is important that you retain the numerous specific needs that comprise each primary need to be leveraged for more detailed analysis later. Many of these needs are in the customers' own words, and provide great insight into each primary need. If one of the primary needs was "Advanced User Training," then the individual needs that comprised that group will be helpful when the service team looks to create new customer training content.

5. Conduct the broad customer rating email survey

Getting to this point requires a significant amount of time and resources. Your new primary needs table can be used immediately, but by conducting one final step you will be assured of getting the most out of your VOC research efforts. With this step you will create your market opportunity map.

This last phase involves surveying a large audience of customers within your target market and asking them to rate each primary need on two criteria: importance to them and your company's performance in delivering on that need. Email the survey to a large enough group to ensure 50 to 300 responses

– the more responses the better. Make sure to cover a comprehensive cross section of your target market.

Here is a four-step process for conducting the email survey.

1. Find an online survey company. If you're surveying a global market, select a vendor capable of handling an international program. Translate as needed. Always track the survey recipients so you can sort the results based on demographic variations if necessary.

Some leading companies that conduct these types of surveys include Survey Monkey, Typeform, Google Forms, Zoho Surveys, Survey Gizmo, Survey Planet, Campaign Monitor, Zoomerang, GetFeedback, Checkbox, eSurveysPro, SoGoSurvey, and FluidSurveys.

2. Create the email survey. Use best practices in the email design to help ensure high open and click through rates (see Solution 4 *Generating More Leads*). Ask each respondent to rate your final 12 to 25 primary needs per the Likert scale.

For each need, you'll ask them to respond to two questions:

"On a scale of 1 to 10 with 10 being most important, how important is this need to you?"

"On a scale of 1 to 10 with 10 being outstanding performance, how does the product you are currently using perform regarding this need?"

While you are in this process of surveying a wide range of your customers, consider adding a third question: The Net Promoter Score (NPS) question. Your NPS score will provide a general snapshot of your company's service performance in just one question. The question is:

"How likely are you to recommend ABC Custom Truck Works to a friend or colleague?"

Then subtract the percentage of "Detractor" customers who rated you 1 to 6 from those "Promoter" customers who rated you 9 or 10 and you have your score. Passive ratings of 7 or 8 are not involved in the calculation. Above 50 is generally considered good.

Keep in mind you are surveying a subset of your overall market in this VOC research, so you are not obtaining the NPS for a full cross section of all customers. Still, you will gain value from adding this one additional question.

Most companies who conduct NPS research do so annually to track performance changes.

3. Send the email survey. Send the survey out to as large an audience as you can. Cover your customers within your target market. The response rate to your email survey will depend on your end market, the title of the person you are trying to reach, and the closeness of the relationship you hold with your customers. You can expect a two to five percent response rate. That will rise to eight to 12 percent when you add an incentive. If you anticipate that even with an incentive, you will not get enough responses, consider preceding the survey with one phone call asking for their support. Even if you only leave a message, you will greatly increase your response rate. Use the same email best practice techniques you would for a marketing campaign (see Solution 4 Generate More Leads).

4. Scrub results and normalize the data. Once you have your data, build your market opportunity map (Figure 2.3). This will provide a clear picture of your areas of strength that you should promote more heavily, areas where you need to improve your offerings, and the priorities that are truly important to the target market.

Eliminate responses that follow a pattern that suggests the respondent did not take the survey seriously (all 10's, all 1's, alternating 1 and 2, etc.). This happens more often when you offer an incentive, and less often if you make a phone call to your customer before you send the email.

To create a usable market opportunity map, normalize the data so it plots correctly on a 2x2 grid. Normalize the data by making the Y axis min and max equal the smallest and largest average number of any importance rating, respectively. Similarly, the maximum and minimum average values found in any performance rating become the max and min for the X axis. If you have 25 primary needs, you will plot 25 points on Figure 2.7, delivering your results in Figure 2.8. With the needs plotted, add in the two lines to divide the quadrants.

How to Normalize and Plot the Data

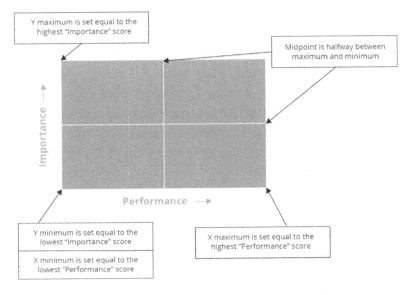

Data Plots for Market Opportunity Map

Weaknesses	Strengths
◎ Price appropriate for service and capability	◎ Full coverage service plans
◎ Labor pool of experienced workers for overflow ◎ Highly maneuverable parking	◎ Integrated trailer braking system Rapid unload, ◎ load capability ◎ Highly configurable and changeable bed layout
Monitor	**Over Emphasized**
◎ Rental programs for work overflow ◎ Extremely easy to keep spotless ◎ User friendly cabin	◎ Emergency support 24/7 ◎ Attractive, classy, functional parking flashers ◎ Safe fuel transportation ◎ Facilitate impressive branding

Importance ⟶
(customer rating of importance regarding that need)

Performance ⟶
(customer rating of satisfaction regarding that need)

◎ Figure 2.8 Plotted data points on your Market Opportunity Map for ABC Custom Truck Works landscaper market.

57

Figure 2.8 shows the results of plotting the average value for each of the 12 to 25 primary needs of ABC Custom Truck Works' market.

Some needs are on the borderline of moving from one quadrant to another, and other needs rank very low in importance. Both results are normal and acceptable. In the example, ABC Custom Truck Works should not disregard the "User Friendly Cabin" need simply because it rated the lowest in importance. All primary needs and are important. There might be 10 percent of potential customers in ABC's market that won't buy a vehicle if it doesn't have a top notch, user friendly cabin. The market opportunity map simply shows the importance of needs as they relate to each other. The plotted version of Figure 2.8 is typically not shared with anyone outside the VOC research team. It's better to show the data represented as shown in Figure 2.3 to your company departments.

ABC's completed market opportunity map (Figure 2.3) represents a clear picture of market needs and priorities. When reviewing this chart, consider the four quadrants of the market opportunity map as described in Figure 2.9.

Description of Market Opportunity Quadrants

	Weaknesses	Strengths
Importance → (customer rating of importance regarding that need)	Customers are not very satisfied with these important needs. Improve your performance as soon as possible.	Customers are relatively satisfied with these important needs. Promote your capabilities here.
	Monitor	**Over Emphasized**
	Customers are not very satisfied with these needs, but the needs are less important to them. There might be hidden opportunities here.	Customers are relatively satisfied with these less important needs. You might not need to put as much effort into improving or promoting these needs.

Performance →
(customer rating of satisfaction regarding that need)

◎ Figure 2.9 A guide for interpreting each quadrant of the Market Opportunity Map.

Your VOC project might be small, and may not require this comprehensive AMS approach. Sometimes all you need is to visit with a few customers. But if uncovering *all* your fundamental customer needs is critical, this process will deliver valuable guidance for many departments in your company.

Voice of the Market (VOM) Research

VOM takes a broader view than VOC research. VOM considers market drivers, competitive landscape, pricing, market growth rate, and channels. VOM research provides information about the overall market and competition that guides company strategy, and helps you better utilize your VOC data. It is most effective to present your VOC research as part of an overall VOM analysis.

The primary components of a thorough VOM analysis include:

- VOC analysis
- Market sizing
- Market growth rate
- Market channels
- Competitive analysis

Market Sizing

With the first component – VOC analysis – covered previously in this solution chapter, we continue on with Market Sizing.

An obvious key component of voice of the market research is the sizing of the market. Markets can be described as shown in Figure 1.4. When researching the market size of a target end market, focus on either the Serviceable Available Market (SAM) or the Serviceable Obtainable Market (SOM). See Solution 1 *Finding your Best End Markets* for more on the use of Figure 1.4.

Market Potential Definitions

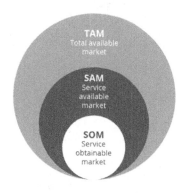

© Figure 1.4 A common depiction of the market universe.

To determine the market size, research trade associations that cover your target end market. Trade associations have a vested long-term interest in providing accurate data to the companies within their target market. Other sources, such as market research firms, conduct research annually (as opposed to continuously as the trade associations do) and their goal is to sell reports. I have found that market research firms provide wildly optimistic forecasts in hopes of selling their report to those in search of wildly optimistic forecasts.

You will also need to conduct your own research. Consider using NAICS analysis through resources such as D&B Hoovers. NAICS is the North American Industry Code System where nearly every business has a code that describes their industry. Although called the "North American" Industry Code System, it is a global database. Hoovers enables you to conduct your own research. Find the NAICS codes for companies in your target end market and identify all other companies with that same NAICS code. NAICs are not always accurate, so scrub your lists carefully.

Market Growth Rate

Compound Annual Growth Rate (CAGR) is a market growth rate analysis that is analogous to the way money grows in a bank via interest rate. If a $1 billion market grows by five percent each year, then in five years the CAGR expands to $1.28 billion.

Shrinking markets are often filled with companies on tight budgets, so it is less likely that these companies will purchase a high-dollar product or service. Conversely, companies in growing markets are more likely to make investments in high-dollar equipment. That's the fundamental reason why banks and investors want to know the CAGR of your target market.

Larger markets often have analyst reports that provide past CAGR and forecast future data. But – as mentioned above – beware of market research firms who tend to inflate CAGRs to sell reports. Historic CAGR data will be accurate, but for predictions you're better served getting forecasted CAGR data from more objective sources, like trade associations.

Market Channels

The topic of channels can be wide ranging, but VOM analysis looks at a narrow perspective of customer preferences. You need to understand the ways in which prospects and customers prefer to purchase products or services - from the original equipment manufacturers (OEM), retailers, value-added resellers, or distributors.

For high dollar sales, some buyers prefer to purchase as much as possible from a single source – the top of the pyramid. If you are the full system provider, then these buyers will tend to prefer to buy from you. If you are a component supplier to a system, then the buyer will tend to want to purchase from the system integrator. In this case, you will need to be ready to sell to those atop the pyramid. Your sales channel should be aligned with how the buyer prefers to purchase.

Competition Analysis

Companies with healthy commercial engines conduct competitive analysis[3] constantly. Keep your competitive data current and accurate.

Competitive Analysis Using Outside Resources

When you need a deep dive into the competition, decide if you will do the work internally, or outsource a portion to an outside market research firm. There are benefits to both approaches. When conducting the work yourself, there is no need for education on the market or the products. You and your staff know the competitors, and will generally be quick to identify what's important. Conversely, an outside marketing agency typically has a standard approach to conducting objective competitive research and is adept at it. They can be more skilled at obtaining competitive information using approaches that may be unfamiliar to you.

Competition: Product Comparison

The format *Consumer Reports* uses (black and red circles partially or completely filled in) is particularly effective in providing quick, clear information on product comparisons. Since creating a Consumer Reports-like table can pose formatting challenges in most document creation applications, I use a simple 5-star system as a visual way to compare. It is easy to create and read. Figure 2.10 is an example of ABC Custom Truck Works.

Primary Needs Competitive Comparison

	Ours	Theirs		
	Landscaper line	A	B	C
Service Needs				
Full coverage service plans	****	*****	*	**
Emergency support 24/7	***	***	*	*
Rental programs for work overflow	*	*	*	*
Labor pool of experienced workers for overflow	*	*	*	*
Transport Needs				
User friendly cabin	**	*	*****	***
Highly maneuverable parking	*	*	***	****
Integrated trailer braking system	****	**	*****	*
Attractive, classy, functional parking flashers	***	*	****	*****
Facilitate impressive branding	***	*	***	*****
Performance Needs				
Rapid unload, load capability	*****	**	*	***
Safe fuel transportation	**	*	*	****
Highly configurable and changeable bed layout	****	***	*****	*****
Price appropriate for service and capability	**	*	*	*
Extremely easy to keep spotless	*	*	***	***

◎ Table 2.10 An example for ABC Custom Truck Works of the Primary Needs Competitive Comparison Table, utilizing a simple 5-star rating system.

The star approach provides the reader with a visual way to compare competition. Don't just compare random features, but instead focus on comparing *primary customer needs*. This helps you keep the customer viewpoint at the forefront and prevents becoming sidetracked by unimportant competitive issues or inconsequential features. It also avoids designing the chart based on your products, which will give you an overly optimistic rating. Use primary needs as your starting point - it will improve the integrity of your analysis.

As illustrated in Figure 2.10, ABC Custom Truck Works has a current advantage in *"Rapid unload/load capability."* ABC should promote this advantage heavily. They also have an opportunity in the unmet needs of *"Rental programs for work overflow,"* and for *"Labor pool of experienced workers for overflow."* None of the competition performs well in these categories, so ABC Custom Truck Works can differentiate itself by creating new support programs. They should also promote "Service plans," and "24/7 support" – areas in which they have reasonable strength compared to the competition.

Competitive Pricing and Win Rate Analysis

Providing a price comparison table is valuable for trend analysis. Such analysis can be tough to put together for some high dollar complex system where it is common to have many different possible configurations. You are often left with an "apples to oranges" competitive comparison. Still, reviewing competitive pricing on an ongoing basis is important. Make sure to set up a system to track competitive prices on jobs you win and lose, keeping notes on configurations and options.

Win rate is another way to gauge the competitiveness of your pricing. A quick way to calculate win rate is to take the number of closed sales divided by the number of new sales-ready projects that were presented to you. Although win rate can vary by industry and strength of competition, most B2B companies with comprehensive win rate tracking strive for a win rate of 50 percent or better with acceptable profit. A win rate below 30 percent could mean your prices are too high, but that is only one potential cause. Resolve other potential factors such as inadequate sales training, ineffective messaging and collateral, insufficient solutions offered, or poor reputation before lowering prices too much.

Data analysis isn't enough to truly understand win rate and pricing. Marketers should talk to and travel with successful sales people to participate in the sales process, understand market dynamics, and uncover root causes for lost orders. Experience the competitive battles to get a true sense of how and why your organization is winning or losing orders.

Sales people will often push for price reductions since they face price pressure every day from potential customers and competitive offerings. But in reality, the problem is always more multi-faceted than simply pricing. For high dollar products and services, the company and salesperson that wins the order creates the perception of value, gains credibility, reduces risk, and builds a vision of success in the potential customer's mind. Help your sales staff by providing new tools and training to create better value in the potential customer's eyes (see Solution 6, *Building a Great Sales Team*).

Competitor SWOT Analysis

The SWOT (strengths, weaknesses, opportunities, and threats) analysis is another effective way to evaluate each of your competitors.

Strengths: A competitor's strengths, as perceived by the customers. What unique capabilities set this competitor apart from others? What are the primary reasons prospects purchase from them? Consider the competitor's attributes, such as their ability to provide value, the intellectual property they hold, their accessibility to the market, their ability to innovate, and their marketing and sales ability.

Weaknesses: A competitor's weaknesses, as perceived by customers. What is likely to cause them to lose business? How do you win orders versus this competitor today? Consider their shortcomings in their ability to provide value, accessibility to the market, ability to innovate, and marketing and salesmanship ability.

Opportunities: The opportunities that lie ahead for this competitor to exploit. What trends or market conditions could prove favorable to this competitor? What capabilities or market positions do they possess that can help them grow their business? What opportunities do their strengths provide?

Threats: The threats this competitor faces. What trends or market conditions could prove unfavorable to this competitor? What are their competitors doing that might negatively impact them? What threats do their weaknesses pose?

Also consider the following items as they relate to your most successful competitors.

- Channel strategy
- Key market differentiators
- Unique selling proposition
- Ways they win against you and how you win against them (see Solution 6 *Building a Great Sales Team*)
- Market share
- Growth rate
- Service level

Using the VOM and VOC Research

Properly compiling and presenting your VOM/VOC research can energize your entire organization. The information lets production know you have a firm grasp on the market and can sustain the unit volumes. Engineering will be inspired to improve and replace products. Sales will adjust their approach to better align with the customers. Leadership will confidently create customer-centric strategies and programs.

The full VOM/VOC report should contain:

1. Research approach, team, reasons it was conducted, ways it should be used.
   Explain that the focus is on identifying customer needs by uncovering the voice of the customer, but also includes VOM information that presents an overall picture of the market and its customers.
2. VOM overview
   VOC results, competitive analysis, market sizing, market growth rate, market channels.
3. VOC detail

Discussion of the research technique to highlight its thoroughness, primary needs table (Figure 2.2) and market opportunity map (Figure 2.3).

4. VOM detail excluding VOC

    Step through the competitive analysis, Competitive Comparison Chart (Figure 2.10), market sizing and CAGR, and channels.

5. Go Forward Recommendations

    Discuss how the information will be used by marketing to strengthen messaging, improve lead generation campaigns, create more relevant content for lead nurturing, and enhance sales training. Make recommendations on ways the report can be leveraged in other departments such as new product development. Suggest each department study the details of each primary need to determine how best to apply the information in their areas.

Consider putting together a summary version of the VOM/VOC report to be shared with everyone in the organization. Highlight the key points and focus on primary needs, the customer personas, and the ways in which each individual can play a role in fulfilling them.

Summary

The basis of the buying and selling relationship is the fulfillment of needs. Your customers need products or services to help them do their jobs, and you must know what those needs are so you can effectively fulfill them. Needs analysis is fundamental to many parts of your business. Understanding and developing strategies to act on customer needs will set you apart from the competition.

The information you gain by uncovering the voice of the customer will help you sustain your business and inspire the leaders in your organization. One word of caution: as valuable as the data is, it is not static. It evolves over time as the needs of your customers change. Plan on conducting the process again in three years – or sooner if you're in an industry where technology changes rapidly. Your customers are always evolving, and you must commit to changing with them if you hope to succeed in a competitive economy.

Solution 2 References

1. Applied Marketing Science, Waltham, MA, http://www.ams-inc.com/. A good reference paper is *The Voice of the Customer,* Abbie Griffin, John R. Hauser, ©1993, The Institute of Management Sciences/Operational Research Society of America 0732-2399/93/1201/0001$.1.25, http://www.mit.edu/~hauser/Papers/TheVoiceoftheCustomer.pdf
2. The explanation of the AMS approach is used by permission of Applied Marketing Science, Gerry Katz, vice chairman and board member for AMS.
3. *How to Conduct Competitive Research*, blog, by the staff at Inc., who references Ken Garrison, chief executive officer of the Society of Competitive Intelligence Professionals, http://www.inc.com/guides/2010/05/conducting-competitive-research.html

Solution 3: Creating Great Messaging

When it comes time to write copy, many marketers grab a pen, paper, and start writing. For some, maybe that works. However, strong brands and category leaders are backed by advanced marketing teams that understand how compelling messaging helps fuel the commercial engine.

Your messaging is one of the key building blocks of your marketing and sales commercial engine. It is used to create all external and some internal collateral, and should be embedded in sales training. It is connected to who you are, what you represent, and your company vision/mission statements – your brand. It tightly connects to the customer needs of your target markets.

Path to a Strong Commercial Engine

◎ Figure 1.1 Messaging is a major building block to a healthy commercial engine (image repeated from Solution 1).

Messaging is a set of high-level points or ideas used to create content for an audience to remember and hopefully act upon. Messaging provides the guideposts for your communications, not verbatim copy.

Many manufacturing companies place much of their energy on product design and production. They don't see messaging as vital to their business success. They fail to carefully create, organize, or use it. The result? Content creation takes a long time, and the delivered message is inconsistent. Though common themes may sometimes reappear, the lack of consistency has a negative impact on brand and business.

It can take over seven interactions with a potential customer for them to consider becoming a lead.[1] You'll need even more touchpoints if your messaging is not consistent. Cutting through the hundreds of ads, logos, and offers your target audience is exposed to every day takes compelling and consistent messaging.[2,3] Formally establishing key messaging points enables anyone in the organization – from a junior marketing associate to the VP of Marketing – to quickly create effective content.

Print your messaging, have it pinned on cubicle walls of marketing and sales staff, and ensure it is evangelized by leadership. Constantly leveraging your messaging strengthens your business.

The Benefits of Messaging Hierarchy

Your company's messaging is an interconnected collection of ideas. It starts when you build your vision/mission statements – setting a philosophical foundation. From that point you begin the creation of messaging with the company brand messaging, then move to end market and product messaging, and eventually to individual promotion messaging.

This hierarchal structure, as shown in Figure 3.1, carries your themes and ideas throughout, presenting cohesive company meaning to both internal and external audiences.

Messaging Hierarchy

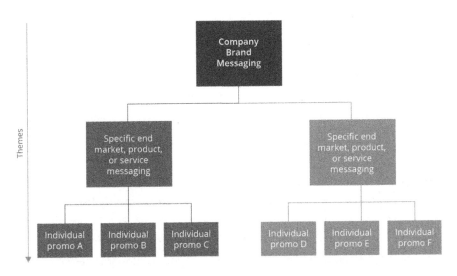

◎ Figure 3.1 Messaging hierarchy drives message consistency and your brand.

But how do you create the various levels of messaging your company requires. Where do you start? By using a proven tool and process that ensures you develop appropriate messaging at every level.

The Barbell Messaging Creation Exercise™.

Over the years I a process I call *The Barbell Messaging Creation Exercise™*, or Barbell for short. It's called a Barbell because the visual form on the worksheet is shaped like a Barbell and it also makes your messaging stronger.

The Barbell is used to create messaging for **all levels of the hierarchy** – from the company brand messaging, to product messaging, to individual promotional pieces. The Barbell concept is my version of a standard marketing approach that has been around for decades: *Move the audience from a current belief and behavior to a future belief and behavior*. The outputs of the exercise are a Unique Selling Proposition (USP) and support points.

Barbell Message Creation Concept

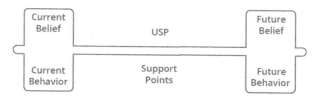

◎ Figure 3.2 The Barbell Message Creation Exercise™ helps you create great messaging by moving the audience from current belief and behavior to future belief and behavior via the Unique Selling Proposition and the associated support points.

The Barbell exercise is used over and over throughout the messaging hierarchy, from company brand messaging atop the hierarchy tiers to specific promotion pieces at the bottom. The USP and Support Points developed by each Barbell are used to create content. This message creation process will improve your messaging, whether you are a seasoned pro or a new marketer.

Note: **Messaging involves themes and ideas – not copy**
You are not creating content or copy with the Barbell. The results are *not meant to be used verbatim*. The USP's and Support Points you develop set the overall themes for your content creation and help you efficiently write the specific copy for the piece you are creating.

When it comes time to write a piece of marketing or sales material you will use the output of the Barbell – the USP and support points – to craft your copy and guide the graphical design.

The Barbell exercise is a single page worksheet as shown in Figure 3.3. The layout helps keep you on task, allowing you to see the whole process on one page. You can move around and refine any portion while you work through the process. It's is easy to learn, and once mastered, becomes a key tool for creating messages.

Barbell Template

Current Belief (4)

What do people currently believe about the subject?

Do they even know it exists?

What are the pre-conceived notions that we are fighting in the field?

What weaknesses are we trying to overcome?

Current Behavior (2)

What reaction is caused by the current belief?

How do people respond to the current belief in the marketplace?

What: What exactly are we trying to define? What subject are we describing? (1)

Vehicle: What is the medium that we will convey the message to the recipient? Website, literature, ad, etc.?

Who: Who is the primary audience?

Tone: What do we want to sound like? This dictates word choice and overall feeling we want to convey.

Unique Selling Proposition (USP) (7)

This is the bridge, or vehicle that will get you from the current to the future. This single promise is the primary outcome from this exercise. It will drive all communications relating to the subject. It is not a tagline.

Support Points (6)

1. Support point 1. These points are connected to the future beliefs and are the means to move people from the current to future belief. The facts and data that make the future beliefs real and back up your USP. Sprinkle these facts within your document as ways to solidify the USP to your audience. These bullets reflect support point 1

2. Support point 2
   These bullets reflect support point 2

3. Support point 3 (if necessary)
   These bullets reflect support point 3

4. Support point 4 (if necessary)
   These bullets reflect support point 4

Future Belief (5)

Ultimately, what do we WANT people to believe about our subject in an ideal situation.

These beliefs can have some emotion in them. Consider starting each sentence in your mind with, "I believe ..."

These are not features, they are benefits the customer will believe if your USP and Support Points do their job.

Future Behavior (3)

How do we want people to react or what action do we want people to take towards our subject. THIS IS THE OVERALL GOAL.

© Figure 3.3 The Barbell Messaging Creation Exercise™ worksheet.

As you follow the numbered sequence of the Barbell exercise, keep your statements concise and to the point. Describing your thoughts in succinct phrases is challenging, but necessary if you hope to produce usable results. Create a first draft with your cross functional team. You can refine later by yourself or with the help of another expert. A completed Barbell is shown in Figure 3.4 for ABC Custom Truck Works. You can find the Barbell template at https://fairmontconcepts.com/tools-templates.

Follow these steps when working through the Barbell Exercise.

1. Purpose of the messaging

WHAT: What is the topic of the messaging? A new product? A promotion? Are you creating a new company website, promoting a new high-tech product, or creating a webinar?

WHO: Determine your target audience. Sounds obvious, but I've seen marketers consistently miss this step and then struggle to create their piece. Your target audience might be the specific end market leads in your database, or existing customers who might want service options, or potential customers attending a trade show. In addition, consider what role the audience tends to have – messaging to the CEO is different than messaging to a purchasing agent. It is important that you carefully determine who will be consuming the messaging. The more narrowly defined your target audience, the greater the chance your messaging will resonate with them.

VEHICLE: How are you going to deliver your messaging? Will it reach the audience via your website, an email, an advertisement, a trade show display?

TONE: What tone do you want your message to have? The tone must be appropriate for the application. Depending on the application, it might be authoritative, technical, sexy, elite, strong, trustworthy or whimsical. Your tone is different if your buyer persona tends to be an engineer, as compared to an artist, small business owner, or CEO of a large firm.

2 & 3. Current behavior and future behavior

How is the target audience behaving now? How do you want them to behave in the future? Future behavior is connected to your CTA (Call to Action).

This section typically includes one concise bullet for the current and one for the future behavior. Examples of the current behavior of a potential customer are:

"I will not fill out the contact information card on your website."

"I will not consider your company as a vendor."

"I will walk by your trade show booth without engagement."

Examples of future behavior of a potential customer after your messaging has done its job are:

"I will fill out the contact card."

"I will call ABC company." "I will inquire at your trade show booth."

"I will sign up for the webinar."

In high dollar sales, you don't want to be unrealistically aggressive, such as listing a future behavior of, "Buy all of my products at full price." Think about the call to action that advances the project.

4 & 5. Current belief and future belief

Again, keep these statements concise and to the point. Current belief statements should be limited to 6 to 12 items and your future belief statements should answer the current belief statements. You may insert some emotion into these statements.

A current belief should describe the attitude of your audience today – how they see your company and offerings today and what problems they face.

Here are some possible current beliefs about ABC Custom Truck Works.

o   I don't know who ABC Truck Works is.

o   ABC is too expensive.

o   A new landscaper truck won't make my job easier.

Here are other current beliefs associated with the typical problems and needs of a landscaper.

o   I must keep my workers safe.

o   I need to complete jobs faster.

o   Idle labor kills my profit.

o   I can't configure the truck myself.

o   I must have complete reliability.

A future belief is what you want the target audience to believe after they have consumed your messaging. Developing your current and future belief statements require careful thought. You are not focusing on features, but instead are looking to communicate an understanding of the benefits your product or service offers.

As you create these statements, imagine starting each phrase with "I believe..." Examples of desired future beliefs include:

- I'll have great ROI with this truck.
- I will complete jobs faster.
- The new design will save project time and gas.
- ABC will help me configure the flatbed properly.
- This equipment will help keep my workers safe.
- I can get high-end jobs.
- ABC vehicles are reliable.

Make sure you are answering the current belief statements with your future belief statements.

6 & 7 Support points and the USP

It's time now to create the output of the Barbell exercise. You will use the messaging of items 6 and 7 when creating copy. Develop the support points and the unique selling proposition together, while constantly referencing the future belief section.

Develop two to five factual support points. These points reflect on your future beliefs and back up your USP. Each of the support points has sub-points and facts that provide further detail.

The unique selling proposition, sometimes also called a unique singular promise, is a short phrase that summarizes the support points and forms the bridge between the current and future beliefs. You will be developing the USP along with the support points, shifting between both as you work to conclusion.

The more iterations you put into your USP and support points, the better your results. It's common to come back to your completed Barbell the next day and refine it further. By revisiting the document, you'll find you can shorten the phrases, clarify the intent, and delete unimportant items. The more concise it is, the more useful it will be when the time comes to create marketing content.

Note: **Messaging is about benefits and value**

Ultimately messaging is about benefits and value derived from features and capabilities that solve a potential customer's problem or improves their situation. Your messaging needs to be truthful, not hype or exaggeration that will ultimately compromise your credibility. Work hard on your Barbell and you'll find that truth. Focus on benefits where you excel, and where those benefits are supported by features and capabilities.

Example Barbell

ABC Custom Work Trucks modifies pickup trucks and vans for electricians, landscapers and carpenters who then perform contract work for private residences and businesses.

ABC's goal is to create messaging for a new line of landscaper flatbed pickup trucks. The company's high-end custom trucks are typically 15 percent more expensive than competitive offerings, so their messaging must show the value and ROI that a more capable – and higher priced - product provides.

Looking at ABC's messaging hierarchy, they are going to create messaging for the 2nd level, *Specific End Market or Product Messaging* (the middle tier of Figure 3.1).

They start by collecting their company brand messaging (the messaging level above this tier level), technical specs, competitive information, Feature Function Benefit documents (described at the end of this solution chapter), and all other relevant information. They are especially interested in the voice of the customer data. They send the collected information to their team made up of marketing staff, sales reps, and technical experts. A few days later, they meet for the first time to create a Barbell draft.

It took a second meeting followed by some individual work by the team leader to refine the Barbell to the level of Figure 3.4. The result delivers a USP and three sets of prioritized support points the team feels will work well as the basis for creating compelling landscaper flatbed truck copy.

Barbell Example - ABC Custom Truck Works

Current Belief (4)

I don't know who ABC Custom Truck Works is

Any flatbed will do the job for me
There is no technology in a flatbed landscaper truck

A new landscaper truck can't make my job easier

I will never get an ROI on a high end landscaping truck

I don't need a fancy service plan

A truck can't promote my brand

I don't know how to configure the truck myself

ABC is too expensive

Current Behavior (2)

Do not consider or contact ABC Custom Truck Works.

What: New line of high-end landscaping flatbed pickup trucks

Vehicle: General marketing pieces regarding the new trucks. This is not for a specific promo piece, but is for the general landscaping truck product line

Who: Commercial landscapers $1 to $5m/yr, US only, serving private residences and commercial properties

Tone: Trustworthy, dependable, thoughtful design

---

(7) Complete landscaping jobs faster with the latest ABC Custom Truck

---

Support Points (6)

1. New technology reduces project time
   Quick load tractor design cuts load/unload time in half
   Low profile flatbed reduces load space for work on busy streets
   Integrated flashers keep workers safe and look great
   Aerodynamic fairing saves 5% on fuel and provides logo location

2. I can trust ABC Custom Truck Works
   A leader, with hundreds supplied in this region
   Since 1985. Designed and manufactured by ABC
   Hundreds of custom options to fit your specific business needs
   Great 3 year service plans, emergency towing, 24/7
   Proven ROI of 2 years under medium usage

3. Improve my business
   Curb appeal for word of mouth: Look like a step above the rest
   Expand into profitable high end homes and commercial
   Shorter project time: lower labor cost, more jobs per day
   More profit per job

Future Belief (5)

ABC makes the best landscaper trucks

ABC is a leader in customizing landscaping trucks with hundreds of options

Great new technology: Quick-load design will save me time on the start and end to every job, fairing saves gas

The integrated road flashers look terrific and will make my workers safer

Signage branding options will raise my brand image, help me expand to the high end clients, and charge more

I'll have a great ROI

The 3 year service plan saves me money and keeps me running

They'll help me configure it just right

Future Behavior (3)

Contact ABC Customer Truck Works about their new landscaping truck

© Figure 3.4 An example barbell exercise for messaging for a new line of landscaper flatbed vehicles from ABC Custom Truck Works.

Once you and your team master the Barbell Exercise, you can use it to create the USP and Support points for every level of your messaging hierarchy. It becomes the crucial first step you take before you begin creating any type of marketing content. One Barbell can be used for many pieces of content, as long as the topic remains the same.

Company Brand Messaging

Company brand messaging is your highest messaging tier. It is usually more complex and extensive than other messages.

The company's brand messaging includes foundational themes found in your vision/mission statements. This brand messaging explains to the marketplace the reason you are in business and outlines your fundamental attributes. It is an expression of your company's direction and what you want to say to your target end markets. It is used when creating messaging for the company website, corporate brochure, corporate video, investor presentations, annual report, or ads promoting brand awareness.

Use the Barbell to create this messaging with your company leaders to ensure strategic accuracy, and widespread adoption.

Your company should print out your company brand messaging and provide it to commercial leaders and executives. I call company brand messaging "Blue Statements." The name is intended to be memorable and to make sure everyone knows they are special. When completed, I recommend you organize the messaging onto a single sheet of paper.

I have found that most companies can break down their company brand messaging into three categories. Three are enough to encompass a company position while being easily remembered and referenced. It can be difficult to boil down to only three, but enforcing this discipline ensures you select only the top ideas.

Start by meeting with company leaders and commercial managers to identify the three main statement topics. Manufacturing companies often choose three out of these ideas: company credibility, technology, leadership, service, offerings, performance/productivity, and ROI.

Once the three company brand topics have been selected, work with the team to flesh out each. You will use the Barbell exercise three times to create the three sets of USP and support points for the company brand messaging – the Blue Statements. Here is an example using ABC Customer Truck Works.

ABC wants to create new company brand messaging, a.k.a. Blue Statements. They come up with three topics that match their company attributes and strategy: 1) Project completion speed, 2) Greater performance through advanced technology, and 3) Company credibility - culture, stability and service

These three topics will be their set of company brand messages – their Blue Statements. ABC then conducts the Barbell Exercise for each of the following three Blue Statements. They then put the results of all three Barbell exercises onto one sheet of paper.

Example of Company Brand Messaging

ABC Custom Truck Works

Company Brand Messaging

Trust ABC to make your custom truck your most valued asset

Complete work faster "Faster work means more work"	Technology and performance "Technology and convenience born from experience"	The Company "Trust ABC Custom Truck Works"
Rapid unload, load capability	**Our technology**	**Service**
· Air assist lift gates on trailers with safety proximity sensors	· Custom configurations for . every need	· Full coverage service plans
· Automatic wheel chucks	· Pre-engineered - not one offs. If you need it, we've done it	· Emergency 24/7 support
· Flexi-bed: most versatile equipment hold down	· Exclusive technology - 14 patents proven to help you	· Rental programs for work overflow
· Flexi-net: instant fuel hold down system		**Our expertise**
· Small tool quick access system	**We sweat the details**	· 30 years experience Landscaper trucks and trailers,
	· Countless small details learned over the years	· Plumber vans, Carpenter vans and trucks
Keep 'em safe	· Driver conveniences include the most user friendly cabin, integrated trailer braking	· All engineering and customizations done in-house
· High-vis parking flashers		
· Automatic emergency braking		**Your local business partner**
· Lane change proximity warning on all vehicles and even trailers	**The look you need**	· Tri-State coverage: New Jersey, New York, Connecticut
· No-roll parking	· The most branding options - your truck is your billboard	· 5 full service and sales locations
· Safe fuel transport	· Vehicle is "dressed for success"	· In-house financing
		· Hundreds of testimonials

◎ Figure 3.5 Example of ABC Custom Truck Works company brand messaging, which I call "Blue Statements."

ABC now has the Blue Statements that will be used to create brand-related collateral, and the themes from these three statements will filter down into all levels of the messaging hierarchy. As you can see in Figure 3.5, each column is the result of a Barbell message creation exercise. The first column, for example, used a Barbell to create a USP of "Complete Work Faster", and two support points were created, each with facts to back up the support points. Another Barbell was used to create the 2nd column, and another for the 3rd. A blank template for company brand messaging follows.

These are not tag lines or phrases to be used verbatim. They are ABC's company brand themes. For convenience, download a blank template (See Figure 3.6) at https://fairmontconcepts.com/tools-templates.

Company Brand Messaging Template

[enter: Topic of this messaging, such as "ABC Inc."]

Brand Messaging for the Company

[enter: Overall Unique Selling Prop]

| [enter: Brand statement #1] | [enter: Brand statement #2] | [enter: Brand statement #3] |
| ["USP for statement #1"] | ["USP for statement #2"] | ["USP for statement #3"] |

Support Point 1
(fact supporting blue statement 1)
· Bullets substantiating the
  support point
·
·

Support Point 2
· Bullets substantiating the
  support point
·
·

Support Point 3
· Bullets substantiating the
  support point
·
·

Support Point 1
(fact supporting blue statement 2)
· Bullets substantiating the
  support point
·
·

Support Point 2
· Bullets substantiating the
  support point
·
·

Support Point 1
(fact supporting blue statement 3)
· Bullets substantiating the
  support point
·
·

Support Point 2
· Bullets substantiating the
  support point
·
·

Support Point 3
· Bullets substantiating the
  support point
·
·

Support Point 4
· Bullets substantiating the
  support point
·
·

◎ Figure 3.6 A template for your Company Brand Messaging.

The statements reflect the company's capabilities in a broad sense and speak to all target markets. The three Blue Statements representing the company brand messaging is a company-wide strategic communication tool and should be updated every few years. Themes will follow the message hierarchy and cascade down to product and then to promotional messaging as shown in Figure 3.1.

Note: **Creating your vision/mission statements**

A mission statement explains a reason for a company's existence, usually in one sentence. A vision describes a desired future state, and is usually a few sentences or short list of concise statements.

Every company should identify and communicate their reason for being to their staff and to the marketplace. If you don't have vision/mission statements, it's time to develop them. Effective vision/mission statements should contribute themes to your highest tier messaging – your company brand messaging.

Usually the senior staff or company owners create the vision and mission statements, not marketing. If you are involved in the creation of these statements you can utilize the Barbell exercise to create the message themes. When it comes time to create the statements, view them as a conversation with all members of your team, your best customers, your target end market prospects and customers, your bankers and investors, and your partners (suppliers, indirect sales channels).

Things to consider as you develop your vision statement include:
- Stress substance over vague statements
- Think far into the future
- Concentrate on realistic expectations and avoid ambitious goals
- Align with the needs of your best customers
- Boil your philosophical ideas and values down into short statements that will support a brand image and will inspire buy-in from the staff
- Consider how you want your staff, your customers, and society to feel

It is important that the vision/mission statements are owned by the company leaders, and accurately reflects your company. If not, disseminating them will do more harm than good – especially in the eyes of your employees. If you need inspiration, check out the websites of Fortune 500 companies for thoughtful examples.

Specific End Market, Product, or Service Messaging

These messages are in the second tier of Figure 3.1. They relate to the voice of the customer and explain the ways in which your product or service solutions benefits them. These messages are used in product line catalogs, product line brochures, target end market buying guides, and ads promoting customer experience.

Individual Promo Pieces

These are messages in your third and final tier. They are used for promotional pieces, specific product campaigns, or activity messaging. They are used in promotional emails, direct mail, social media, trade show messaging, and flyers. They incorporate themes from the two higher tiers.

Content Creation – Using your Messaging

Once you develop your messaging (the USP and Support Points) with the Barbell exercise you can begin creating the actual content and copy for the specific marketing pieces you need. T

The Barbell doesn't make copy, it provides themes used to create the copy. The USP and Support Points you developed from your Barbells are the ingredients to the piece you are creating. When you stand back and look at your piece, you should be able to check it against your Barbell. You should see that you have communicated visually, verbally, and emotionally the essence of the USP. You should see your support points translated into compelling phrases, pictures, and feelings.

Note: **Writing copy**
Writing copy is an art of persuasion. As Benjamin Franklin said, "If you would persuade, you must appeal to interest rather than intellect."

Effective copywriting starts with the output of a Barbell exercise – the USP and support points. With these messages in hand the creation of the content is significantly easier and faster. Copywriting should focus on the reader, not your company or offer. Be humble, listen to your audience, care about them, and then write.

Headline: Spend most your time here.
- 80 percent of the impact of a piece comes from the headline. Don't bunt – swing for the fences.
- Short phrases, especially those that are sound bites or tag lines in larger font, are recommended. Studies show a typical reader can take in eight words in a single glance.
- Usually the headline highlights the single biggest benefit for the reader. Ask yourself why your offer matters to the reader. Intrigue them to want to read more.

Main body: Keep it short.
- Solve problems, overcome objections
- Tell stories, use analogies, discuss product origins, explain the testing or challenges overcome. Never talk down to the reader.
- Clearly explain why should they buy – What's in it for them.
- Use power words like: you, your, vivid, lifelike, imagine, healthy.

Call to Action (CTA): Frame the CTA as a benefit to the reader.
- Learn how...
- Design a new...
- Take advantage of...

If writing copy is not something you are good at, consider using a professional copy writer to improve the effectiveness of your copy. It can make all the difference in the success of your marketing activities. Writing effective copy takes time. Great copy gets understood and retained. The rest is noise.

Going back to our example, the USP in Figure 3.4 reads, "Complete landscaping jobs faster with the latest ABC Custom Truck" This USP might not be appropriate text for a TV ad, but you must find a way to incorporate the core messages. The same concept applies to the support points.

To create effective and consistent copy, grab your Barbell, review previous content from you and your competitors on the subject, and get to it. You'll find that content creation is faster and easier. Your marketing VP or junior marketer can now create decent, if not excellent, content.

Note: **Feature, Function, Benefit worksheet**

The Feature, Function, Benefit (FFB) document, is a classic and effective marketing tool that has been around for decades because it works. It is an internal document that translates technical features into customer benefits. I often create an FFB before beginning a Barbell Exercise. Figure 3.7 shows a template for developing an FFB.

Feature, Function, Benefit Template

[Product of service name]		
Feature	Function	Benefit
Group 1 [name of group 1]		
1. [enter feature 1] 2. [enter feature 2] 3. Etc.	1. [enter function of feature 1] 2. [enter function of feature 2] 3. Etc.	1. [enter the benefit of feature 1] 2. [enter the benefit of feature 2] 3. Etc.
Group 2 [name of group 2]		
4. [enter feature 1] 5. [enter feature 2] 6. Etc.	4. [enter function of feature 3] 5. [enter function of feature 3] 6. Etc.	4. [enter the benefit of feature 3] 5. [enter the benefit of feature 4] 6. Etc.
Other		

Table 3.7 A basic FFB layout.

To create an FFB sheet, gather a cross functional team that includes technical experts, product managers, and knowledgeable marketing, sales, and service staff. Have everyone work independently to list as many features about your product as possible. To aid brainstorming, consider questions like: What are the key features of the product, who will use it, what does it do, what technology did we employ or develop making it, what are the user needs, how will it be stored or transported, how is it serviced, how is it different, what does it replace? Then, collect the list of features and start working across all three columns. This FFB approach is easy, intuitive, and fun.

Table 3.8 shows an FFB example for ABC Custom Truck Works.

Feature, Function, Benefit Example

Landscaper Flatbed Trucks - FFB		
Rapid unload/load capability (Primary Need)		
Feature	**Function**	**Benefit**
Air assist automatic tailgate	Optional trailer feature. Press button to safely lift & drop gate in seconds. Locks. Handles irregular topography, won't hit workers.	Workers don't lift heavy gate/ramp Can be doing other things - saves time on each job.
Integrated wheel chucks	4 seconds to chuck and un-chuck tires. Chucks are held in wheel well during travel. Worker presses button, chucks drop down to pavement in front and behind tire. Retract: chucks pull away from tires as long as truck doesn't begin to roll.	Shortens the transition time associated with starting and stopping each job, which is a major cost for landscapers. Saves time on the job. Reduces costs associated with paying labor between jobs.
Highly configurable and changeable bed layout (Primary Need)		
Flexi-bed hold down system. A connection point every 4 inches.	Holds down any equipment securely, quickly and easily, including odd shaped equipment.	Easily hold down equipment of any shape. Don't waste time or money fastening down odd shaped equipment at the end of a job. Get to the next job quickly.
Safe fuel transportation (Primary Need)		
Flexi-bed gas container system	Bungie netting that safely holds 2.5 to 5-gallon fuel tanks in place. Holds 1 to 6 tanks. Fast to secure and access.	Safely and quickly store any shape fuel can for transport. Take all the fuel you need for the day – no need to stop and refill cans. Saves time and headaches and ensures safety.
Etc.		

Table 3.8 Feature Function Benefit example table for ABC Custom Truck Works' new line of landscaper flatbed trucks. The features are categorized, where possible, under the appropriate primary need.

Summary

Messaging is an often-overlooked ingredient to driving the success of the commercial engine. Devoting time to create strong messaging is an important, foundational element to lead generation and closing sales. Consistent messaging resonates with your potential customers, provides your own staff with direction, and greatly speeds the time it takes to create effective content.

Solution 3 References

1. *Why It Takes 7 to 13+ Touches To Deliver a Qualified Sales Lead (Part 6: Case Study)*,
    Laura Beasley, President of Beasley Direct and Online Marketing, for the Data
    and Marketing Association Blog, August 3, 2016,
    https://thedma.org/blog/marketing-education/why-it-takes-7-to-13-touches-to-
    deliver-a-qualified-sales-lead-part-6-case-study/

2. *How Many Ads Do You See Each Day? Fewer Than It Seems (I Think)*, David M. Raab,
    Blog, Customer Experience Matrix, September 2015,
    http://customerexperiencematrix.blogspot.com/2015/09/how-many-ads-per-day-
    do-you-see-fewer.html

3. New Research Sheds Light on Daily Ad Exposure, Sheree Johnson, September 29,
    2014, SJ Insights, https://sjinsights.net/2014/09/29/new-research-sheds-light-on-
    daily-ad-exposures/

Solution 4: Generating More Leads

If you've been involved in sales or marketing for any length of time, you've no doubt found that consistent lead generation is difficult. Studies show six out of ten B2B marketers find generating high quality leads is their biggest challenge.[1] Similarly, our *MarketMD Health Check* reveals that ineffective lead generation is usually one of an organization's top priority issues. Finding leads you can convert into business is tough, but it's not impossible... if you follow some basic steps.

Path to a Strong Commercial Engine

Ⓒ Figure 1.1 Increasing leads is part of step 4 in the process of great marketing (image repeated from Solution 1).

Figure 1.1 drives home the point that before you go out searching for more leads, make sure you've selected the best end markets to pursue, uncovered the needs of those end markets, and created messaging and content that will resonate. Only then are you ready to focus a portion of marketing resources, like a rifle shot, specifically at your target segments. The rest of your marketing resources should concentrate on awareness, like a shotgun blast, promoting your brand and seeking leads from all markets (see Figure 4.1 that follows). The rifle shot provides profitable business, and the shotgun blast provides business diversity and potential growth opportunities. The split of funds and resources is typically 50/50.

Two Types of Lead Generation Campaigns

General Awareness Campaigns   Specific Target Campaigns

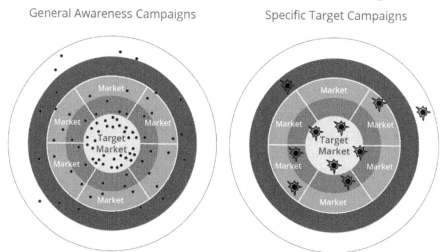

Figure 4.1 Illustration of the inherent imprecision of brand awareness (left) and targeted (right) lead generation activities.

But even when you aim lead generation efforts at your target markets with a focused rifle shot, you will sometimes end up hitting adjacent markets. For example, if a company like ABC Custom Truck Works, who manufactures custom work vans and pickup trucks for residential and commercial tradesman, launches a lead generation email campaign to landscapers, their message might still reach some carpenters or electricians. Similarly, their general brand awareness marketing activities, such as print ads, would be seen by people both in and out of their target markets.

This solution chapter primarily focuses on the rifle shot approach where you are looking to generate leads within your target end markets.

The Buyer Journey Funnel

Managing leads and customers is complex. Without a clear set of terms for the many stages a buyer goes through, your people can get confused and you risk valuable leads fall through the cracks.

Typically, companies describe their funnel as a "sales funnel." At Fairmont Concepts, we believe the traditional view of a "Sales Funnel" is too restrictive, since it doesn't take into account front end marketing efforts and back end customer support. The process doesn't begin when a lead is dropped into the hands of the sales team nor does it end when a sale is made.

We prefer to look at a company's funnel through the buyer journey framework. The buyer journey approach expands the traditional "Sales Funnel" into a "Buyer Journey Funnel," divided into *three distinct segments*:

1. The Marketing Funnel Segment (marketing team responsibility)
2. The Sales Funnel Segment (sales team responsibility)
3. The Customer Funnel Segment (customer service responsibility).

The Buyer Journey Funnel best represents the comprehensive nature of the commercial engine and assigns responsibility to each of your commercial engine teams – marketing, sales, and customer support. This approach enables you to provide the right interaction at the right time, delivered by the right staff.

The Commercial Engine
Three Segments of the Buyer Journey Funnel

© Figure 4.2 The complete Buyer Journey Funnel.

For your commercial engine to work properly from lead generation to customer loyalty, you must recognize and support the three distinct funnel segments within the overall Buyer Journey Funnel. In most companies, each funnel segment is managed by different departments. Lumping segments together will reduce ownership, accountability, and continuous improvement.

Note: **TOFU, MOFU, BOFU**

Content marketing experts describe the 3-parts of the company funnel differently than I suggest here:

Top of Funnel (TOFU): Generating awareness from your total available market and obtaining subscriber leads.

Middle of Funnel (MOFU): Once you've obtained a lead's contact information, including a phone number, you can qualify their interest. Qualification enables you to provide content and interactions targeted to their needs.

Bottom of Funnel (BOFU): You are selling a solution.

Although quite useful for mapping the buyer journey, these stages don't span the entire commercial engine from lead generation to customer loyalty, nor are they titled in a way as to clearly define departmental responsibility.

Lead Management Terms

Lead management includes the marketing funnel segment and the sales funnel segment – interactions from the first contact up to the point of closing the deal. There are many different lead management terms in use today. My recommended terms align with the three funnel segments of the total Buyer Journey Funnel.

Lead Management Terminology

Funnel	Name	Description
	Prospect	Companies and contacts in your total available market with the potential to become a lead. They have not given you permission to market to them. They might or might not be aware of your company or offering.
MARKETING FUNNEL Goals: Generate and nurture leads	Subscriber Lead	A lead who has given you permission to market to them. You only have their email address and need their name and phone number to move them to an Open Market Lead (OML).
	Open Marketing Lead (OML)	A lead who has given you permission to market to them. You have a phone number and name, but you have yet to reach them to qualify them as a Marketing Qualified Lead (MQL) or Open Sales Lead (OSL). This list should be kept as small as possible.
	Marketing Qualified Lead (MQL)	This lead has given you permission to market to them, you have spoken to them to qualify them, but they are not yet ready to move to the sales funnel because they are not yet considering or in the buying cycle.
SALES FUNNEL Goal: Obtain order	Open Sales Lead (OSL)	A sales lead that has been sent to the local sales person responsible for closing business to be qualified. Sales has not yet had an opportunity to qualify. The qualification process might send the lead back to marketing as an MQL or kept with sales as an SQL. This list should be kept as small as possible.
	Sales Qualified Lead (SQL)	A lead that has been qualified as sales ready – they are considering entering the buying cycle. These leads are in the hands of the sales people responsible for closing business.
	Sales Forecast Opportunity (SFO)	Sometimes called "opportunities," these contacts are in the buying cycle. They have a prognosis date, revenue prediction, product list, and probability of closing. Probability of closing is set to a percentage.
CUSTOMER FUNNEL Goal: Earn loyalty	Customer	Someone who has purchased from you.
	Loyal Customer	Customer who continues to buy all they can from you, is impervious to competition, and recommends you to others.

◎ Table 4.3 Lead Management Terminology

In my experience, companies typically have four to eight times more contacts in their marketing funnel segment than their sales funnel segment (can be more if they are not diligent about removing dead projects).

Your Baseline Data and Industry Benchmark Data

Leads fuel your commercial engine. There are a vast number of lead generation options available to you, but like most marketing leaders you face spending constraints. This means you need to select the most cost-effective lead generation activities.

Where Do You Spend Your Marketing Dollars?

Consider your current marketing mix. How much are you spending on digital versus non-digital? Inbound versus outbound? How much do you spend on each specific activity and what is the return? Understanding the answers to these questions will allow you to select the lead generating activities with the best ROI.

Ten years ago, your marketing mix would typically be at least 80 percent non-digital. Just twenty years ago, it was 100 percent non-digital.

Marketing Operating Expense Mix

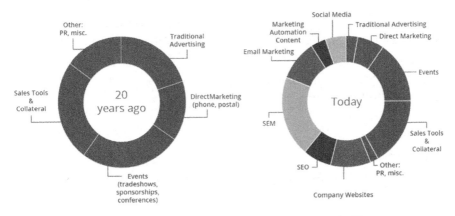

○ Figure 4.4 An example showing a shift in marketing operating expense compared to 20 years ago.
Today over half is digital.

Before the explosion of marketing options arrived with the internet, manufacturing marketers spent their budget on collateral, ads, trade shows, speaking engagements, PR, direct mail, and cold calling. Today, marketing departments spend on average just over half of their lead generation budget on digital marketing, most of that on inbound activities. Budget dollars have not changed significantly, but the mix has shifted in response to buying behaviors and preferences.

Digital information is so useful to consumers today that the average B2B buyer is approximately 60 percent through the purchase decision before engaging a supplier sales rep. That's why you need to create a compelling reason for potential customers to find you online and include you in their search and discovery process. Buyers tend to gravitate to the thought leaders who freely deliver valuable and relevant information. In today's internet-dominated environment, marketing people don't promote products with digital marketing, they educate and consult with the buyer to understand their issue and help them decide on the best purchase.

Marketing activities can be broken down into digital/non-digital and outbound/inbound marketing. Outbound marketing is based on interrupting the prospect to get them to behave or feel a certain way, and inbound marketing is based on providing the prospect with valuable content to attract prospects to engage with you.

Non-digital

o Outbound

Advertisements (print/radio/TV), trade shows, PR, cold calling, speaking engagements (conferences, open houses), sponsorships

o Inbound

Magazine articles, case studies, technical articles, word of mouth referrals, indirect partner leads

Digital

o Outbound

Email marketing campaigns to subscribers and rented lists

o Inbound

Website, SEO (Search Engine Optimization, getting your site found by organic search results), blogs, social media posts and forums, videos, webinars, mobile marketing, SEM (Search Engine Marketing such as pay per click or banner ads)

Calculations for Measuring Lead Generation Efficiency

When leads are down, chances are your revenue forecast is down as well. A drop in the revenue forecast can spark the leadership team to ask you to cut expenses while simultaneously getting more leads. You find yourself looking for the most economical method to generate leads. To make appropriate decisions, you need to know your average cost of generating a lead by source.

For high dollar sales of about $150,000, I have seen the average cost per lead range between $150-$300. Manufacturing companies selling $1 million products or selling to a small number of Integrator OEMs will see a much higher average cost per lead, while those with sub $20,000 products will have a lower average. Understanding your average cost per lead is necessary when measuring for lead source effectiveness.

Average marketing cost per lead =
Total annual marketing OpEx spend
Total number of annual *new* leads generated (all lead qualities)

Average marketing cost per high quality lead =

<u>Total annual marketing OpEx spend</u>
Total number of annual *new* sales ready leads (Sales Qualified Lead + Sales Forecast Opportunity)

These crucial ratios provide your baseline. Compare the cost of each individual lead source against the average to rate marketing activity effectiveness.

Note: **What if sales and leads are down and I have no budget?**
Every marketing manager has faced the situation when leads and sales are slumping, budget is maxed, and no additional funds are available. That doesn't mean your hands are tied. Pursue activities that require time, not money. Here are the two places I'd start:
1. Start by mining your database of current sales qualified leads. Then move to marketing qualified leads. Push as many as possible down their funnel segments. Starting here – with the leads you already have – is always the best place to start. Warm calling will get the fastest results.
2. Initiate activities with your indirect partners (distributors, dealers, agents, finders) to reach their current potential customers.
    Other less effective options are to cold call untapped prospect lists. Plan on making at least six attempts to reach each contact. Your average will be around three calls. Conversions to a qualified lead will be low, but you will get some leads. Also, go to previously unattended trade shows in your market as an attendee (not an exhibitor) to identify and talk to as many prospects as possible. This tactic can be especially effective at the end of the day when the show traffic slows and booth staff is available. Finally, send out press releases and write articles for trade publications to stimulate to interest in your offerings. This won't have an immediate effect, since it takes months for the piece to run, but it can help down the road.

Benchmark Data

Table 4.5 shows typical benchmarks I have seen surrounding the lead generation process for small to mid-sized companies selling high-dollar products in manufacturing. This data relates to products with an average selling price (ASP) of approximately $150,000.

Lead Generation Benchmarks

Example: $150,000 average selling price and $10,000 aftermarket annual income:		
Description	Benchmark	Data range and comments
1) Average marketing cost per new lead	$250 per lead	$100-$300. Marketing costs include staff.
2) Average marketing cost per high quality lead	$800 per lead	The range is $450-$1200
3) CAC - Customer Acquisition Cost, or Average total marketing cost per unit sale	$6,000 per unit sale	The range is $4,000-$12,000. This number helps you calculate CLV (see next row), and gives you an idea of what you can afford to give an indirect partner as commission if they generate the lead that becomes a sale.
4) CLV - Customer Lifetime Value	$75,000 profit	Measures bottom line income. Assumes 45% gross margin, annual aftermarket $5k for 10 years, and subtracts out customer acquisition cost $10k and cost to serve $5k.
5) Lead quality breakdown SFO = in buying cycle SQL= considering entering cycle MQL and Subscriber = interested but not in cycle Other = unlikely to enter	7% +/- 3 23% +/- 5 60% +/- 10 10% +/- 5	25 to 30% of new leads generated will be ready to immediately enter the sales funnel as SQLs and SFOs. Calculate this number for your company, as it is valuable when evaluating the success of lead generation campaigns.
6) Average lead velocity to close 60 days 90 days 365 days	1 to 2% 2 to 3.5% 2.5 to 5%	If a new lead turns into a sale, how long does it take?

Table 4.5 Lead generation benchmark data for high dollar B2B sales.

For companies selling commodity products or very small companies[1] the benchmark numbers can be quite different. For example, a small company selling commodity products would see an average cost per lead significantly lower than the $250 I show in the previous table.

Take the time to calculate your version of Table 4.5 since it is valuable when evaluating campaign results.

It's often not easy to determine lead source. For example, a new lead might have been prompted to contact you from a trade publication article, but then filled out the contact information online. Train your marketing and sales staff to ask questions to identify, as best they can, the true lead source.

Here's a sample data set of costs per lead source for a B2B company with high dollar sales:

Leads by Source

	New Qualified Leads	High Quality Sales Ready Leads	% Sales Ready	Activity Cost	Cost/ Lead	Cost/ High Quality Lead
Website conversions	300	90	30%	20,000	67	222
Email campaigns	175	35	20%	10,000	57	286
Trade shows	125	38	30%	35,000	280	933
Cold calling agency	100	2	2%	60,000	600	30,000
Word of mouth referrals	60	24	40%	1,000	17	42
Conference speaking engagements	60	12	20%	2,000	33	167
Webinars w/ Trade Association lists	50	10	20%	5,000	100	500
Social media conversions	35	11	30%	1,500	43	143
Direct mail	32	10	30%	3,200	100	333
Ads, print	10	1	10%	40,000	4,000	40,000
	947	231.6	24.5%	$177,700	$188	$767

◎ Table 4.6 Example cost of leads per source, excluding overhead.

Each lead source category in Table 4.6 can be broken down into more detail. For example, website conversions would include pay-per-click, banner ads, SEO, and more.

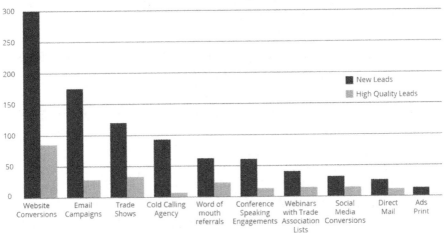

◎ Figure 4.7 Data from Table 4.6 shown in graph form.

Create your version of Figures 4.6 and 4.7, and include the level of detail you need for your analysis. Make sure you span a large enough timeframe - six months at a bare minimum - to get accurate results. Creating these figures with your data gives you a solid foundation for making effective lead generating decisions. You'll be able to compare costs, determine which generate the highest number of leads, and which can deliver short-term results. The data helps you forecast the results of your marketing activity efforts and evaluate performance.

Generate More Leads

With the fundamental baseline ratios and benchmark data for your company in hand, you can now focus on generating more leads. Below is a list of common lead generating approaches for high dollar sales, and the suggested best practices associated with each.

Website Conversion – SEO and SEM

Of the many uses for your website, the most important is to help grow your business by generating leads. Prospects will do more than half of their vendor evaluation online before reaching out to you. To generate more leads, you need to increase website traffic (new unique visitors + returning visitors) and conversions (visitor provides email to become a Subscriber or name and phone to become an Open Marketing Lead).

There are two main ways to generate website traffic: SEO and SEM.

SEO – Search Engine Optimization

Search Engine Optimization (SEO) helps your website show up in a search engine's unpaid results. The major search engines are continually changing their algorithms to ensure search results return the information users want. Google makes minor changes 500 to 600 times a year, and does a major revision once or twice a year.[2] Trying to "game" the search engines with SEO tactics that once worked are now not only ineffective, but they can actually damage your site's ability to be found.

There are legitimate things you can do to increase your searchability – like providing a constant stream of fresh content – but SEO has now become a highly-specialized niche. You're best served by working with a respected SEO professional who keeps up with the latest best practices and can help get your site found through organic search.

SEM – Search Engine Marketing

Search Engine Marketing encompasses many types of online paid advertising. Some effective SEM activities include:

- *Pay per click* (PPC)
  Online advertising is where you pay the host of a website each time a visitor clicks on your advertisement. The visitor is then directed to your website – often to a special landing page designed to match the ad content and solicit the visitor to follow your call to action.
- *Keyword PPC*
  Keyword pay per click SEM involves paying the search engine provider (Google, Yahoo, Bing) whenever someone searches for your keyword, and in return for your payment, they put you on the list in the "Ad" portion of the search engine results page (SERP).

  You place bids for specific keywords or phrases that you believe prospects in your target end markets will use to search the web. The higher your bid versus your competitors the better your chances to rank higher in the ad section of the SERP. Your ranking usually is determined by more criteria than just your bid. For example, Google states that the landing page quality, historical click-through rate, content relevance, and ad formatting also play a part in determining SERP ranking.
- *Pay per impression*
  Pay per impression involves paying each time your ad is shown on a webpage, whether the user clicks on it or not. The idea is that there is value in having the prospect simply see your ad. The pay per impression advertising method is also known as CPM *cost per thousand impressions* (where M stands for thousand) because the payment is often $X per 1,000 views.

- *Banner ads*

  Banner ads are online ads delivered by an ad server and embedded into a webpage. They are image based, as opposed to text only, and can be static or animated. By clicking on the ad, the prospect is usually sent to your website or a specially designed landing page that is part of your website.

- *Remarketing or Retargeting*

  These two SEM advertising services are provided by Google and others. They enable advertisers to show their ads to users who have already visited their site while browsing the web.

  For example, once a prospect visits your site using Google, a cookie is dropped onto the visitor's computer. When that person visits another website using Google, your ad might show up there as well. Your ad follows the prospect around, popping up occasionally on other websites they visit.

- *Geo Fencing*

  This advertising technology involves paying for a message or ad to be sent to a prospect's smart phone when they enter a certain geographic area. This is a form of location based services (LBS). You establish the geographic area by GPS or RFID. For example, you might tell trade show attendees your booth number when they enter the trade show hall. You can learn a lot about your prospect's behavior by utilizing this rather intrusive approach. Geo fencing is more relevant to B2C marketing but can be helpful for high dollar B2B marketing.

The SEM analytics available today are extensive. They can provide important insight into your marketing performance and prospect behavior, especially powerful when coupled with A/B testing - sending different versions of your email, changing only one element. The best way to leverage search activities is to work with SEM and SEO professionals who stay on top of the latest trends and tactics in the field.

Email Campaigns

Many marketers remain big fans of email campaigns. In the high-cost world of marketing, email campaigns are inexpensive, integrate easily with other marketing activities, and can deliver or link to a wide variety of content. Email campaigns also offer a lot of analytics into buyer behavior, such as whether they opened the file or clicked on a call to action link. Although email overload is real, if done well, marketing email is still a highly effective, proven lead generation method.

Make sure all your email campaigns follow the Anti-Spam regulations (defined in the CAN-SPAM Act) as required by the Federal Trade Commission (https://www.ftc.gov/tips-advice/business-center/guidance/can-spam-act-compliance-guide-business).

> In short:
> Don't use false or misleading header information ("From:"), don't use deceptive subject lines, don't sell or transfer any email to another list, identify the email as an ad, tell recipients where you're located, provide means to opt out, honor the opt out, and monitor what others are doing on your behalf.

Many who sell email lists state that, "All contacts have opted-In." The contacts on the list didn't opt-in to receive information from you - they opted-in for someone else. Few people opt-in to receive everything from everyone, and if they did they are likely not good prospects.

Although purchasing lists for email campaign blasts is not illegal, most reputable marketing agencies will counsel against it. The risks are high when sending emails to recipients who have not opted-in to engage with you.

A Legitimate Way to Rent an Email List

There is a way to ethically and effectively email prospects who haven't directly opted-in with you. Rent from a reputable organization who can prove they scrub their lists, meet all regulations, follow email best practices, and will send the email co-branded. With this approach, you send your content to the seller who sends your content to *their* list – to prospects who have opted-in to *them*. Your logo is displayed along with theirs. They may introduce your email or the content might be presented exclusively from you.

The list seller is ultimately responsible for adhering to the FTC's CAN-SPAM regulations and email best practices. It is their list to properly and legally manage, not yours, so you have no liability. You usually have to pay for each send, and so costs per campaign can get a little pricey.

Sending Out Large Campaigns

Don't send email campaigns from your company or personal outlook account, even if you are sending to your own subscriber list. If you make a mistake and your email blast gets you blacklisted, then you have caused long term damage to your company or personal email account. A better way to handle email blasts to a large list is to use a third-party email client, sometimes called a Mail User Agent (MUA). Your MUA will help (but not guarantee) that you stay within the regulations and best practices. A few popular email client services that can help you create, send, and manage your email campaigns are: MailChimp, iContact, Campaigner, Constant Contact, GetResponse, AWeber, Pinpointe, and Benchmark Email.

Most email marketing services provide monthly pricing since multiple mailings are common. Typical charges from email service providers are quite inexpensive - $10 to $20 per month for 1,000 sends, and $50 to $200 per month for 10,000 sends.

There are other advantages to using a third party to send out mass emails. They handle large lists easily by coordinating the send with various servers. Most MUAs can easily conduct A/B testing of a subset of your list (you should have nearly 1000 contacts for each test for accurate results) and provide detailed analytics on open and click-through rates as well as special analytics not available when you send on your own. Some MUAs will change the email format for those recipients who block HTML display, improving your chances they will be viewed and opened. MUAs will likely offer email capture forms, email templates, IP address tracking, and auto bounce handling.

Note: **Artificial intelligence and marketing campaigns**

Heavy use of artificial intelligence (AI) for lead generation activities is inevitable. We are in the early stages of AI, but it will eventually change the way marketers work every day.

Machine learning will help find consumer patterns more quickly for prospect list generation, execute A/B testing on nurturing campaigns, handle initial digital communication with prospects and qualify them, and improve SEM. It will do all of this within established spending limits, and will eliminate mundane activities from the marketer's plate. AI will help marketing teams scale up to handle large prospect, subscriber, and marketing qualified lead pools with small teams of staff.

AI will help humans communicate the way they want, and more quickly. In the near future, people will talk more than they type because it is faster and easier. AI will instantly understand what is spoken and respond with a mix of words and, more importantly, images – people process pictures much faster than other input methods. The consumer/marketer exchange will become more efficient.

Marketers will always establish the guard rails for the machine/human interaction, and any conversation that doesn't stay inside the lanes can be escalated to a person. It will be fascinating to watch as machine learning evolves to provide consumers with better service while helping you make your marketing system more efficient.

Benchmark Data for Email Success

Open, click through, and conversion rates are the primary means of measuring email campaign success. Open rate measures the number of emails opened by recipients. If the recipient opened the email, then you can assume they consumed at least part of your message. Click through rate measures the number of recipients who clicked on the link within your email. In this case, the recipient has clearly consumed your message and exhibits some level of interest. Usually, the link will go to a page of your website or a specially designed landing page within your website that contains your promotional offer, file download, and contact info collection form. Conversion rate is the percentage of recipients who not only click through, but also followed the CTA, provide their contact information, and became a lead.

Typically, good email open rates range from 14 to 35 percent to a targeted list of contacts who have opted in, click-through rates from two to six percent, and conversion rates 0.2 to 0.5%. Smaller companies with highly targeted lists tend to deliver higher open and click through rates.[3]

Email campaign benchmark targets to a targeted list[1,3,4]

Open Rates	At least 14%
Click through rates	At least 2.5%
Conversion rates	At least 0.3%
Unsubscribe rates	Below 1%, target below 0.3%
Abuse rates	Below 0.03%, target below 0.02%
Bounce rates (hard + soft)	Below 0.1%, target is below 0.05%

If you are within 25 percent of these numbers, seek minor tweaks through A/B testing. If outside that band, conduct a deeper analysis of your campaign to make sure you are targeting the right audience with relevant content. Unsubscribe rates should be under one percent, and abuse (someone clicks you as spam) under 0.03 percent for your own list of contacts who have opted in. Bounce rates should be under 0.01 percent. Bounces can be hard (the email address is not valid or an unexpected error occurs) or soft (the email inbox is full or temporarily unavailable). If you have a bounce rate over five percent your account can be suspended by your MUA.

Note: **Test often**

Successful lead generation takes a great deal of trial and error. Use the benchmark data as targets, but successful marketing departments don't stop there. They drive a culture of continuous improvement: testing, measuring, adjusting. The goal is to maximize success, not reach benchmark numbers.

Whenever possible, conduct A/B testing to learn what works with your specific audience. Change one variable at a time and make sure you have enough of a pool to show a statistical difference. If your list is large enough to support A/B testing, randomly select two equally sized subsets of your master list and conduct A/B testing before hitting the whole list. Attributes to test include subject line, preview text, offer, offer placement, CTA hyperlink button placement, body copy, download speed, time to send, day to send. For example, testing might reveal that video at the top of the email improves success.

There are free calculators on the web[5,6] to help you determine statistically significant results to verify you are conducting relevant A/B testing. Make your decisions based on accurate information. Don't bother A/B testing on a list with under 1000 names. It is unlikely that the open rate or click through rate will vary enough to prove anything with two pools of 500. Experimenting with the free A/B testing calculators will illustrate that a few percentage point differences in open rates between two email sends is statistically insignificant. A rule of thumb is that the smaller the send list the greater the difference between A and B results must be to provide statistical significance. Test, fail early, adjust.

Although generating leads is the goal here, those who open or click through but do not fill out the contact information have still seen your message. In today's world of integrated campaigns, nearly all interactions help move potential customers closer to becoming leads.

Since 2014, total digital activity on smartphones and tablets accounts for over 60 percent of digital media time spent in the U.S..[7] This means your emails must be created using *responsive design* so they will view appropriately regardless of device - computer, tablet, or smartphone.

Email Best Practices

Expert opinions vary on the best ways to craft a successful email campaign, and best practices will change over time. In each campaign, there are hundreds of choices to be made, each one having some degree of influence over campaign success. Successful email campaigns – those that exceed benchmark average results – rely on three main elements; the quality of the list, the appeal of the subject line, and the quality of the email body copy. The call to action is considered part of the email body copy.

- *The quality of your list*

The best approach to ensuring you have a quality list is to use only homegrown lists of contacts who have opted in and given you permission to send them marketing material. In today's world of countless email promotions, it is important that you work your list to target those recipients who will find the content of a specific campaign relevant, and don't send to those who won't.

- *The appeal of your subject line and preview text*

With emails piling up in everyone's inbox, people have perfected the art of skimming – looking for a few words that helps them make the decision on whether to commit further to the email. That's why the appeal of your subject line is crucial. Segment your list and tailor the subject line to the preferences of each segment (e.g., provide a different subject line to the business owners on your list versus purchasing managers). Keep the statement short and action oriented. Make the recipient feel special by offering something unique or sending an exclusive invitation. Compelling questions can be effective but don't use all caps or exclamation points (that's SHOUTING). Regularly research spam filter algorithms to ensure your subject line and overall email design doesn't get rejected. For high dollar items, avoid the use of emoji's.

Email recipients scanning new unopened emails will not only see the subject line, they will also see the preview text. The preview text (also called preheader text) are words that appear directly below the subject line in most email apps. It is the second most important key to getting your email opened. Nearly all current email clients and smartphone apps default to previewing the first 30 to 100 characters of your email body text. As you might expect, phones tend to display fewer characters than computers. Sometimes if you don't specifically designate your preview text, the email client will display useless symbols or a phrase like, *"Is this email displaying correctly? View it in your browser."* Always keep your main points up front so the email client doesn't truncate your key message.

- *The quality of the body of your email*

Once you've "hooked" someone into opening your email, the next step is "landing" them – convincing them to take action. That happens with relevant body copy. Pay special attention to your email appearance, the message, the CTA, and the landing page.

The email body can be text-only for a more person-to-person feel, or HTML to give your message a graphical, finished look. Both approaches can be effective. For example, with integrated campaigns I often send an HTML-based email from the company and then follow it up a few days later with a text-based email from an individual (local salesperson, CEO, marketing manager, product manager). Your message must be captivating and offer real value to the recipient. See the Barbell Message Creation Exercise in Solution 3 *Creating Great Messaging* for a proven process on crafting appealing messages. Always prominently display your CTA.

Note: **Call to Action**
Your Call to Action (CTA) is the key to getting email address and full contact information.

Optimize your CTA boxes on your email campaigns and on your website to make them compelling and easy for the visitor to take the desired action. Test various CTA phrases and graphics to determine which result in the best conversion rates. Track the number of people who show interest by following a link, but then fail to pull the trigger and fill out the form. With today's digital analytics tools, you can test, learn and improve conversions.

When creating your CTA, speak directly to the potential customers using second person pronouns (you, your), use action oriented phrases, keep it simple, speak of reader benefits, stay truthful, be encouraging. Use unique button shapes, strong colors, placement, and test for success.

Examples of CTAs are:
Give _____ a try, Request a demonstration, Learn more, Subscribe to get more valuable stuff, Chat now, See how ____ can help, Download a free trial, Download whitepaper, Get your free copy, Read blog, Request a quote, Reserve your seat, Watch this quick video, Subscribe here, Get started, Learn how, Sign in with Facebook, Register for free webinar now.

Email Frequency

There is much debate over how frequently you should send your emails. Some marketers say that you will obtain twice the click through rates by sending 16 to 30 emails a month versus one to two emails a month. [3] For high dollar sales in the manufacturing field those numbers are high and would turn off most buyers. I recommend two to five interactions per month for marketing funnel leads. The solution chapter on lead nurturing, Solution 5 *Nurturing your Existing Leads*, covers the topic of email frequency in more detail.

Direct Mail

Direct mail pieces are postcards, letters, or packages mailed to prospects in your target market or contacts in your CRM through a postal service. Both my personal experience and those of other marketing agencies have convinced me that the lead generation effectiveness of direct mail campaigns is on the rise. Reasons include:

- Direct mail can be sent to a purchased or rented prospect list without worrying about CAN-SPAM regulations.
- The US Postal Service says that 98 percent of people sort through their mail daily – a powerful statistic, especially when considering that average email open rates are around 17 percent.
- A well planned direct mail campaign will normally achieve a three percent or higher *conversion* rate – 10x the conversion rate of an email campaign making it worth the added expense.[8,9]
- The personal touch of a piece of mail can be strong and memorable. The prospects must physically touch it even if they decide to throw it away.
- People trust mailed content more than an email.
- The amount of direct mail a manager receives each week has been steadily dropping as the proliferation of email campaigns increases making each physical piece of mail stand out.

Direct mail is 100x more expensive per send than an email, but it can differentiate your message from the crowd and get an equivalently higher response, so you end up with a similar cost per lead.

Here are ideas to help your direct mail piece stand out:

- *Handwrite*
  Consider handwriting the name and address, or use a high-quality handwriting font to remove the industrial, mass produced look. Don't use a window box in the envelope.
- *Postcards*

You can save postage and increase effectiveness with postcards. Your message is in the open and the prospect can see it even if they are throwing it away.

* *Priority envelope*
Sending a USPC, FedEx, UPS, or DHL priority envelope will have a much higher chance of being opened than a letter.

* *"Lumpy" mail*
If you can afford it and have a small but high-quality prospect list, consider making the mail piece 3D in some way. Lumpy mail has near 100 percent open rates, but will be 10x to 20x more expensive than a letter. Lumpy mail might include a small branded memento or something even more unique to drive home your message.

Costs of direct mail pieces vary as postal rates change. Including bulk rate, printing, and addressing, post cards are $0.50 to $0.70 each, letters are $0.90 to $1.25 each, and lumpy mail is $6 to $15 each (excluding cost of contents).

Using a printing service that can preaddress and presort your envelopes will get you a lower postal rate.

The keys to a successful direct mail campaign are the same as for email campaigns: the quality of your list and message. Attractive graphics and design are important, but not as much as a targeted list and compelling message.

Results from direct mail are inherently more difficult to track than email since you can't know who actually looked at your piece, who filed it, who shared it with someone else, or who simply tossed it in the trash. Unlike digital campaigns, if they respond to your direct mail by calling your company you won't necessarily know that it was your direct mail that spurred them to act. Have your CTA point people to a website landing page designed specifically for that direct mail piece so that you capture lead source statistics, and make sure to train your marketing staff to ask for the true source of the lead upon receipt of each phone inquiry.

Cold Calling

Cold calling to a large, generalized B2B prospect list is a high effort, low return endeavor.

* 90 percent of cold call recipients do not engage

- Cost per lead using an outside telemarketing agency is two to three times higher than average, costing $500 to $800 for delivering an appointment.
- Lead quality is low. In my experience, only six percent of all leads are buyer journey funnel quality, as opposed to an average of 25 to 30 percent of leads generated by other means.

You can improve the effectiveness of cold calling by making it a part of an integrated marketing campaign. For example, you might choose to send a direct mail – preferably lumpy mail – prior to the phone call. With lumpy mail, the costs are so high that you are usually forced to pursue a small, highly-scrubbed, list. With so few targets, make the follow up cold calls yourself to avoid the costs of hiring an outside telemarketing firm.

Word of Mouth Referrals

For large dollar sales, word of mouth (WOM) referrals generate the highest quality leads. Unfortunately, the volume is relatively low, and it's difficult to increase it quickly. WOM lead volume is tied to the overall performance of your company, to your net promoter score (NPS), and to your brand recognition.

For high dollar sales, it is sometimes possible to stimulate WOM activity by creating a referral program where your customer receives a gift, commission, or a discount on their next purchase for recommending you to others.

Another form of WOM is through finders. I define a finder as a person who is not a full agent representing your company, but simply one who is in your market and might come across opportunities. A finder might be a freelance sales agent, service provider, or respected expert who frequently interacts with your prospects. Publicize that you will accept leads from any source, and will pay a finder's fee (a flat fee or a percentage of the first purchase price up to some amount) for any lead that becomes a booked order within 24 months of lead registration. A common commission structure is 0.5% to 2% with a max of $5,000.

Tradeshows

Attending trade shows to generate leads can be costly but effective for businesses in many industries, including manufacturers selling high dollar products.

Tradeshows provide more benefits than just lead generation. They provide face-to-face interaction with a wide representation of the market where you can gain insight into prospect needs, customer needs, and new market opportunities. You can also obtain valuable competitive intelligence. If you have exhibited at a show before, you can accurately forecast the number of leads you will get, which helps in the ROI analysis and justification.

Trade show results vary depending on show size and attendee behavior. For example, small shows are usually designed for information exchange and relationship building – attendees seldom buy. Larger shows are full of visitors looking to learn, select a short list of final vendors, and sometimes to buy. These big shows will have vendors in larger booths displaying relevant products and services. High-tech industries and well-established large industries will have multiple trade shows both large and small.

Attending a show in the US with a small 10 x 10-foot trade show booth and simple pop-up portable display typically costs $3,000 to $12,000, including floor space rental and facility charges. With larger 30 x 50 booths, your costs increase to around $60,000. Double that if you will be demonstrating industrial equipment requiring rigging for delivery to the floor and trades for equipment installation and tear down. You will also have to add labor and travel expenses for your staff. Shows are expensive, so make the most of them.

Attend the Right Shows

Before signing up as an exhibitor for a new show, have your top sales and marketing people walk the show first, study the attendee and exhibitor lists, evaluate the best floor locations and exhibitor booth sizes, not direct competitors attending, and evaluate their success.

Create the Right Booth

Two factors are most important when designing your booth: booth ambiance and message attractiveness. The booth must be interesting and inviting, and needs to tell a story on its own, like a museum display. Use the Barbell Message Creation Exercise found in Solution 3 *Creating Great Messaging* to help you develop the best message for each show. You have just a couple seconds to get the passerby's attention, so make sure your booth is inviting and your messaging is persuasive and concise.

Use a Multimedia Presentation

Design your content for those prospects who respond to sight, sound, or touch. Pay special attention to the visual, as it is the number one sense visitors will use at a show. Video is a must - even for a small pop-up booth - as it provides movement, acts as a sales prop, gives an impression of credibility, and helps clearly communicate your message. If your offering supports it, consider giving live presentations at large shows. Presentations create interest and excitement, will generate more leads, and increase awareness to bystanders who are not ready yet to become a lead.

If your booth is big enough, set up an event to draw a crowd - a product unveiling, guest presenter, or celebrity. Live stream the event on social media to make it appear even more special. Show events with cameras tend to stop passerby's in their tracks.

Logo Giveaways

A great way to extend the reach of your message is by offering carefully branded trade show giveaways such as bags, pens, or laser pointers. My favorite is a high-quality plastic or canvas logo bag with a shoulder strap. The quality is important. A low-quality bag will be replaced by a better bag from another booth. If you provide a shoulder strap or strings and other booths supplying branded bags do not, you'll find prospects will stuff the non-strapped bags into yours – leaving your brand out there walking the hall for all to see.

Don't Leave Literature Out for the Taking

Although literature should be available in the booth for sales people to use when selling, I do not believe in having literature out and available to be grabbed by the casual passersby or handed out by booth staff. You want to make contact and collect information so the person becomes a lead, not to have the prospect walk away with your literature feeling they now have everything they need from you. Most literature doesn't even make it to the prospect's office, but instead ends up in the trash at their hotel or home. If someone asks for literature, tell them you'd be happy to send it to them so they don't have to carry it around the show. Get their contact information and qualify them.

Set Goals and Incentives

Your entire trade show team – all booth staff – needs to know the show goals and should be updated on the progress each day. Providing incentives for leads generated or sales made are key. My personal favorite is to pay each staff member $3 or $4 for each lead they obtain - an effective way to maintain momentum and energy. Does such an incentive risk generating too many low-quality leads? No. I have seen over and over that if a prospect is willing to let you collect their contact information, then they are just as likely to be a hot opportunity as any other lower qualification. The percentage breakdown remains consistent whether you stop them in the aisle to talk or they approach you to talk. If they are not interested, they won't let you gather their information.

Work the Show Hard

We have all been to trade shows and seen salespeople sitting near the back of the booth reading the paper, eating a sandwich, chatting on their cell phone, or working on their computer. The booth is not a staff cafeteria or personal office area. All people supporting your trade show booth (sales, marketing, technical, executives) need to be well-trained on how to stand, how to approach a prospect, how to qualify in 60 seconds, collect a lead, and make your booth environment welcoming and efficient. Have a meeting each morning with all show staff before the start of the show to review and prepare. Review goals and booth rules.

Your delightful, enthusiastic, and welcoming staff should have an icebreaker comment as well as a physical component or sample (not a piece of literature) to help stop likely prospects in the aisle as they pass your booth.

Note: **At trade shows, qualify in 60 seconds**

Tradeshows are expensive, and when the aisles and your booth get busy your team must run at peak efficiency to maximize lead volumes and sales opportunities. In my experience, the target time to qualify a prospect during busy traffic times is 60 seconds. Train *all* booth staff on qualifying.

1. *Break the ice.*

"Are you familiar with < product or service you're promoting, or your company name > ?" If they answer "yes," then ask them how. If they answer "no," then ask them what is it that they do at their place of work. Don't ask them, "May I help you?" The most likely reply is, "No."

2. *Answer no more than 2 or 3 questions.*

If you are lucky, the prospect will have a question or two sparked by your intriguing booth display. As you briefly answer these questions insert some key credibility building statements to educate the prospect. Remember your purpose during this first interaction is to qualify him or her as a lead. After answering a couple of questions take control of the conversation. Ask their reason for attending the show, whether they have an application for products and services like yours, their business and role at the company, whether they have budgeted for purchasing this year, and if they are attending alone.

3. *Collect their information.*

Once you get an indication that the prospect could be a lead, interrupt the conversation long enough to politely ask to collect contact information. If the show is set up with badge scanning, run their attendee badge and take notes. If the show does not provide lead scanning and printing capabilities, collect the attendee's business card and staple it to a sheet of paper to enable note taking. Use the five key points of qualification – budget, application, need, timing, and familiarity - to help guide the conversation. More on this later in the solution chapter. Also, be thorough in writing down any pertinent information about the conversation so that the next interaction does not start from scratch.

All visitors considering entering the buying cycle (open sales leads - OSLs) should be immediately taken to the appropriate salesperson on the show floor. If the salesperson covering the visitor's territory is working the booth, take the prospect over to them and hand them the lead form. The salesperson should then requalify and convert them to a sales qualified lead (SQL) on the spot, or reject down a level as a marketing qualified lead (MQL). If the local salesperson is not at the show or is busy, then take the visitor to the next available top salesperson and fax the lead form to the salesperson at the end of the day so they can call the following morning.

An empty booth can be intimidating for a passerby. When things slow down, send some of your people back to the hotel, schedule VOC interviews with your customers in the booth, and keep low quality leads longer than usual.

Use Social Media at the Show

Integrate a social media plan tightly with your show. Discuss upcoming show schedules, talk about the booth message, post live video feeds of a walk through the booth, post video of customers who stop by and help promote their business, and put up blog posts about the show. Make it an exciting event for your followers.

Invite Loyal Customers – They Are Your Best Sales Tool

A trade show is a great opportunity to thank your key customers, have them meet staff, learn more about their current needs, and take them to dinner. Your loyal customers can be your best sales people, so getting them to talk to buyers about their experience with you is the most powerful selling tool you can use.

Invite Potential Customers to Your Booth

Be sure to invite to your booth hot potential customers who have indicated that they are already going to the show, and monopolize as much of their time as possible upon their arrival. If they are not already planning on attending, it is best not to encourage them to come where they will see competitors. Instead, set up site visits to meet with these high potential opportunities, either at their facility, a local customer facility, or at your facility. As for lower quality subscribers and leads, invite them all. Moving them along the buying cycle is more important than keeping them away from other competitors at the trade show. Try to create an incentive to entice subscribers to come to your booth.

Trade Show Follow Up

Effective follow up is the key to trade show success. Your sales team should already have their SQLs from the show, and they must maintain appropriate levels of contact. Marketing has the show generated MQLs, and immediate follow up is vital. Many of your competitors will be lethargic in their follow up, and a third of all leads won't be followed up on at all. Follow up as fast as possible with relevant discussion by phone and a welcome pack with literature by mail.

Trade shows are expensive, but the ROI is easier to predict than many other activities. Make the most of these costly investments.

Conference Speaking Engagements

Nearly all end markets have conferences, seminars, and networking gatherings - often given by trade associations. Having an expert from your company speak at one of these gatherings can be an excellent source of lead generation. If you can't find a speaking opportunity, create one at a hotel or university. They are relatively inexpensive with your primary cost being travel and the staff resource time.

Speaking at conferences can be a hit or miss activity. Sometimes a conference is well attended, but with few prospects. Other times the conference might be smaller, but contains good quality prospects that are a captive audience for your presentation. Prospects who attend speaking engagements are typically very open to becoming a lead and absorbing your message.

Keys to Successful Presentations.

- Make sure your presentation has a well thought out message, even if the content is technical.
- Ensure that every participant at a conference walks out with material about your company. Many conferences now offer a flash drive or internet link where attendees can download conference information. Relying on someone to find and download information related to your talk is too passive. Hand it out to them upon your conclusion.
- Consider every attendee a lead, so after the speaking engagement contact all of them with the goal of qualifying them.

When networking, take notes about all conversations and exchange business cards. Work the room. It might be that for a technical presentation you are not allowed to "sell," however, that doesn't stop you from having engaging conversations before and after you present.

The day after the conference, send a personalized email to every attendee and include comments you may have exchanged in a conversation. This email should come from the presenter, not the marketing department. In most cases, you will be the only presenter at the conference to do this.

Webinars

Webinars can be effective in generating low and mid quality leads, but relatively few leads instantly become sales ready SQLs. Webinars are affordable and are effective in building brand awareness, thought leadership, and filling the marketing funnel. They have a long shelf life, and continue to build your brand via downloads. You can use a webinar as an email campaign or social media download offer, and leave it accessible on your website to attract visitors and enhance SEO. In addition, one webinar can often be repurposed into many individual pieces of marketing content.

An effective way to generate webinar leads is to partner with trade associations. They typically charge between $2500 and $9000 to host your webinar, act as the moderator, and promote your webinar to their circulation list. You should also promote your webinar via email, social media, SEM, your website, and with your partners.

Trade associations give your webinar credibility and marketing reach. A successful webinar might bring in 80 to 200 leads providing a good cost per lead. About half the people who sign up will actually attend, and only 60-70 percent of attendees will stay for the entire webinar (sometimes less than half). Regardless, you have captured their contact information and a reasonable level of permission to market to them. Follow up with webinar leads in the same, aggressive manner as you would a trade show lead, even if they don't attend the webinar or download it later.

Indirect Partners

Indirect channel partners can play an integral role in lead generation. Just like you, your indirect partners are striving to increase the volume and velocity of their marketing and sales funnels. Here are a few ways to leverage your indirect channel to generate leads:

- Provide an incentive for new lead generation.
- Share in the cost of an aggressive lead generating campaign to be executed by your indirect channel. Options might include an email, warm calling, direct mail, or integrated campaigns that might include some combination of these activities.
- Demand, encourage, or sponsor an event to take place at your indirect partner's facility, such as an open house, seminar, or demonstration day.
- Create a competition among channel partners to see who can generate the most leads over a certain period.

Landing sales is often the focus of OEMs with their indirect partners, but generating leads is just as important.

Social Media

Social media can be an effective lead generator. Blogs and social media platforms with large amounts of highly relevant content foster credibility and establish you as a thought leader. Social media should be tied to your messaging and brand. The SEM options in social media have exploded in the past few years and many have found advertising through social media, especially Facebook and LinkedIn, to be extremely effective and affordable (low cost per lead). Lead generation through LinkedIn and YouTube are available. An effective social media system will increase your reach.

You must take a disciplined approach to maintain a regular schedule of content creation, so embed it as an ongoing task for your marketing team. You can ease the burden by becoming adept at repurposing existing content.

Note: **List of networking social media sites**[10]
A general list of popular social media sites listed by monthly visitors includes: Facebook, YouTube, Instagram, Twitter, Reddit, Vine, Ask.fm, Pinterest, Tumblr, Flickr, Google+, LinkedIn, VK, Classmates, Meetup.

The volume of visitors should not be your primary concern when choosing where to engage. For example, you might find LinkedIn to be more effective in reaching your target B2B audience, even though other sites have more traffic.

Sales Navigator

LinkedIn's Sales Navigator can be an effective platform for lead generation. For a monthly fee, you use their search programs to perform demographic market research within the large LinkedIn database to find, contact, or keep up to date with potential customers. You then use the LinkedIn mail system (InMail) to initiate contact. Unlike other list generating approaches, Sales Navigator allows you to leverage your own LinkedIn connections as well as the connections of the people you are connected to and use that information to break the ice. LinkedIn says you are 5x more likely to schedule an introductory appointment with someone if you have a mutual personal connection.

Blogs

Blog posts provide an opportunity to stake your position as a thought leader. It allows you to provide a continuous stream of relevant content to subscribers and those who find your content through internet searches (SEO). Building credibility through thought leadership is a vital component in getting a prospect to become a lead and moving potential customers along the buyer journey funnel segments. Thought leadership comes from providing content that educates and informs, not content that sells. There are other places on your site where you can sell your product or service.

Blogs embedded into your site also significantly improves your SEO. Each new post registers as a website update. Frequent website updates, increased traffic, comments, links, downloads, and the usage of keywords in the body copy all enhance SEO. Search engines rate well-written content high, so posts should be interesting and relevant. Posts should focus on a single idea, geared towards the needs of your best end market prospects. The latest research reveals that longer blog posts (2000+ words) attract more readers.[18] Blogs, like webinars, have a long shelf life, and can continue to lure subscribers long after posting.

Use analytics to gauge your response to different types of content to ensure you stay relevant. Assign someone to monitor conversations on all social media sites and develop an action plan to handle interactions – both good and bad.

YouTube Channel

A series of YouTube videos following a single thread are highly effective. YouTube is a frequently used search, so it is an attractive platform for communicating with prospects. Thanks to advances in technology, creating video content has become simpler and less expensive. You can also buy ads on YouTube which can be another effective option.

YouTube allows you to create a custom branded channel. For most small to mid-sized manufacturing companies, a branded channel can be a great option. Company YouTube channels provide a consistent experience for your users, easily integrate with your other social media activities, expand your social media reach, and cross promote your website. Information on setting up a company YouTube channel is readily available by searching *YouTube company channels.*

Print Ads

Printed advertisements are top of the marketing funnel media, used more for brand awareness than lead generation. Ads are expensive versus other marketing activities and have a long timeline between creation and placement, and so are not cost effective for short term lead generation.

Putting it all together - Integrated campaign examples

Although individual activities can generate leads, best practices suggest that integrated campaigns deliver much better results. Deliver a common message through multiple touch points. Below are examples.

Example 1: Integrating Direct Mail with Email from a Rented List

This campaign is focused on reaching prospects who are not in your CRM. Combining direct mail, an HTML email and a text based email provides three touch points.

  ·   In preparation, rent the list of prospects who have opted-in from a reputable source such as a trade association. This list provider will mail your direct mail piece and send your email out from their MUA. Create messaging via the Barbell exercise (Solution 3 *Creating Great Messaging*) that will be consistent throughout the three pieces.

From the messaging, create the HTML email, the text email, direct mail piece, and social media posts. Create scripts for your marketing staff to loosely follow when a call comes in as a result of this campaign.

1. Send a direct postcard to the rented prospect list under your brand. Unlike the email sends, the direct mail piece does not have to be sent under the trade association's brand, though they will probably want to send the mail for you rather than give you the full list of addresses.

Include a CTA that drives recipients to a unique landing page designed only for the postcard. This allows you to track direct mail results. Include your phone number as well, though it will be harder to always identify the direct mail as the lead source when they call in.

2. Two days after expected <u>delivery</u> of the direct mail, send an HTML email to all who have not responded with messaging that is consistent with your direct mail piece. Include a slightly different landing page location to track performance separately from the direct mail postcard. The emails will be sent under the list renter's brand with your brand also prominently displayed.

3. Two days after delivery of the HTML email, send a text email from the local salesperson to any prospects who have not yet responded. The CTA drives the audience to the same landing page as used for the HTML email.

Over five days the audience will have received three communications with the same core messaging.

Example 2: Integrated Electronic Campaign to your Subscribers

This campaign uses digital marketing techniques to move subscribers to become marketing qualified leads (MQLs). In preparation, create an eBook, white paper, or other electronic document that has interesting content for your target audience. This content will be available for website download to those who follow the CTA. Create a series of five or six posts for placement on various social media platforms. Create three variations of banner ads to be used on the social media sites, partner websites, and for remarketing. Create an email blast intended for subscribers and MQLs. Create the landing page that will carry the CTA for the content piece download.

1. Use social media teasers to inform followers of the upcoming content piece. Two posts are sent two days apart.

2. Two days later announce the availability of the content piece on social media, your website, email blast to your CRM, banner ads, and remarketing. Purchase SEM keywords associated with your campaign.

3. Continue social media sends every other day until you've exhausted your posts.
4. Send an HTML-based email blast announcing the content piece to all subscriber leads, MQLs and SQLs.
5. Place banner ads with trade associations and partners to run for four weeks.
6. Begin your four-week Google remarketing campaign so visitors to your site will see your banner ad show up on the other websites and Google SERPs (search engine results pages) they visit.
7. Two days after the start of your remarketing campaign, send a text-based email blast to subscriber leads and MQLs.
8. Three days later and one week after that, change the banner ad.

By the conclusion of this integrated campaign, the prospects will have had many possible interactions with your company, experienced a common message through many activities, and had many compelling chances to become a lead.

Example 3: Integrating Direct Mail and Phone Campaign to a Created List

Create your own list of prospects using a source such as D&B Hoovers, SalesGenie, Manta, or LinkedIn. In this example, find the NAICS codes of your existing ideal customers using Hoovers or SalesGenie, and then find other companies with similar demographics and that same NAICS code.

Note: **What are NAICS codes?**[16]

Most US companies who use financing and most international companies who export have a 6-digit North American Industry Classification System (NAICS) code that classify their main industry segment. The codes are self-assigned and based on the organization's top revenue generating activity. Here are two examples of 6-digit codes under the high-level category of "Utilities."

221114, Solar Electric Power Generation
221115, Wind Electric Power Generation

There are 20 two-digit code categories (see below), and a total of 1065 six-digit categories. Here are the two-digit categories.

Code	Industry
11	Agriculture, Forestry, Fishing and Hunting
21	Mining
22	Utilities
23	Construction
31-33	Manufacturing
42	Wholesale Trade
44-45	Retail Trade,
48-49	Transportation and Warehousing
51	Information
52	Finance and Insurance
53	Real Estate Rental and Leasing
54	Professional, Scientific, and Technical Services
55	Management of Companies and Enterprises
56	Administrative, Support, Waste Management, Remediation Services
61	Educational Services
62	Health Care and Social Assistance
71	Arts, Entertainment, and Recreation
72	Accommodation and Food Services
81	Other Services (except Public Administration)

Follow this link to get to the NAICS FAQs: https://www.naics.com/frequently-asked-questions/

For this campaign use traditional marketing approaches – direct mail and phone. You don't use email blasts because the recipients have not opted in to receive marketing material.

Use a shotgun blast approach with postcard direct mail, and then rifle shot to the best prospects with lumpy mail and cold calling. In preparation, Segment the list into those who will receive just the postcard direct mail piece (90 percent of the list) and those who will receive the lumpy mail and cold calls (10 percent). Create messaging for the postcard and lumpy mail packaging that is consistent. For the post card, consider inviting prospects to attend an event, such as a conference, open house, demonstration, tour, or customer visit. If you cannot conduct an event, consider a download that has proven to be valuable to those in the target end market. The CTA is to RSVP via email or phone. Create the script that will be used by the cold callers and the landing pages for the postcard and lumpy mail CTA.

1. Send the postcards to 90 percent of the list and lumpy mail to 10 percent. In step two you will be making phone calls to the recipients of

the lumpy mail, so if you cannot keep up with the call volume of step two, break the lumpy mail sends up into waves of appropriate size.

2. Place phone calls to the lumpy mail recipients two days after receipt. Leave a scripted message for those you don't reach, and place four rounds of calls in total – one on every other day – and leave a second message only on the last call.

You can expand on these three examples significantly to mix any of your lead generating activities. Well-crafted integrated campaigns will boost your lead generation results.

A question often arises over how to handle contacts who did not respond. The temptation might be to remove them from future campaigns, but you are better off continuing to market to them. Remember, it can take over seven interactions to get a prospect to become a lead. Don't throw out prospects who were not responsive, but do discard those who ask to not be contacted or who opt-out. Each campaign provides more brand recognition and can move you to front of mind when the prospect finds a need for your products or services. This is especially important with any prospects you've identified as clones of your best customers. These are the ideal candidates – the people you really want as customers. It can take years to cultivate a lead out of them, so be patient because they're worth it.

The Lead Management System

No matter how you design your lead generation system, you will not get your needed results unless you tightly manage the process. There are simply too many people involved and with too many opportunities to drop the ball. Marketing and sales staff must be trained, and CRM software must be tweaked into a comprehensive and effective system – a system that fits the behaviors of your buyers and your company structure.

The following lead management system has proven effective for manufacturing companies selling high dollar items. It matches typical buyer journey stages introduced in the beginning of this solution chapter, and will also be integral to nurturing leads as covered in the next chapter (Solution 5, *Nurturing your Existing Leads*).

Total Buyer Journey Funnel

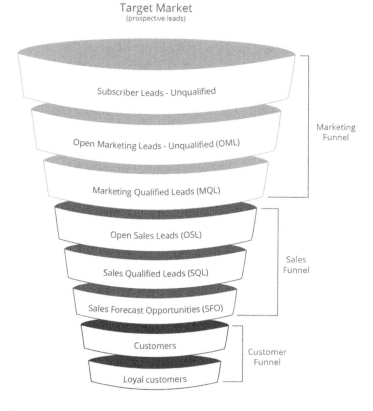

Figure 4.8 The total buyer journey funnel. For lead generation, we focus on the marketing funnel.

Figure 4.8 expands on the three funnel segment idea illustrated in Figure 4.2.

- The marketing department manages **The Marketing Funnel** to generate leads and nurture leads to a higher status.

- The sales department manages **The Sales Funnel** to win business and to return leads not sales ready back to marketing for nurturing.

- The customer service department manages **The Customer Funnel** to serve the customer with ongoing aftermarket products and services, move customers back into the sales funnel when an opportunity for a large sales re-emerges, and nurture customers to become loyal advocates.

The best way to illustrate this lead management system is to take a project from start to finish with a hypothetical customer who touches every step.

Using the Three Funnel Segments – the Otis Example

The marketing department at ABC Custom Truck Works conducts a lead gen campaign and receives an email address from Otis Black Dog Carpentry. Otis enters ABCs Marketing Funnel Segment as a subscriber lead.

Step 1 – Subscriber Lead: Since Otis has given ABC permission to market to them, ABC's marketing department nurtures the subscriber for a few weeks with compelling and educational digital content. Otis eventually follows a CTA on an ABC nurturing email and fills out their contact information to receive a case study. The download requires submission of name and telephone number. Otis now becomes an open marketing lead (OML).

Step 2 - OML: An ABC marketing representative calls Otis within five minutes of receiving their contact information because research shows that if marketing responds within five minutes then there is a 90 percent chance of reaching the contact (Figure 4.9). During the conversation, ABC's rep discovers the contact's role in the company, Otis' basic needs, and their purchasing timeframe.

The ABC marketing rep does not judge Otis to be considering entering the buying cycle, and so qualifies Otis as a marketing qualified lead (MQL). If the marketing rep had identified them considering or in the buying cycle, then the qualification would have been as an open sales lead (OSL). If the rep had considered them to have no chance of ever being a customer or advocate (e.g., contacted you by mistake), then the lead is removed from the CRM and placed in a "Dead" directory.

Fast Response Improves Contact Rates

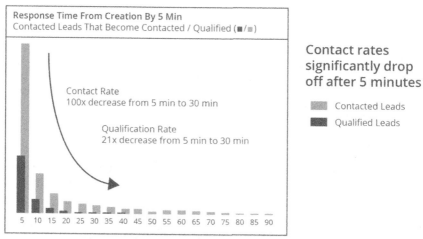

Response Time From Creation By 5 Min
Contacted Leads That Become Contacted / Qualified (■/■)

Contact Rate
100x decrease from 5 min to 30 min

Qualification Rate
21x decrease from 5 min to 30 min

5 10 15 20 25 30 35 40 45 50 55 60 65 70 75 80 85 90

Contact rates significantly drop off after 5 minutes

■ Contacted Leads
■ Qualified Leads

Source: 2007 Original Kellogg/MIT Study, Dr. James Oldroyd

Ⓒ Figure 4.9 Data from the 2007 Oldroyd study shows the importance of contacting new inquiries quickly. Whether you are making the initial response (black bars) or a second call to qualify (gray bars), near-immediate response to buyer initiated contact pays off.

Step 3 – MQL: As a marketing qualified lead, Otis remains the responsibility of the marketing department and is nurtured. Otis receives regular, relevant content each week. Eventually, reports from ABC's marketing automation software show an increase in downloads and website visits by Otis, which triggers ABC marketing rep to call and requalify. During that phone call, the marketing rep deems Otis to be considering entering the buying cycle and elevates Otis to OSL status.

Otis moves along the Buyer Journey Funnel from the market funnel segment to the sales funnel segment.

Step 4 – OSL: As an open sales lead, the local salesperson responsible for closing business receives an alert of a new sales ready lead. The salesperson reviews the notes in CRM and contacts the OSL to evaluate. Otis is called "open" because sales has the choice of accepting the project as a sales qualified lead (SQL), or rejecting it to return Otis back to marketing an MQL. After the conversation with Otis, the salesperson judges that Otis is considering entering the buying cycle and qualifies them as an SQL.

Step 5 - SQL: When sales accepts the lead, it becomes sales ready as a sales qualified lead. Otis is now in the sales funnel segment, and sales takes on primary responsibility for working the project. Marketing continues to send appropriate content to them (double checking with sales before sending any content that might interfere with the selling process). The project heats up, and the salesperson goes to visit Otis to further advance the sale.

Step 6 – SFO Stages: During the visit, ABC's salesperson determines that Otis is in the buying cycle, and ready to receive a quote. Therefore, Otis is elevated by the salesperson to a level of sales forecast opportunity (SFO). As required, the salesperson inputs the probability, the estimated revenue amount, equipment list, and prognosis date for closure into the CRM. Sales sets the probability to 25%. Once the Otis project is an SFO it is on the radar of the production team to make sure the product can be ready if the sale closes.

After presenting the quote to Otis, ABC's salesperson moves the project from 25 to 50 percent probability of closing. Since the product quoted to Otis is standard product, the production and sales management teams decide to consider Otis as 50 percent of an order, combines it with another similar 50 percent probability order, and begins to build one unit "to forecast" to be completed by the earlier prognosis date of the two.

Over the next week, the Otis project continues to heat up and Otis begins pursuing funding. The salesperson moves Otis to 70 percent probability of closing and adjusts the prognosis date after an encouraging face-to-face review of a revised quote. ABC's production and sales management take notice. Two days later, Otis signs the quote and gives a PO number to the salesperson. Now Otis is set to 90 percent probability of closing in the CRM. Production has been tracking the progress, and has equipment scheduled to be ready by the delivery date.

Step 8 – Customer: Otis provides the down payment, product is shipped to them, and they officially become a customer. They enter the customer funnel segment, and the primary department responsible for supporting them is now customer service. Under the guidance of the customer service department, the product is commissioned, the customer trained in operation, maintenance, and parts ordering, and over time the Otis' satisfaction grows. Customer service and marketing continue to nurture Otis toward loyalty. Marketing sends user-related content every three to five weeks. Sales checks in periodically on Otis as well.

Step 9 – Loyal Customer: Sixteen months later, ABC places Otis on the list of loyal customers because it is now apparent that Otis buys all they can from ABC, is impervious to competition, and recommends ABC to others.

Qualifying leads

To properly qualify your leads, you must employ a standard process that everyone can follow or your marketing and sales funnels will not be valid. Unreliable funnel segments make it impossible to forecast production and will cause you to lose orders.

Some companies employ an advanced classification system called Lead Scoring. Funnel segment position is determined by points the lead collects from consuming certain content, answering questions about their intentions, or following certain behavior patterns. Lead scoring works well for large companies with hundreds of thousands (or millions) of potential customers. However, for small to mid-sized companies selling high dollar items, a numerical lead scoring system is often more trouble than it is worth.

A simpler approach to lead qualification involves five basic considerations. It is a qualitative, judgment based system as opposed to a quantitative, number based system.

1. **NEED**: Does the prospect have an application/need?
2. **TIMEFRAME**: Is the prospect working to a schedule, or did he or she offer a sense of urgency?
3. **FAMILIARITY**: Is the prospect familiar with your products or those of competitors?
4. **BUDGET**: Does the prospect have, or can he or she obtain a budget?
5. **AUTHORITY**: Is the contact person the decision maker?

Some marketers use an acronym BANT to help staff remember the criteria of Budget, Authority, Need, Timeframe. This acronym is certainly helpful, but it has two problems. First, it does not start with the most important criteria: need. Second, it does not consider familiarity. A prospect who is already familiar with your offerings or those of your competitors is further along the buyer journey than one who is not. If you decide to use an acronym, I suggest BANT-F.

The goal for your staff during qualification is to gain as much information on the five criteria as possible. That is often difficult, but they should be trained to pick up hints that will allow them to make a subjective judgement. In most cases, the best you can hope for is that your initial qualification is *generally right* most of the time. Your lead nurturing system should correct misdiagnosed qualification levels.

Funnel Segment Velocity

It's important to calculate and track the velocity of sales through your sales funnel segment. I have seen high-dollar projects typically move through the sales funnel segment at the following rates:

- 1 to 2% of all new qualified leads close within 60 days
- 2 to 3.5% close within 90 days
- 2.5 to 5% close within one year

It's not difficult to calculate these numbers for your business. They can vary depending on the type of business, average selling price, end market, channel, and geography (US percentages are usually higher than EMEA, for example). The numbers reflect only qualified leads and omit subscribers and social media followers.

The combination of lead volume and lead velocity determines the health of your buyer journey funnel and is an accurate predictor of future revenue. If your funnel is dry and you need two more sales in the next 60 days to hit your target and your 60-day close rate on new leads is two percent, then you need 100 leads - quickly.

Note: **Lead Velocity Rate Calculation**[11,12]
Lead velocity rate (LVR) is a forecast metric that can be combined with lead volume to predict future business.

LVR = (Qualified leads [MQLs, OSLs, SQLs, SFOs] received this month – qualified leads received last month) / qualified leads received last month.

You can break down the LVR analysis into two metrics, one using MQLs (marketing funnel segment) and another for SQLs and SFOs projects (sales funnel segment). A positive number suggests sales should go up, if your sales team remains equally efficient. A negative number suggests sales will go down.

The economy can impact lead velocity and volume. Your lead-to-close velocity will change depending on whether people are generally spending money on high dollar items. Plot your sales against market health indicators (Capacity Utilization and Purchasing Managers Index numbers, published by the Federal Reserve each month, for example) to see if your business is tracking to national or regional trends. This will provide a better idea of whether your performance is a result of your execution or the business climate.

- Capacity Utilization is a measure of total manufacturing output. It hit a low of 63 in 2009. A measure 77 or above is very good, and 80 or above is considered boom time.[14]
- Purchasing Managers Index[15] is an indicator of economic health of the manufacturing sector. Similar to an NFL quarterback rating number, the PMI is a composite of multiple inputs. The single PMI number calculated from five other numbers: new orders, inventory levels, production, supplier deliveries and the employment environment. PMI of 50 percent is considered an indication of strong economic health.

Summary

If it is true that nothing happens until a sale is made, it is then equally accurate to say a sale can't be made until you have a lead. Lead generation is rated consistently as the biggest issue facing sales and marketing teams. As we've discussed, there are multiple ways to fuel your lead generation engine. Not every option is right for you. Be aware that lead generation is an ever-changing process, and ways of attracting new leads will shift as new tactics and technologies evolve or buyer preferences change.

Peel back the layers of every successful company and you are likely to find a robust, effective lead generation process residing at its core. That is what you should aspire to in your organization.

Solution 4 References

1. *Demand Generation Market Survey, 2017 Report,* Hubspot, Kipp Bodnar, https://offers.hubspot.com/2017-demand-generation-benchmarks-report
2. *Google Algorithm Change History, Moz,* https://moz.com/google-algorithm-change
3. *What's a Good Email Open Rate & Click Rate? [Benchmark Data],* Ginny Mineo, HubSpot, https://blog.hubspot.com/marketing/email-open-click-rate-benchmark#sm.0001nzqpaz131bctgtmoq4ryeqmk4
4. *Email Marketing Benchmarks,* MailChimp Resources, 2017, https://mailchimp.com/resources/research/email-marketing-benchmarks/
5. *Sample Size Calculator,* Creative Research Systems, http://www.surveysystem.com/sscalc.htm#one
6. *A/B Split Test Calculator,* Zettasphere, http://www.zettasphere.com/abcalculator/
7. *The US Mobile App Report,* Adam Lella and Andrew Lipsman, 2014, a whitepaper, comScore.com., http://www.comscore.com/Insights/Presentations-and-Whitepapers/2014/The-US-Mobile-App-Report?cs_edgescape_cc=US
8. *Direct Mail Statistics,* Data & Marketing Association, data were for 2016, https://thedma.org/marketing-insights/marketing-statistics/direct-mail-statistics/
9. *30 Direct Mail Statistics for 2017, Compu-Mail,* https://compu-mail.com/blog/2017/07/14/30-direct-mail-statistics-for-2017/
10. *Top 15 Most Popular Social Networking Sites (and 10 Apps!),* Dreamgrow.com, Priit Kallas, February 17,2017, https://www.dreamgrow.com/top-15-most-popular-social-networking-sites/
11. *Why Lead Velocity Rate (LVR) Is The Most Important Metric in SaaS,* Jason Lemkin, SaaStr, 2012, https://www.saastr.com/why-lead-velocity-rate-lvr-is-the-most-important-metric-in-saas/
12. *Lead Velocity Rate,* Geckoboard, https://www.geckoboard.com/learn/kpi-examples/saas-kpis/lead-velocity-rate/#.WeJaRmhSxnI
13. Fairmont Concepts calculations collected through the MarketMD™ Business Health Checkup.
14. *Capacity Utilization,* US Federal Reserve, https://www.federalreserve.gov/Releases/g17/current/default.htmhttps://www.federalreserve.gov/releases/g17/current/
15. *Purchasing Managers Index,* Institute for Supply Management, https://www.instituteforsupplymanagement.org/
16. NAICS stands for North American Industry Classification System. Launched in 1997 as an improved system over the SIC system. https://www.naics.com/frequently-asked-questions/
17. The Digital Evolution in B2B Marketing, Driving Marketing Performance with Multi-Channel Content, Communications and Analytics, CEB now Gartner. https://www.cebglobal.com/marketing-communications/digital-evolution.html

18. *The Character Count Guide for Blog Posts, Videos, Tweets & More*, April 25, 2017, Lindsay Kolowich, https://blog.hubspot.com/marketing/character-count-guide

Solution 5: Nurturing Your Existing Leads

Lead generation is expensive and difficult – but so necessary to the health of your commercial engine. Only ~25 percent of new leads are sales ready.[1] Many of the others can be converted into sales opportunities if you effectively nurture them.

One report shows that lead nurturing can increase your sales opportunities by 20 percent. Incredibly, the same survey revealed that nearly seven of the ten companies fail to nurture their precious leads. [2] Many organizations struggle with lead nurturing and our MarketMD health checkup respondents consistently rank lead nurturing as a top weakness.

Lead nurturing is the act of providing relevant content and interactions to move buyers along their buyer journey efficiently so that they will purchase from you. Nurturing programs have two goals – keep buyers in and move them through your funnel segments as fast as possible. Reaching these two goals gives you a healthy buyer journey funnel and a strong commercial engine.

Nurturing involves converting leads into opportunities, opportunities into customers, and customers into loyal advocates.

Since this solution chapter focuses on improving lead nurturing, I will primarily be discussing the marketing funnel segment where we focus on converting subscribers and marketing qualified leads into sales ready leads, and the sales funnel segment where we concentrate on closing orders.

Every study on lead nurturing shows how important it is to commercial engine health.

- Companies who nurture leads generated **45 percent** higher lead generation ROI.[3]

  Takeaway: Unlike new leads that come in sales ready, nurtured leads have had time to get to know you. Nurturing builds your credibility and raises the confidence buyers have in you, resulting in getting more sales out of your lead generation activities.

- Nurtured leads have a **23 percent** shorter sales cycle.[4]

  Takeaway: Nurturing leads gains credibility. A new sales qualified lead (SQL) will close faster if it has arrived at this stage via nurturing rather than entered the funnel as an SQL.

- Companies increase their number of sales opportunities by **20 percent** with lead nurturing.[1]

  Takeaway: To close more business you need more sales ready leads. Nurturing delivers more sales ready leads – a key to business health.

- Over **60 percent** of B2B marketers have not established lead nurturing.[3,6]

  Takeaway: Despite the cost of generating leads and the potential for increasing the number of sales opportunities, most companies still fail to nurture their leads.

- **36 percent** of all leads in B2B companies are never followed up on.[5]

  Takeaway: Wow. Many companies feel it is futile to devote much time to all but the hottest of leads - resulting in organizations "burning" more than a third of their leads. Creating an ongoing lead nurturing system is now affordable enough to work leads of all quality.

- Only ~**25 percent** of leads are sales ready.[2,5,7]

  Takeaway: Most people interested in your products or services are not yet ready to buy. Don't bog down your sales team with leads that are not sales ready.

- It takes **7 to 13+** touches to convert a lead into a sales-ready opportunity.[7]

  Takeaway: Without a nurturing program, your lower quality leads can be wasted. This highlights the traditional marketing Rule of 7, suggesting it takes at least seven marketing interactions or touches to get someone to take your desired action. Some data suggest it is more like 13 or more touches. But don't stop there – create a continuous program for reaching out to leads and only remove a lead if you have clearly established they have no potential to buy or advocate for you, or they opt-out. The process of nurturing leads in a high dollar sales environment can span years, so be patient.

- **68 percent** of companies have not clearly established their Buyer Journey Funnel.[3]

  Takeaway: Without identifying the various stages of the buyer journey, you cannot know the appropriate interaction to engage the potential customer. Companies overburden sales teams with non-sales ready leads, while simultaneously missing future business by not nurturing lower quality leads to the sales ready level.

The message is consistent: Most companies don't focus enough time and effort on lead nurturing, despite obvious lucrative benefits.

Note: **Nurturing isn't selling.**
Nurturing is educational. You inform the buyer, answer questions, and pique interest. It is an opportunity for you to build trust and set yourself apart from the pack. Selling is different. When a salesperson gets to the point of actually "selling" the solution by asking for money in return for the promised benefits and value, all the nurturing should have already taken place. For high dollar sales, successful nurturing programs help the potential customer along the buyer journey toward purchasing your product or service, but don't attempt in any way to close the sale.

The Anatomy of a B2B High Dollar Buyer Journey

The buyer journey is the consumer's progression from curious prospect to loyal customer. The buyer journey for high dollar sales can sometimes be long – often lasting years – and is not necessarily sequential. The buyer can jump forward, move back, or leave your funnel all together.

Buyer journey stages help you match the needs and behavior of a group of buyers as they move through their purchasing process. Too little granularity in your journey stages and you won't be able to provide the content or interaction buyers need at a point in time. Too much detail and your nurturing program will become overly complex and difficult to execute.

For manufacturers selling high dollar products, the total Buyer Journey Funnel has three funnel segments (marketing, sales, and customer segments). **Two buyer stages** exist in each of the three funnel segments. Figure 5.1 shows how the buyer stages align with each segment of the Buyer Journey Funnel.

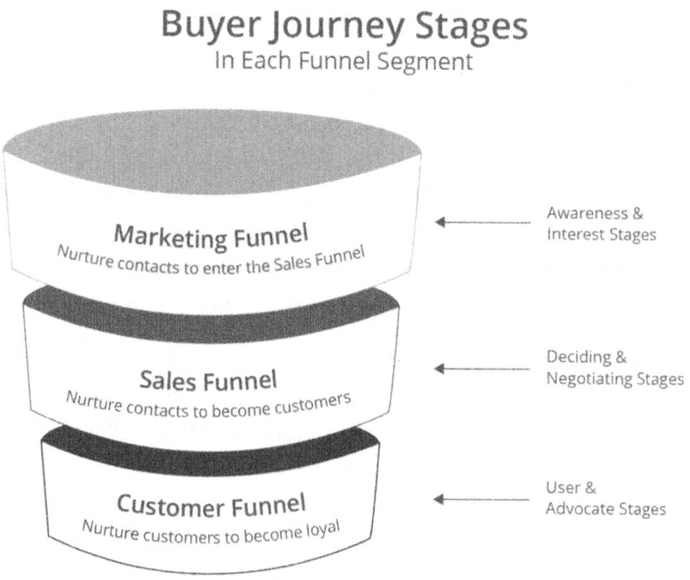

Figure 5.1 Six Buyer Journey Stages, two in each funnel segment.

Figure 5.1 shows the buyer journey stages that best match B2B buyers of high dollar items. It's important to keep the three funnel segments – marketing, sales, customer– separate so that you can maintain focus and accountability to each. This enables you to maximize the velocity through each funnel segment while not allowing any valuable contacts or customers to leak out.

As buyers move through their journey stages, they also advance through your market segments. Each step requires different contact frequency and types of content. Figure 5.2 shows the framework of a typical nurturing program and how to interact with the buyer at each stage of the journey.

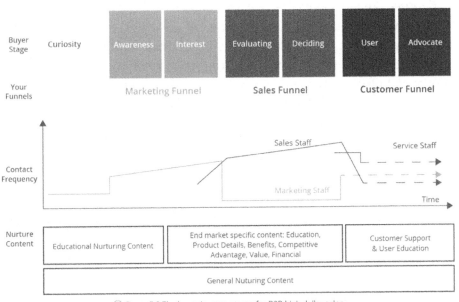

Figure 5.2 The buyer journey stages for B2B high dollar sales.

The potential customers in your target markets begin with some **curiosity** about their problem and your solution. They ultimately become a lead and enter the Buyer Journey Funnel. Here are descriptions of the elements of your nurturing framework as illustrated in Figure 5.2.

Buyer Stage: In the top row of Figure 5.2, you can see that the overall buyer journey consists of six stages in three funnel segments. The longest possible path is when a curious potential customer enters as a lead who has gained *Awareness* of your products, and ends up eventually as a loyal *Advocate*.

Your Funnels: Each of three funnel segments – marketing, sales, and customer - contain two stages of the buyer journey. Focusing on each segment separately allows you to assign responsibility – and demand accountability – at each stage of the journey. It also enables you to provide relevant nurturing content to buyers as they evolve.

The focus in each of the marketing funnel segment is to nurture the lead to become sales ready. The goal of the sales funnel segment is to close the order. The goal of the customer funnel segment is to move a customer to the point of becoming a loyal advocate (customer loyalty is covered in Solution 7 *Creating Customer Loyalty*).

Contact Frequency: In the first two stages of the journey, marketing is responsible for gradually increasing the frequency of contact as the lead becomes more engaged. Two to five interactions per month are common, but the number can be higher if the lead triggers further contact through their actions. As I discussed in Solution 4 *Generating More Leads*, some marketing experts suggest five to 10 times more frequent contact, but I have found buyers of high dollar products and services are turned off by such constant bombardment.

When the lead becomes sales ready, it is moved to the sales funnel segment where the sales people responsible for closing business take over. In the sales funnel segment, marketing's nurturing frequency is greatly reduced and tightly coordinated with sales, especially during the deciding stage. Sales contact frequency increases through the sales negotiations and closing.

In the customer funnel segment, the service or aftermarket department is responsible for nurturing as the role of marketing and sales teams lessens.

Mature Content: As buyers move from one stage to another, their needs and behavior change. In the marketing funnel segment, buyers are investigating and learning about their problem and possible solutions, and they need general educational content. As they move to the sales funnel segment, they require more specific information about the products, including comparisons and benefits. In the customer funnel segment, the information includes general content and user and service related content.

Many pieces of content or types of interaction can span more than one stage. Content or interactions might be digital (emails, downloads, website visits) or non-digital (phone calls, face to face meetings, trade shows). Contact can be triggered by the buyer or initiated by the seller, or sent by the seller on a predetermined schedule.

Align Your Lead Management System to Buyer Stages

Many nurturing programs fail not because of a lack of effort, but because the company cannot efficiently handle the volume of interactions. As time passes the number of leads you are managing grows (which is a good thing). You'll have four to eight times more leads in your marketing funnel segment than in your sales funnel segment, and these leads need nurturing. If you don't put together an organized and streamlined system, your attempts to nurture will fall short or break down as the number of contacts in your CRM increases.

To have an organized nurturing system you must align your lead management activities precisely around the buyer stages. This allows your marketing and sales teams to clearly understand how to move leads through the funnel in their CRM, and what to call each stage. For example, a new, low quality lead that only provides an email address should reside at the lowest level of your lead management system (subscriber) and buyer stage system (Awareness), as shown in Figure 5.3.

Figure 5.3 Matching your lead management system to the buyer stages will help you keep your nurturing system organized.

Marketing funnel segment: The Awareness stage contains subscribers. The Interest stage contains MQLs.

Sales funnel segment: The Evaluating stage contains SQLs. The Deciding stage contains SFOs.

Customer funnel segment: The User stage contains customers not yet loyal. The Advocate stage contains loyal customers.

Understanding the relevant stages that contacts occupy and aligning your CRM software and staff resources to address them accordingly is key to an effective and efficient lead nurturing program.

Your marketing staff – including your "tele-sales" or "inside sales" groups - should handle the marketing funnel segment. Sales staff responsible for closing business should manage the sales funnel segment. Service staff should have the lead responsibility for the customer funnel segment.

Some manufacturing companies assign sales the responsibility of qualifying new inquires and nurturing leads, while marketing has the sole task of generating new inquiries. This approach is not recommended. Your sales staff cannot respond fast enough to a new inquiry (within 5 minutes is best), is not in position to consistently nurture the large number of leads (due to appointments and interruptions), and must stay focused on the difficult task of closing business (to keep the revenue stream coming in). Initial qualification and nurturing of leads is best handled by marketing staff who reside in an office and can handle the complex schedules.

If you sell only through indirect channel partners, or you have a hybrid system between direct and indirect channels, then your nurturing structure might need to be different. However you organize, you must match lead management stages to buyer journey stages or you risk organizational confusion.

Creating your Nurturing Program

There are four key points to consider when creating your nurturing program:

- *Create general and end market specific programs*
  Just as with lead generation, you should employ the shotgun and rifle shot approach to nurturing - generalized nurturing applied to all end markets and custom nurturing applied to target end markets. Shotgun marketing strengthens your company by generating brand awareness,

market diversity, and growth opportunities. Rifle shot marketing strengthens your company through pursuit of the greatest immediate profits.

- *Start small and build from there*
  Nurturing programs can quickly become complex and nearly impossible to execute even when using marketing automation software. Begin with small programs and build from there as you get your internal processes down.

- *Stay buyer focused*
  Invest the time to fully understand your market before creating or improving your nurturing program. Research customer needs, review company brand messaging (Blue Statements) and end market messaging, create buyer personas, and understand content delivery preferences.

Figure 5.4 describes the buyer stages and buyer behavior, needs, and questions at each stage along the buyer journey. Your goal is to align your interactions and content as the potential customer advances through your funnel segments.

Buyer Profile by Stage

Buyer stages	Awareness	Interest	Evaluating	Deciding	User	Advocate
Buyer behaviors	Investigate challenge and solutions	Explore solution strategies and vendors	Create short list of vendors, finalize solution strategy	Negotiate with final vendor(s)	Employ the solution, receive benefits or frustrations	Ambassador for the solution, impervious to competition
Buyer needs	Needs to gain deeper understanding of challenge	Needs to clearly define issue and research initial solution options	Research all solutions, get funds	Justification, right value, reasons to buy, internal sales tools	ROI, training, support, continuous improvement	Sustain relationship, validate my loyalty
Buyer desired delivery	Email, access websites on my own, magazines	Email, website downloads, and phone	Face to face, phone, email	Face to face, phone, and sometimes email	Website, email, phone, face to face	Phone, face to face, website, email
Buyer title	Managers or staff	Assigned person: staff or manager level	Team leader for purchase	Team leader, dept. head, CEO, owner, CFO	Staff & manager where product used, purchasing	Manager where product/service used
Buyer questions	How deep is my problem, what solutions might apply?	Who can help? What approach should I take?	What is price, ROI data? What's your solution, & versus others?	Are you best ROI, vendor, who else uses you, am I at risk?	Are you best ROI, vendor? Are prices right for all items?	How can we work together to improve?
Your most valuable content	Educational content on problem and solutions	Expert content: Whitepapers eBooks Analyst reports Case studies Webinars Phone call	Compare models ROI analysis Webinars Buying guide Visits Service options Phone call	Trial downloads Live demos Phone call Visits Service programs Loyalty program Compare vendors	User guides Manuals Aftermarket and upgrade flyers User group invite Loyalty program	User guides Manuals Aftermarket and upgrade flyers User group invite Loyalty program Special benefits
Your lead stages	Subscriber Lead	Marketing Qualified Lead (MQL)	Sales Qualified Lead (SQL)	Sales Forecast Opportunity (SFO)	Customer	Loyal Customer
Your funnels	Marketing Funnel		Sales Funnel		Customer Funnel	

Figure 5.4 A generic buyer profile by stage.

Buyer Behaviors: Closely observe your potential customers to determine buyer behaviors. Are they investigating with intent to educate themselves? Are they creating a specification to solve their issue? Are they seeking funding? Are they selecting a vendor?

Buyer Needs: Consider what would be most helpful at each stage to determine buyer needs. Early on, subscribers and MQLs in the Awareness and Interest stages need things such as a better understanding their problem and possible available solutions. Later, SQLs and SFOs in the Evaluating and Deciding stages want to compare solutions, obtain financing, and purchase the solution with the best ROI.

Buyer Desired Delivery: Buyers want to get their information differently at each stage. Buyers prefer digital communication when conducting research in the early stages. When they move to evaluating and deciding, they expect to interact face-to-face.

Buyer Titles: Titles of the buyers you are dealing with will sometimes change during the stages as well. Early on you will most likely be dealing with buyers and lower level members of the purchasing group – especially if the company you're dealing with is large. As they move along the buyer journey into the later stages, you could find yourself working with the Director of Procurement, Owner or President.

Buyer Questions: Buyer Questions are particularly important. Your nurturing program will be more successful if you are able to answer buyer questions and objections with relevant content. Try to anticipate the questions and objections the buyer might have at each stage.

Your Most Valuable Content: What type of content do you believe will be most important to the buyer at each stage.

Aligning with Buyer Behavior, Needs, and Questions

Using the Buyer Profile by Stage table, you can then map out the appropriate contact and content plan for each stage. Use a cross functional team to take the following actions to help you pull together the content you will need and to map out your contact scheduling.

1. **Assess content you have and need**
2. **Map the content and apply date and action triggers**
3. **Create content as needed**
4. **Execute, track, and continuously improve**

The manual system described in this book uses spreadsheets to organize, prioritize, and track a nurturing program. Software as a Service (SaaS) products are available from many software suppliers that help automate, organize and execute lead nurturing. Most of the following vendors offer content management, marketing automation, and collaboration features:

HubSpot, Marketo, Adobe Campaign, Pardot, Act-On, ActiveCampaign, and Intercom, Right On Interactive, Net-Results, eTrigue, ClickDimensions, inBOX25, Listrak, GetResponse, Maropost Marketing Cloud, iContact Pro, Autopilot, ThriveHive, LeadSquared, SharpSpring, Lead Liaison, Vbout.com, ActiveDEMAND, Real Magnet, Blueshift, Wishpond, OutboundEngine, DSS™ (Dynamic Self-Syndication™), Exponea, and Informz.[8]

1. *Assess Content You Have and Need*

Companies are consistently surprised at how much content they already have on hand. Some may have been used in the past for marketing events or campaigns and require only minor rework to be ready to go. Other material can be hidden away in other departments originally intended for other uses (such as service manual or technical presentation) and require repurposing to make it ready for promotional material. It's worth the effort to hunt down existing content, as it will save time and spark content ideas.

Below is an example from ABC Custom Truck Works that illustrates how to collect and rank your current content and then scour your company for other material that can be the ingredients for new content.

First, ABC created a Nurturing Content Library as shown in Figure 5.5

Nurturing Content Library

ABC Custom Truck Works nurturing program (example)

Content Name or Title	Content Type	Trigger - Date based or Action based	Target Market	Stage	Content Location	Expectation of Recipient	CTA or goal	Value to Recipient	Add'l Effort to Meet Expectation
Newsletter - ABC Custom Truck Works	Email	Date: Q1 - January	All Markets	All	G:\Mktg \Newsletters	Learn about the Industry, us, our products, culture, events	Phone call	3	1
Tradeshow Invite in NJ	Email	Date: 3 weeks prior	All Markets	Subscriber, MQL	G:\Mktg \Tradeshow-Inv	Learn why I should go	Accept & fill out CTA form	3	1
Demo Days Event in NY	Email	Date: 4 weeks prior	All Markets	Subscriber, MQL	G:\Mktg \DemoDays	See products/people, Interact with experts and peers	Accept & fill out CTA form	8	1
Complete Jobs Faster	Video	Date: Q2	All Markets	Subscriber, MQL	G:\Mktg \Ecampaign1	Easy to run video, informative, interesting	Download	7	1
Happy Holidays greeting	HTML graphic	Date: Q4 - December	All Markets	All	G:\Mktg \Ecampaign4	Nice, respectful, positive well wishing	Open	3	1
New lead Thank you response and lit pack	Email	Action: Receive new lead	New unqualified lead	All	G:\Mktg \Ecampaign4	Instant acknowledgement that I contacted you	Open	3	1

© Table 5.5 An example of a Nurturing Content Library. ABC Custom Truck Works catalogs and rates all existing content.

Most of these columns are self-explanatory, except perhaps for Trigger, Expectation of Recipient, Value to Recipient, and Additional Effort to Meet Expectation.

- *Trigger*
  A trigger is an event that initiates the delivery of content or interaction. They are either date triggered or action triggered. Date based triggers revolve around timing, and are sometimes called Drip Marketing. For example, sending a monthly newsletter or sending a flyer four days after a webinar are two examples of date based triggers. Action based triggers are where you respond to a buyer action with some type of interaction or content. An example is initiating a phone call to a lead when they download the Buyer's Guide paper or eBook.
- *Expectation of recipient*
  List what the buyer expects to gain from the content. The more detail you can come up with, the better you can design the interaction to meet or beat buyer expectations. What questions or objections might they have, what problems are they facing, what do they need?
- *Value to recipient (1 to 10)*
  On a scale of 1 to 10 with 10 the highest, rate the value of the interaction to the buyer. To determine a rating, you can have several market knowledgeable people rate the content independently, compare results, and come to a final rating. If you find too much disparity in opinions, contact willing customers and ask them to rate the content. You should rate an interaction high if the content is popular, and very high if the interaction tends to prompt the buyer to move to the next stage.
- *Additional Effort to Meet Expectation (1 to 10)*
  On a scale of 1 to 10 with 10 the highest, rate the amount of time, resources, and money required to develop the content. Set the rating levels in whatever way is most useful. For example, you can rate items ready to go or already in use as a 1, something requiring five to ten hours as a 5, and something that will take many days of staff time and tens of thousands of dollars (such as a new corporate video) as a 10. You might also rate things based on cost (such as brochure printing or contracting with an outside resource such as a writer, graphic designer, landing page developer, or mail user agent for email sends). It's a relative scale,

meaning that you are only trying to rate activities against each other to help you make decisions.

Once you complete your Nurturing Content Library table you can begin searching for material that can be used to create new content. Again, I'll use ABC Custom Truck Works as the example.

ABC's marketing staff has completed their analysis and rating of existing content, and so now turn to scour their company in search of unused content. They know many documents might be able to be repurposed into new content. They meet with the service team to review manuals, how-to guides, and service procedures. They discuss with engineering and product management types of research and analysis that might be repurposed to give credibility to your design or explain a complex product benefit. They talk with other marketers and sales people to see if they have ever created something for a one-off issue – such as a unique sales tool, effective email correspondence, or customer testimonial – that could be used on a broader scale.

Table 5.6 shows a list of unused content that is currently available to ABC that might prove valuable for nurturing.

Content Previously Unused for Nurturing

	All Markets	Landscaper	Carpenter	Electrician
Literature	- Company Overview brochure	- Vehicle brochure - Case study: Jones Corp.	- Vehicle brochure	- Vehicle brochure
			- Van accessory flyer	
		- Truck accessory flyer		
Papers/ eBooks	- Service manual - Safety is built in eBook	- Trailer ramp technical paper		
Video	- Corporate	- Trailer video	- User video: Smith Inc.	
Human	- Script lead qualification - Script for warm calls			
Others	- *Modern Trade Vehicles* articles in magazine - Direct mail postcard	- Direct mail postcard		- Webinar on electrician vehicles

Figure 5.6 ABC Custom Truck Works example of unused content.

ABC's list is promising. Some of the pieces can be made ready for use with a few modifications, such as the Jones Corporation case study. The trailer ramp technical paper and webinar will need more work, but can be repurposed eventually. The group discusses and resolves any differences in their ratings and then sorts the data per the column *Value to Recipient*. See Table 5.7.

Content Name or Title	Content Type	Trigger - Date based or Action based	Target Market	Stage	Content Location	Expectation of Recipient	CTA or goal	Value to Recipient	Add'l Effort to Meet Expectation
Landscaper vehicle lit	Brochure	New Landscaper lead, send with literature pack	Landscaper market	MQL	G:\Mktg\new	Valuable info specific to my use. Professional, Not too salesy	Phone or email	8	0
Call script for warm calls	Phone	Q3	Leads > 60 days old	MQL	G:\Mktg\Req...	Professional, help me learn	Advance to sales ready	8	1
Electrician vehicle lit	Brochure	New Electrician lead, send with literature pack	Electrician market	MQL	G:\Mktg\new	Valuable info specific to my use. Professional, Not too salesy	Download	7	0
Trailer overall video	Video	2 weeks after initial qualification	Landscaper market	MQL	G:\Mktg\new	Allow me to compare and assess. Clearly represent vehicle	Download	7	0
Carpenter vehicle lit	Brochure	New Carpenter lead, send with literature pack	Carpenter market	MQL	G:\Mktg\new	Valuable info specific to my use. Professional, Not too salesy	Download	6	0
Van accessories flyer	Flyer	Upon download or buyer initiated phone call/email	Carpenter and Electrician	MQL, SQL	G:\Mktg\new	Explain what's available on each vehicle, show value to my work	Open	6	1
Truck accessories flyer	Flyer	Upon download or buyer initiated phone call/email	Landscaper and Carpenter	MQL, SQL	G:\Mktg\new	Explain what's available on each vehicle, show value to my work	Open	6	0
Corporate video	Video	1 week after move to Deciding	Carpenter market	MQL	G:\Mktg\new	Why should I do business w/you?	Download	6	0
Jones Corp story	Case study	Upon download or buyer initiated phone call/email	Landscaper market	MQL	G:\Mktg\new	Read real world usage of product	Download	6	2
User Video - Smith Inc.	Video	1 week after move to Deciding	Carpenter market	SFO	G:\Mktg\new	See real world usage of product	Download	6	7
Service manual	Technical paper	TBD - repurpose this	All	SFO	G:\Mktg\man...	Deeper understanding of maintenance and operation	Download	5	10
Electrician vehicle webinar	Webinar	TBD - repurpose this	Electrician market	MQL	G:\Mktg\bro...	Valuable info specific to my use. Professional, Not too salesy	Accept & fill out form	5	7
Safety is built in ebook	eBook	User downloads something regarding any vehicle	All	SQL	G:\Mktg\scri...	Understand how technology and design makes my workers safer	Download	4	7
Modern trade vehicles article	Reprint	4 weeks into Deciding stage Coordinate w/sales	All	MQL	G:\Mktg\bro...	Unbiased article by 3rd party learn about today's vans	Download	4	0
Lift ramp paper	Technical paper	TBD - repurpose this	Landscaper market	SQL	G:\Mktg\wid...	Understand how to complete jobs better/faster	Download	4	9
Landscaper mailer	Direct mail	Internal trigger - start of integrated campaign	Landscaper market	MQL	G:\Mktg\bro...	Learn about benefits, provide download resources	Phone or landing pg	3	8
General mailer	Direct mail	Internal trigger - start of integrated campaign	All	MQL	G:\Mktg\bro...	Make me aware of you in case I need your products	Phone or landing pg.	3	5

© Table 5.7 ABC Custom Truck Works documented content library with value and effort ratings. They have circled the pieces they are likely to use for their new program (circled).

ABC selects 10 items that they feel have the best ROI as candidates for their new program (shown circled in Table 5.7) To download go to https://fairmontconcepts.com/tools-templates. Each is valuable to the customer and has a low resource drain to complete. They plan to revisit the list and pursue other items later as resources become available.

2. *Map the Content and Apply Date and Action Triggers*

Before you finalize all content, map out your drip marketing schedules, triggers, and follow up to triggers. Creating your plan first ensures you don't waste time repurposing or finalizing any content that will not be used.

Creating a lead nurturing plan that includes a general end market plan (shotgun) and one end market specific plan (rifle shot) can be a complex process. To simplify the process, start by laying the rough plans out on paper. Here's an example.

Nurturing Program for All Contacts in CRM

January	February	March	April	May	June
· Email send - Newsletter · Email send - Invite to an event (Subscriber and MQL only)	· Email send - General products eBook download (Subscriber and MQL only)	· Email send - Magazine article download	· Email send - Corporate video · Phone - Begin reclassification calls as follow up (MQL only)	· Email send - Service flyer dowload · Phone - Continue calls (MQL only)	· Email send - Video download · Email send - Flyer download · Phone - Finish calls (MQL only)

Nurturing Program for Target Market #1

January	February	March	April	May	June
· Direct mail send - Campaign #1, Part A (MQL only)	· Email send - Campaign #1, Part B (MQL, SQL) · Email send - Campaign #1, Part C (MQL, SQL)				· Email send - Campaign #2, Part A (MQL, SQL) · Email send - Campaign #2, Part B (MQL, SQL)

◎ Figure 5.8 A Nurturing Program that addresses both the general and target markets. All markets receive general content, and the target market receives both the general and the end market specific content.

Using Figure 5.8 as a guide, lay out your <u>annual</u> plan (as opposed to the six-month example) for the general market and for one target market. Using this visual format helps you space your lead interaction appropriately using a variety of content types and delivery vehicles.

- *Schedule your annual nurturing plan for the general market.*
  Start with the general market plan by laying out a schedule for the entire year using date based triggers only. In this drip marketing approach, note the intended audience(s) for each piece – subscriber, MQL, SQL, and/or SFO. This allows you to make the content relevant to the buyer stage(s).
- *Schedule your end market specific content.*
  Once you complete your annual drip marketing campaign intended for the general markets, move to your target end market plan. In this step, schedule individual pieces of content or campaigns using *only* date based triggers.
- *Incorporate your action triggers activities.*
  Add your response activities to buyer actions. For example, if a subscriber follows a CTA on your email by exchanging their name and phone number for an eBook download, make them an open marketing lead and call to qualify them as an MQL or OSL. The subscriber trigger is the download, and your response is the qualification call.

Lead nurturing won't happen unless you plan and prepare. Follow the steps above to plan the full year of drip marketing and specific campaigns and then prepare as much of the content as you can to ensure you're ready when the time comes to send. You can always adjust your plans as the year progresses and market dynamics change.

Note: **Gated Content**
Gated content requires contacts to provide something in order to receive content from you. It is most common that someone following a digital CTA must enter their email, name, company name and phone number to receive a download. Use gated content to obtain necessary information or to confirm that an event has occurred. Here's an example.

A subscriber lead has not provided you a name and phone number. Your goal is to obtain this information so you can qualify them by phone and move them along the buyer journey. Therefore, you provide gated content you think is valuable to them, and when they click on the CTA to obtain the content they must enter their name and phone number to receive it.

Avoid using gated content with MQLs, SQLs, or SFOs since they have already provided you with name and email. Advanced computer platforms enable you to set up accounts that allow previously signed in and approved visitors to access gated information without re-entering contact info.

Once you've developed your annual plan, enter it into a table similar to the one shown in Figure 5.9.

Drip Marketing Schedule - General Market

	Content Name or Title	Content Type	Trigger - Date based or Action based	Target Market	Stage	Content Location	Expectation of Recipient	CTA or goal	Buyer Action Trigger
	B	C	D	E	F	G	H	I	J
2	Newsletter - ABC Custom Truck Works	Email	Date: January 16 - Q1	All Markets	All	G:\Mktg\Newsletters	Learn about the industry, us, our products, culture, events	Phone call from them	1
3	Tradeshow Invite in NJ	Email	Date: January 30 (this is 3 weeks prior to event)	All Markets	Subscriber, MQL	G:\Mktg\ShowInv	Learn why I should go	Accept & fill out CTA form	1
4	Demo Days Event In NY	Email	Date: May 15 (this is 4 weeks prior to event)	All Markets	Subscriber, MQL	G:\Mktg\DemoDays	See products/people, interact with experts and peers	Accept & fill out CTA form	2
5	Complete Jobs Faster	Video	Date: April 10 - Q2	All Markets	MQL	G:\Mktg\ECampaign	Easy to run video, informative, interesting	Download	3
6	Happy Holidays greeting	HTML graphic	Date: December 6 - Q4	All Markets	All	G:\Mktg\ECampaign	Nice, respectful, positive well wishing	Open	-

Follow up to Triggers

	Content Name or Title	Content Type	Trigger - Date based or Action based	Target Market	Stage	Content Location	Expectation of Recipient	CTA or goal	Buyer Action Trigger
1	Call to qualify or re-qualify using BANT-F	Phone call script	Action: any situation where qualification is needed	All Markets	Subscriber, MQL	G:\Mktg\ScriptQualif	Have questions answered, be handled by appropriate person	Qualify	-
2	Send event details	Email	Action: Responds to our invitation to NJ tradeshow	All Markets	Subscriber, MQL	G:\Mktg\Newsletters	Any further details would be helpful.	Confirm attendance	-
3	Send accessories flyer	Email	Action: They downloaded video Complete Jobs Foster	All Markets	MQL	G:\Mktg\Newsletters	Receive other relevant info pertaining to completing jobs	Download	1

© Figure 5.9 The nurturing plan for ABC Custom Truck Works general market.

The top section of Figure 5.9 (the annual drip marketing schedule) shows the plan for sending out date triggered content. For a response to a CTA (column I) refer to the appropriate action trigger number (column J). The corresponding required interaction response to the buyer action is shown below in the lower section (Follow up to Triggers).

For example. Let's follow the *Complete Jobs Faster* email sent to ABC's marketing qualified leads. It includes a CTA offering a video download.

- *Pre-scheduled email send*
  Row 6 shows that ABC sends out an email to MQL leads in all markets offering recipients a video download.
  Trigger:
  The recipients who follow the CTA and download the video (cell I6) trigger response number 3 (cell j6).
- *2nd email send that is a follow up to trigger*
  ABC's marketing team goes to the *Responses to Triggers* table and executes activity 3 (row 13) by sending an email it believes will be of interest to those that downloaded the video. It includes a CTA offering an accessories flyer download.
  Trigger:
  For MQL leads that follow this second CTA (cell I13) and download the flyer, marketing follows trigger 1 (cell J13) and calls them.
- *Phone call to requalify as a follow up to the 2nd trigger*
  Those MQLs that followed both CTAs and downloaded the video and the accessories flyer have exhibited a high level of interest. Therefore, marketing calls the contact to requalify them (row 11), hoping to elevate them to sales ready status.

Once you have organized your annual nurturing plan, you are ready to prepare all content.

3. Create Content as Needed

Keeping your content fresh and relevant can seem like a daunting task, but leveraging the prep work you performed in steps 1 and 2 simplifies the process. You know precisely what content you need, and can go about repurposing content or creating new content as needed.

Here are a few tips to help you as you move through the creation phase.

- Always try to answer the questions buyers need answered before they will advance from their current stage.
- Look first to repurpose before creating new content.
- When creating recurring content (blog posts, newsletters), follow the formula: *"Where audience X gets content Y for the benefit of Z."* It's easy to get off track when you find you need to create new content, and having a template for your recurring content is helpful.
- Use the Barbell Message Creation Exercise (Solution 3 *Create Great Messaging)* when creating content that is highly valued by the recipients.
- Marketers never waste a good conversation by having it in private. Train your marketing and sales staff to be on the lookout for recurring questions from potential customers and customers that spark new content creation, or interesting conversations that your target audience would like to hear.

You can assign the responsibilities of creating or repurposing content to various members of the marketing department or assign one person to focus on content creation and meet one-on-one with staff for ideas. I have seen both approaches work. What doesn't work is assuming your nurturing content will remain relevant, fresh, and effective without concerted effort and managerial focus.

Keep a master library like the one shown in Table 5.5 to document the status of all content. Add columns assigning owners and due dates.

4.   *Execute, Track, and Continuously Improve*

Executing a nurturing program involves scheduling your drip marketing content and responding to triggers. Create an editorial calendar to manage drip marketing. Use a whiteboard, an Excel spreadsheet, or employ a service such as Trello, Divvy HQ, GetFlow, CoSchedule, or Gather Content. Most Marketing Automation software packages (listed above) provide an editorial calendar planning feature. Maintain a rough annual plan and detailed three-month plan at all times.

Track important indicators to alert you when your nurturing program is bogging down and slowing your funnel velocity. You should be able to get all the metrics you need if you employ a CRM system with embedded marketing automation. To ensure the data is accurate, stress proper and consistent data input to the marketing, sales, and service staff.

Here are fundamental nurturing metrics most companies are able to execute.

Nurturing Program Metrics

Topic	Metric
Funnel velocity	What is the average time spent in each of the 3 funnels? - You might want to use a 30 or 60 day running average to soften spikes.
Marketing funnel movement (quantity, not time)	How many subscribers provided phone and name to become OMLs this month? How many MQLs have become sales ready? - Compare to plan, compare to prior year. These are fundamental, high-level nurturing KPIs. Data is usually very easily obtained from a CRM.
OML response time	How many calls made within 5 minutes of contact becoming OML, and how many attempts per week if no contact made? - Response speed is key to drastically improve success in making contact. If contact is not made, are we continuing to try at our predetermined rate?
Email success	Track versus benchmark data (i.e., open rate, click through rate, competed CTA rate). - See Solution 4 for email campaign benchmarks.
Contact unsubscribes percent	How many new this month, and compared to prior year? - Some unsubscribes (.3 to 1%) are OK. Shows your nurturing system is helping to keep your CRM healthy.
Website downloads - unsolicited	Number of downloads per month. - This is an indicator of potential customer interest if they are already in your CRM. It is also an indication of SEO performance if they are not in your CRM.
Nurture interactions per month	Number of marketing funnel interactions? Sales funnel interactions? (will be much lower than marketing funnel) - Keep your program alive. Compare to last year and to plan.
Phone call to MQLs	Requalifying MQLs by phone each year? - Might limit to three call attempts, leaving message first and last time. Can be outsourced.

◎ Table 5.10 Fundamental nurturing metrics.

You must track metrics to obtain business status and to drive positive behavior. Eliminate metrics if they don't result in an action when the number moves away from optimal. Every metric shortfall should spark a countermeasure, even if it is only to "watch the number for several more cycles to determine if it is a blip or a trend." Staff closest to the metric should record the data and supply countermeasures if the number falls short. The supervisor or department head should report the results and countermeasures at the agreed upon frequency.

Effective marketing is about adapting to the ever-changing market conditions. Nurturing programs are key examples of that statement - they require constant adjustment. For the sake of continuous improvement, employ A/B testing whenever possible before launching emails, constantly collect questions from the marketplace coming in to customer facing staff, ask for feedback, send surveys, and have open conversations with those potential customers willing to participate about your marketing efforts. It's not easy to stay relevant while addressing thousands of contacts, so design in your continuous improvement feedback loops.

Summary

Revenue may be the lifeblood of your organization, but leads provide nourishment to keep that blood pumping. For that reason, it's imperative that you get the most out of your leads. Ignored leads result in slow funnels, a bad reputation, and revenue shortfalls - which can ultimately doom a company.

Ensure a steady flow of solid opportunities by providing the information and interaction your contacts want, when they want it. A well-designed and efficiently executed nurturing program is the best way to make that happen.

Solution 5 References

1. *30 Thought-Provoking Lead Nurturing Stats You Can't Ignore,* by Pamela Vaughan, HubSpot, January 18, 2012.
    https://blog.hubspot.com/blog/tabid/6307/bid/30901/30-thought-provoking-lead-nurturing-stats-you-can-t-ignore.aspx

2. *Calculating The Real ROI From Lead Nurturing*, Demand Gen Report, 2014, white paper, http://www.demandgenreport.com/industry-resources/white-papers/204-calculating-the-real-roi-from-lead-nurturing-.html and https://www.hubspot.com/marketing-statistics

3. *Lead Generation Benchmark Report,* MarketingSherpa, 2012, Lead author Jen Doyle, http://content.marketingsherpa.com/data/public/reports/benchmark-reports/BMR-Lead_Generation.pdf

4. *Hard Date to Justify your Marketing Automation Investment,* blog post, citing Market2Lead, David Raab, 2010, http://customerexperiencematrix.blogspot.com/2010/09/hard-data-to-justify-your-marketing.html

5. *Lead Response Management Study,* InsideSales.com, 2013, https://www.insidesales.com/insider/lead-management/5-products-that-help-you-stop-losing-leads/

6. Fairmont Concepts calculations collected through the MarketMD™ Business Health Checkup.

7. *Why It Takes 7 to 13+ Touches To Deliver a Qualified Sales Lead (Part 6: Case Study),* Laura Beasley, President of Beasley Direct and Online Marketing, for the Data and Marketing Association Blog, August 3, 2016, https://thedma.org/blog/marketing-education/why-it-takes-7-to-13-touches-to-deliver-a-qualified-sales-lead-part-6-case-study/

8. *Best Marketing Automation Software 2017,* blog from G2Crowd, https://www.g2crowd.com/categories/marketing-automation

Solution 6: Building a Great Sales Team

Most research shows that buyers are nearly two-thirds the way through their purchasing process before they contact vendors. So, does that minimize the importance of having an effective sales team?

Absolutely not.

The buyer still must get that final third of the way to make the purchase – the most critical part of the journey. Brand, marketing, and product offering can get you the opportunity, but sales capability determines whether you close the deal.

The higher the purchase price the more important the selling skills – and this book is focused on big ticket B2B sales. An effective sales force can make the difference between making the sale and watching a competitor snatch away the purchase order.

This solution chapter is addressed mostly to sales management – the group responsible for building an effective sales team. However, the marketing organization also plays an important role in helping to make the sales team successful, so their roles and responsibilities in helping to build great sales teams is discussed where appropriate.

Winning against your competition is always a key goal for your sales people. Some do that effectively, while others struggle mightily. Closing the deal rarely comes down to product knowledge. Instead, getting the sale is the result of selling skills. Though some people are born with sales talent, selling skills can be learned. It is the responsibility of sales management to help the sales team develop skills needed to land more business and drive revenue for the organization.

Effective Selling Technique

I have found that it is best not to concentrate on teaching sales people how to quote or how to close. The sales manager is typically involved in these late-stage tasks where hands-on training takes place naturally. The most important skills for your sales team to learn is to focus on the *beginning of the sales process*. The first few interactions are the most important ones, as they either get you on the final vendor list or tossed out of contention.

Three Key Preselling Goals

One of the biggest mistakes low performing sales people make is to start selling the solution too soon.

It's natural to want to quickly highlight the virtues of company and product, but without first understanding the situation and gaining the potential customer's confidence, the salesperson will face a series of objections which can derail the sale and result in an overall lower close rate.

Potential customers are self-serving. They want to know that you understand them before they will be open to hearing about your solution. In addition, if you make the mistake of offering a solution to a problem that they don't have, it can be difficult to ever get them to listen again.

Before selling your solution, you must meet three key preselling goals.

- Uncover needs
- Establish credibility
- Understand the competitive landscape

Once this threefold foundation has been set, the salesperson can move to solving the buyer's needs and demonstrating superiority versus the competition.

Don't Sell Too Soon

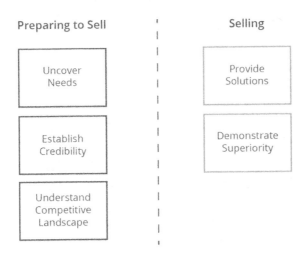

Figure 6.1 During interactions with the customer, top sales people accomplish three 3 pre-selling goals on the left before moving to selling the product and proving superiority on the right.

As Figure 6.1 illustrates, you must first address the three preselling goals on the left. You do this by weaving all three into natural conversations with the potential customer. Only when these three goals are met does the top salesperson move the conversation to the right side and begin the selling process.

Note: **The difference between customer needs and market needs**
In Solution 2 *Uncovering the Voice of the Customer*, I discussed uncovering the needs of your best target end market, an activity the marketing department handles. In this solution, I am talking about the needs of specific potential customers. This is an activity handled by sales people as they work individual sales projects.

One of the surest indicators that a salesperson has jumped from the pre-selling to selling too soon is that they start getting several objections from the potential customer. Training your salespeople to respond to common objections is important, but it is even more important to get them to understand that objections come when your solution doesn't match the potential customer's needs, they don't have confidence in you, or a competitor is in the lead. Top sales people rarely have to respond to objections because they accomplish the pre-selling goals first. More on the handling of objections later in the sales training section of this solution chapter.

The First Sales Call

When a lead comes to you as sales ready, your first conversation with a potential customer is all about them – their wants, their problems, their needs. Their time is valuable, and they are looking to get down to the final list of companies they plan to consider for their purchase. They will be quick to cut you from their list if they don't feel you can help them. Your salesperson must quickly uncover important needs and establish personal and company credibility or you will be excluded from the opportunity.

While making the cut is the primary goal, sales people also have a secondary responsibility to qualify the customer. They need to make sure that a genuine sales opportunity exists. Thus, the first sales call represents an interesting two-way qualification process.

Focus on the Three Main Preselling Goals

This first sales conversation to a sales ready lead focuses initially on uncovering needs and establishing credibility. Understanding the competitive landscape is also important, but if it isn't possible in this first meeting, the salesperson can always find out more about the competitive landscape later in the process.

Response Time

Potential customers today expect fast response on all interactions. Sales people are not always available to make an immediate phone call, but you should strive to have someone get back to prospective customers on any question or request as quickly as possible.[1,2,3]

Avoid Mistakes that Quickly End Your First Call

Avoid these common mistakes that can eliminate your company from further consideration at the outset of the process.

Mispronouncing names: Practice pronouncing the name of the contact and the company a few times before calling. If you are unsure, make a good first attempt as you ask the person at the front desk for the proper pronunciation. If you are connected directly to the contact, simply ask for clarification upon introductions.

Don't assume friendship: Sales people who begin their first dialog with a potential customer using an overly friendly tone make nearly every buyer uncomfortable. It shows arrogance and a desire to be in a place of power above the potential customer – the opposite of friendly. Earn credibility first by being professional.

Don't recite your pitch: Some sales people think they are doing their job if they memorize or read their pitch. This approach rarely works and shows a general lack of respect. The potential customer can tell that you're just delivering a spiel. Have a dialog, memorize short phrases, but keep the tone conversational.

Don't talk too much: Initial calls are about uncovering needs, establishing credibility, and understanding the competitive landscape. Get your potential customer talking - you can't learn these things if you're not listening.

Note: **Example of a first phone call**
The first call from the salesperson to a sales ready lead is similar to a marketing qualification call (see Solution 4 *Generating More Leads*). The following is intended to provide guidelines, not a script. The discussion must be more conversational rather than canned.

"Hello, my name is ____ from ____. You spoke to ____ from my company. My company is a leader in providing _____, and I am experienced in working with companies like yours. I'd love to see if my company can help you. How are you today Mr./Ms. _____?" Clearly describe who you are, that you are responding to their inquiry, and provide one reason they should welcome your expertise. If you are unsure how to pronounce their name, ask for clarification now.

"I understand from your last conversation with us that you are looking to improve your _____. We've had a lot of success helping companies like yours with that very issue. Can you give me a little information on what you are looking for so that I may help you? The salesperson must take it from the top, and not assume the information they received from the marketing or inside sales staff is accurate or complete. Seek ways to uncover needs and include an occasional credibility generating statement.

"How familiar are you with _____? Have you ever seen one in operation?" This dialog thread uncovers how far they are in the buying process, and might indicate the competitive landscape.

"What have you liked or disliked so far in the solutions you have seen?" This question is like the one above, but more focused on getting the potential customer talking about needs and the competition.

"You mentioned the need to reduce downtime with the equipment you have now (shows you listened to the potential customer's problems). That makes perfect sense, as we've seen some of our other customers work on the same problem (establishing credibility). When you look at downtime, what do you include in the cost?"

This illustrates how to expand the importance of a need you know you can solve into as big of a problem as possible. This is an example of turning an implied need into a clearly described explicit need.[4,5]

Building Credibility While Uncovering Needs

Much has been written about uncovering needs, but not enough emphasis placed on the importance of establishing credibility. You won't be able to uncover all needs until you have established enough credibility in the potential customer's mind. Unless potential customers believe you can help, they will hold back many fears and needs.

Weaving brief and relevant credibility statements into a back-and-forth conversation with a potential customer is an essential skill. These credibility statements are mixed into discussions sparked by open ended questions (see Solution 2 *Uncovering the Voice of the Customer* and Neil Rackham's classic *Spin Selling*[4] book). They are not long diatribes extolling the virtues of your company, but instead are brief phrases meant to convey to the potential customer that you can truly help them. To establish credibility, your questions should include key statements about your company's longevity, experience, reputation, and stability.

Show that you have experience with their issue: As potential customer needs become clearer, express in a short reflective phrase how you and your company have intimate knowledge about the problem the potential customer is having, and that you have had success solving the problem with other customers.

Highlight how your offerings directly apply to their situation: Mention the wide acceptance and reliability of your product or service as it relates to the potential customer's problem.

Emphasize that you have extensive experience in their business area: Prepare one or two facts about yourself ready to interject into the conversation, including longevity with the company, industry knowledge, and technical background. These are important, but keep them brief. If the potential customer senses you're bragging, you will lower your credibility.

Show that you know about their company: Perform research on the potential customer's company so you know whether it is large or small, public or private. Check their website for recent press releases that detail important changes, closures, expansions or events. This will enable you to interject something about the potential customer's company that impresses you during your conversation.

Point out that your company is full of experienced professionals: Always highlight the expertise of your company's staff. Explain that they are the best at what they do, are hardworking, strongly supportive, collaborative, and intensely focused on delighting customers. Never make a disparaging comment about your company or co-workers.

Establish that your company is a reputable leader: Include any relevant statistics that demonstrate your company's leadership in the market such as the number of customers successfully using your product or service. Discuss inventions or groundbreaking technology the company has developed.

Illustrate that you have things in common with them: If the opportunity presents itself, create a personal connection in some way through a common experience or professional acquaintance. This needs to occur in the natural flow of the conversation and shouldn't be forced or contrived.

Note: **Uncover all needs, but focus on those you can solve**
After uncovering all the needs of the potential customer, establishing credibility, and understanding the competitive landscape, the salesperson must decide where to focus the potential customer's attention.
- If your company can't solve a specific problem, move on to one you can solve.
- If all your competitors can solve a specific problem equally well, then continue to probe until you find issues that your company excels at solving.
Amplify the customer problems associated with those things where you have a competitive advantage.

Making credibility statements is not about chest pounding. It's about gradually building up a sense of confidence the potential customer has in your salesperson and your company. Potential customers looking to solve a problem will answer a question or two, but to get them to really open up about their problems you must build trust and credibility.

Understanding the Competitive Landscape while Uncovering Needs

Top sales people eventually identify which competitors are involved in a project. Why is this so important? Why not just sell your own product and ignore competitors? Because, if you don't know how you compare to the competition in the buyer's mind, then you might be setting competitors up to win by promoting an attribute where they – rather than you - excel.

For example, if you heavily promote your two-year parts warranty and a low monthly charge for 9am to 5pm technical phone support without knowing one of your top competitors has a three-year parts and labor warranty and no charge for 24/7 technical phone support, then you've created a major problem. The buyer now has obvious reasons to strike you from the potential supplier list. Once your competitor sees your mistake on one sales opportunity, they will promote their advantage even more heavily on the next one. If you ignore the competition and allow competitors to identify and exploit your weaknesses, your market share will steadily decline.

Companies with superior brands and strong market share sometimes profess that they ignore the competition, boasting that they blaze their own trail. But even if they tout this high-level strategy, somewhere in the background there is a team of effective marketing and sales professionals who have done their competitive homework and positioned their "unique" offering to win against competition. Sales is a tough zero-sum game, and you simply can't be confident you'll win unless you know who you are competing against.

Top sales people rarely ask directly for names of competitors. They find out subtly while uncovering needs. If a potential customer makes comments suggesting they have been conducting research into finding a solution, a top salesperson compliments them on their progress so far and asks what they have learned that is of particular interest. A well-trained salesperson can then usually identify which competitors have the characteristics the potential customer reveals.

Sales people can also identify competitors from the questions the potential customer asks. For example, if a buyer asks about a certain feature - such as three-year parts warranty - top sales people know which competitor has that feature.

Even when salespeople know against whom they are competing, they should still refrain from competitor bashing. Instead, they should promote their strengths that address customer needs, especially those that maximize your capabilities and minimize the benefit of competitor's offerings.

Covering the Three Main Preselling Goals Takes Time

The first call is important, but it is just a start. Assuming that both parties pass the other on this two-way qualification, your salesperson is still not likely to be ready to actually begin selling. Successful salespeople will conduct more detailed fact-finding calls working the three pre-selling goals of uncovering needs, establishing credibility, and understanding the competitive landscape before they ever offer a solution.

- You can't provide a solution until you completely understand buyer needs.
- You can't uncover all buyer needs until you establish credibility and get the buyer to open up.
- You can't effectively position your offerings until you know needs and the competitive landscape.
- You can't understand the competitive landscape unless you know the competition well.
- You cannot win an order unless the buyer feels you understand their needs, are a credible solution provider, and have a better solution than the competition.

Preparing Your Team to Sell

Once the three main preselling goals have been met, it's time to sell. Successful sales teams have an effective sales manager/coach to lead them.

Some managers make the mistake of hiring sales people and offering only pure on-the-job training; setting them off with little or no training on the product, market, or company specific selling techniques. This flawed approach results in overly long sales cycles and many lost orders for new hires. An effective sales training system focuses on shortening the sales learning curve, improving win rate, and better serving customers. The sales manager is the key to implementing this more enlightened program.

Sales managers should also be effective sales people who know the market and customers well. Sales reps will respond to leaders who have demonstrated success "on the street." This credibility not only allows them to properly train the reps to improve but can be indispensable in helping reps close business in a team selling situation. Although sales managers have other responsibilities like reporting and forecasting, their top priority – first and foremost – must be to help sales staff close business.

Sales reps often feel like they're out there on an island, doing their work by themselves. Group meetings help make salespeople feel part of a team. Conduct monthly conference calls and semi-annual sales training meetings to build team chemistry and keep everyone informed about the company,

Monthly Team-wide Conference Calls

Gather the sales team once a month to discuss, as a group, better ways to win business. This ongoing interaction helps keep sales people connected to the company and their peers. Peer to peer training instills a culture of excellence in your sales group. Pulling senior sales people out of the field to travel with and help train others is also valuable – but difficult. Regular department-wide conference calls are an effective alternative.

Note: **Logistics of the monthly sales team conference call**
- Use a computer-based conferencing service that allows out of office staff to join by phone.
- Create a full agenda for each meeting.
- Email documents to be discussed before the meeting.
- Monday mornings or Friday afternoons are the most likely times the team is in their office so are ideal times for calls.
- Keep the calls to one hour.

- Make meetings mandatory except for vacations or excused absences (e.g., flight, customer meeting, illness).

Sales people not attending should send their input or comments to the sales manager ahead of the meeting.

The meetings should be judgement-free, open forums for sharing ideas, problems and successes. Avoid including senior leaders from outside the sales team unless there is a specific reason for them to speak. Key marketing people might attend some or all of the meeting, strengthening teamwork, describing events, and coordinating activities.

Part of the monthly call can be devoted to "Sales Stories," where sales people recount how they were able to win an order through teamwork, overcoming an obstacle, or some other technique worth sharing. The sales manager must set up these discussions ahead of time so they stay on point. Prior to the meeting, select the individual who will tell his or her sales story, meet with them to review their story and set the duration. Follow a format that delivers the most relevant information and avoids a long-non-productive-chest pounding narrative.

Sales Stories should follow this structure:

1. Situation
    End market, product or service being sold, competition, customer specific information
2. Obstacle
    What was the primary issue to overcome or significant aspect of the project worth relaying to the team.
3. Solution and result
    Include sales tools, teamwork, and strategy
4. Lessons Learned
    Summarize the key takeaways

Document the sales stories, as they are valuable training tools for young sales hires.

Other topics to cover in the call include product and service updates, company news, high level metrics tied to sales goals, department-wide budget updates, pricing, promotions, and news on the competitive landscape. Keep the meeting brisk and have remote sales people speak as often as practical. Solicit meeting feedback privately to help ensure you are making these get-togethers so valuable that the sales team looks forward to attending.

In my experience, no department has ever benefited more from department-wide monthly meetings than a sales department, so be diligent in holding them.

Sales Training Meetings

Set up annual or semi-annual sales meetings with both junior and senior sales staff present.

Selling is intense – and the meeting needs to be intense as well. Sales people are used to working in short bursts, changing topics during the day as they move from one project to another, not sitting for days in meetings. Have a training activity where they are up out of their chair part of every morning and afternoon (especially mid-afternoon after lunch when people are tired). In general, sales training meetings should be one and a half to two and a half days long. Any longer and the non-sales related meeting topics will slide in while the sales staff's eyelids slide shut.

Focus exclusively on sales training. Training meetings are not opportunities for executives to learn about the market or catch up on the commercial side of the business. Their presence can change the training meeting vibe from useful and motivating to boring and stifled. If you must handle non-sales training related subjects add extra time to the meeting.

But be careful not to dilute the potency of your sales training with too many non-training activities. Ask these questions before adding a topic to your training agenda:

- Will this help motivate the team and help them sell?

  YES: Presentations by the leader of your company.
  YES: Future new products and services. But don't reveal so much that salespeople want to hold back sales in expectation of the new product.
  YES: Training on efficient use of the CRM in the field to help organize project data and free up time to sell.

YES: Explanation on how the executive team uses the CRM data to make important business decisions, such as production volumes, and market trends. This can help the sales team understand the importance of keeping CRM data current.

NO: A discussion of HR's benefits package. Though important, this topic is probably not motivational and better handled on a conference call, with smaller groups or one on one.

- Is this relevant to every salesperson in the room?

  YES: Won order case studies.

  YES: Competitive discussions when the competitor spans all territories.

  NO: A review of sales funnels for each territory. The manager should handle this one-on-one with the sales lead of each territory.

  NO: Expense reviews by territory. The manager should handle this one-one-one.

- Is it something that must be handled face-to-face?

  YES: Role playing on describing a new product. In room peer-to-peer interaction is important.

  NO: Finance presentation on the company's OpEx budget plan and actual. This is better handled on the monthly conference call.

Sales meetings are rare opportunities for managers of various departments who want to get to know the salespeople better. Set up the interaction for breakfasts, lunches, dinner, and entertainment events.

Effective sales training meetings require extensive planning. Sales meetings should be planned and developed by the sales leader, product managers, key marketing staff, and vetted by top sales people for value and relevancy. Conducting a great sales meeting is a team effort.

Consider including these 10 essential components.

1. *Overview pitches for key products or services*
2. *Competition training*
3. *New product training*
4. *Role playing on objections and sales scenarios*

5. Important sales wins
6. Sales Tools
7. Lead management – the marketing, sales and customer funnels
8. Company strategy review from the president or CEO
9. Sales promotions
10. Outside training resources

The Overview Pitch

Although successful sales people never deliver a standard pitch verbatim, they still appreciate being trained on a well thought out overview where they can pick up themes and short phrases. An organized overview pitch is a carefully crafted sales presentation broken down into a 30 second elevator pitch and an expanded version for formal presentations. Both versions key off your messaging and drive home benefits and value. The expanded version can incorporate images, videos or data to back up the key points. All pitches should follow a common format and be easy to remember and deliver.

Example topics for overview pitches are key products, services programs, the company, technological advantages, and other topics that provide you with a competitive advantage and match customer needs.

The overview pitch should flow naturally into a conversation with the potential customer. The entire pitch should not be memorized. However, sales people should commit key phrases and short snippets to memory to be used during presentations to potential customers. During sales training, focus the team on retaining the general elements and key points of the overview pitch.

Here is a sample outline for the elevator pitch and detailed pitch:

1. Elevator Pitch (30 second monologue)

Value Proposition – A short sentence that describes for whom the offering is intended and the primary benefit or value. *"The easiest to use and productive _____ available for the _____ industry."* Or, *"Our product helps _____ people solve _____ by providing _____."*

Credibility – A short sentence as to why the potential customer should listen to the salesperson and why the potential customer should consider the company and products offered. Here are three examples. *"We are the world's largest provider of _____ and have solved _____ for customers just like you for the last 20 years." "We are number one in customer satisfaction according to independent market research." "We spent ____ engineering hours developing and then field testing this new ____, so you can be confident it is robust and efficient."*

<u>How</u> – A one to three sentence description of how the value proposition is delivered. Focus on benefits, not features. *"Using our _____ technology, we are able to produce 3x faster than any other system, yet we have simultaneously reduced the steps in doing this to make it simple to operate. That is how we are the easiest to use and most productive ____ available."*

<u>Objection Prevention</u> (if time permits) – A statement that counters the most common objection the potential customer might have before it comes up. *"Some people might think that the increased productivity and ease of use means the price is not competitive, but as the world leader we have the technology and unit volumes to remain very competitively priced."*

2. Expanded Presentation

Here you step through a, b, c, and d above in more detail, and include relevant sales tools for key points.

<u>Value Proposition</u> – stays the same as above.

<u>How</u> – Provide a list of the top features and the benefit and value they deliver. You can use an abridged version of your Feature Function Benefit (FFB, see Tables 3.7 and 3.8) and add pertinent sales tools to prove the benefits.

<u>Credibility</u> – Include a list of short statements that foster the credibility of the salesperson, the company, or the offering that the salesperson can drop into the conversation.

<u>Objection prevention</u> - Detail the top few objections you predict will be mentioned and craft a thoughtful and persuasive response. Once into this detailed pitch, the salesperson is not trained to bring up objections, but they are trained on how to handle the common ones if brought up by the potential customer.

A well-crafted overview pitch and supporting sales tools gives your salesperson confidence, the key to success in sales. Even the best sales people benefit from thoughtful and well-executed sales pitch training. Use role playing drills to help them master the elevator pitch and expanded presentation and the use of appropriate sales tools.

Note: **Do top sales people memorize their pitches and statements?**

Yes and no. Top sales people memorize short phrases and ideas, and they master how to weave them into ideas they use in conversations. Most don't memorize paragraphs or stories verbatim. The phrases and ideas are ingredients to effective conversations. Your sales training meeting must contain many clear, persuasive, short phrases that drive home important benefits of your offerings and will resonate with the marketplace. Make the sales people use them in the meeting, and praise them when they do. Make sure they leave the meeting armed with the ingredients for effective sales conversations.

Competition Training

Devote time for training on your top two or three competitors as a way to build confidence in your salespeople. Assign sales people to act as keepers of information and expertise for each significant competitor. Sales people interact with competitors directly and indirectly more than anyone else in your organization so they are the best sources of intel on competitors.

The team must keep each other up to date on an ongoing basis, with each member sending competitive information and strategy to the assigned teammate. Assigned salespeople should present a SWOT analysis to the rest of the team at the sales meeting. Concentrate on the competition that spans all or most of the territories. Focusing on a small competitor who acts in only a few territories will mean nothing to most of the sales people, and once a salesperson shuts down in your meeting it is very hard to get them interested again. Focus on commonly occurring scenarios, not one-off occurrences.

Have sales people share stories related to a major competitor – orders won and lost.

Conclude the training on each competitor by answering these three questions to get to the heart of what the salesperson needs to know to win.

1. What is the competitor's message and sales pitch?
2. How does this competitor sell against you? What do they say and what do they do?
3. How do you beat them? What tools and strategies work best against this competitor?

New Product Release or Product Update

Your sales team needs to see that the company continues to invest in creating new offerings. Wherever practical, use your sales meetings to explain product roadmaps and showcase continuous advancements in products and services – even small ones - that build excitement and confidence in sales people. In fact, as described in Solution 9 *Making your Current Offerings More Attractive*, sometimes you don't even need anything new. You just have to probe deeper into the offerings you have to find new benefits.

Sales people need new things to sell to keep interactions with potential customers fresh. They get inspired by new sales tools like brochures, quote examples, technical documents, images, movies, web links, case studies, and overview pitches. At the meeting, use your best sales people to demonstrate how to get the most out of the new products.

Follow these steps when releasing a new product or service or re-training on an existing one.

1. *The need*
   Explain the reason the marketplace needs this product or service. Identify the end markets it addresses. Show that your findings are backed by solid market research.

2. *Technical presentation*
   Make this brief and to the point. Include development team members, how the product was developed/improved, what problems were overcome, and the teamwork and effort that was involved. The technical presentation will build confidence as it shows sales people the effort put forth to bring the product or service to market, the depth of talent in the company, and acknowledges the team behind the scenes who contributed.

3. *Feature, Function, Benefit review*
   Detail the features of the new product and illustrate the ways in which they match customer needs and the benefits and value they provide. Stress benefits over features.

4. *Overview pitch*
   Provide a strong, well thought out pitch for the new product or service. Veteran sales people will appreciate the starting point as they develop

their own presentation, and less experienced sales people will benefit from a detailed game plan.

5. *Collateral and other sales tools*
    Provide new and updated collateral and sales tools.
6. *Commercial information*
    Clearly define pricing, options, discounting, indirect partner involvement, lead times, and any other relevant commercial information. Review a sample quotation.
7. *Competitive review*
    Review how the new product or services measures up to the competition and where it might provide a new advantage.
8. *Objections and responses*
    Boost your sales team's confidence by providing practical responses to the objections they are likely to face. Rely on your experienced, knowledgeable sales people to predict potential customer objections.

Prior to the meeting, have one or two experienced sales people review your presentation and provide you with feedback. This offers you a chance to improve your presentation and gain important advocates.

Role Playing Objections and Sales Scenarios

Role-playing is an effective training tool for practicing sales scenarios and handling buyer objections.

Many sales people hate to role play in front of their peers, but you must make them do it. There is no better way to get them to absorb the sales training content and be ready to apply it than to practice it live in the meeting. Spend hours in your meeting role playing, but break the sessions up into 30-minute segments, interspersed throughout the sessions.

Work hard to set up a non-threatening environment. Explain that acting ability is not important. When they are asked to respond to an objection or a scenario, they can either act it out using another person as the potential customer or they can narrate it.

Follow this sequence.

*   *Collect scenarios and objections*

Before the meeting collect scenarios and objections from the sales team and from technical, marketing, and service staff. Number and print the best of them on paper, leaving room for people to take notes.

- *Describe the exercise*

Be sure to stress that no judgment will be made on execution, no Oscars or Emmys will be awarded, and that the only goal is to help the team learn how to do their jobs more effectively.

- *Conduct the exercise*

Select an objection or scenario, read it, and project it on screen.

Give everyone two minutes to work independently and write down how they would approach the situation: what would they do, what tools would they use and what advancement would they pursue?

Have one salesperson role play their response directly to the sales manager. He or she can choose any presentation method - speaking hypothetically or acting in a more realistic way. They can use tools or just describe what tools they would use. Each rep should take their own notes. Every person should have to respond to at least one scenario or objection at some time during the course of the meeting.

Do not pass judgement. Instead, open a dialog with the entire team by asking, "What did you like about what they said?" and "What would you add (not correct)."

Product managers, technical experts, and service experts might also be in the room to add valuable thoughts from their expert position. Exclude anyone who is not vital to the exercise or the mood will tighten and the outcome will be less than ideal.

Not every rep will come up with the ideal answer, but with the additional input from the rest of the sales team you will end up with a strong result. Have someone document the an effective response and hand it out at the end of the meeting. There can be more than one response to each sales scenario or objection, so the optimum response to the objection is not going to be the only possible effective response.

Note: **Effective sales people avoid objections**

Getting more than one objection from the potential customer in a sales call is a signal that your sales call is not going well. It suggests that either competitors are involved and planting objections against your offering, you haven't established credibility, or you haven't uncovered needs. Effective sales people get few or no objections in the sales call because they have spent enough time on the three pre-selling goals: uncovering needs, establishing credibility, understanding the competitive landscape.

Suggestions for handling objections:

1. Consider why the objection was voiced. Did a competitor plant a seed? Is there a need that you did not yet uncover? Does this potential customer doubt your credibility?

2. If you have a good response to the objection, explain why it is a great point, expand the problem to be even bigger than the potential customer suggested it might be, use the right tools, and solve it. Use clear benefit and value statements with your solution, and move the discussion forward immediately so that the potential customer cannot add more objections.

3. If you don't have a good response, tell the customer you will get back to him or her later.

4. Backtrack to the discovery phase of the sales process and go after the three preselling goals again. You have missed something, so stop selling and start uncovering again.

Important Sales Wins

Selling is more like a sport than almost any other function in the company. Like a baseball or softball batter, salespeople will have more failures than successes. The takeaway? Celebrate and learn from important hits to keep the team motivated.

In your sales meetings, celebrating wins is important, but learning from wins is even better. Select important sales victories that are common to all territories and highlight best practices. Your team can learn from losses as well, so explore them in the same way. However, focus on learning from wins versus losses in a 3 to 1 ratio, so that the learning is positive and motivational.

Encourage comments and input from both junior and senior sales people to maintain a positive, non-threatening environment for dialogue and learning. Start off on the right foot by having two of your sales people have one story each that you want everyone to hear. The story should illustrate a strategy or tactic that provides everyone with a learning moment. Have each presentation end with a general discussion of the best practices that were used.

Sales Tools

You wouldn't send a carpenter to a job site without a tape measure and saw. In the same way, don't send your sales team into the field without proper selling tools and training on how to use them effectively to close deals.

Effective sales tools help sales people communicate key points, provide an ongoing reminder of best practices, build presentation confidence, and help focus their energy. Sales reps will tend to sell into the segments where you have provided the best tools, so make sure your best tools are always designed for your best end markets.

Consider providing the following sales tools.

- *Physical samples*
  If appropriate for your offering, provide something that can be held and touched by the potential customer that relates to an important aspect of your offering. Set yourself apart from the competitors by having an impressive and unique demonstration product. It should be light and, if your sales staff must fly, be able to be sent through airport security.

  People remember things they touch most of all, then what they see, followed by what they hear. Whenever possible, provide your potential customers with a variety of media to help them remember your key points.
- *Printed and downloadable collateral*
  Corporate brochure intended to gain credibility. Product brochures showing benefits and value. Include features only as they convert into benefits and value. Case studies representing your target end markets to gain credibility. Whitepapers covering technical topics.
- *Your company website.*
  Most potential customers use websites extensively to research and compare competitive offerings. If your website has been developed properly and has a significant amount of content, then your sales people can use it as a data resource and a sales presentation tool. Ensure your sales team is adept at locating and sharing content useful in the sales process. Encourage them to give feedback to keep your website up to date and effective.
- *Video and electronic image library*

In my experience with high dollar sales, a thorough video, document, and image library are among the most powerful tools in the salesperson's bag. Provide digital data focused on your company, products, technical specs, and customer success stories.

Although PowerPoint was the sales presentation vehicle of choice decades ago, it doesn't always work in many sales situations today. Either the environment is wrong for projecting or the audience won't tolerate a canned, sequential slide presentation. Provide a variety of sales images, videos, and documents that can be accessed quickly via an easy to navigate format.

- *Team selling*

Team selling is extremely effective in high dollar, B2B sales. Providing demonstrations by experts within your company shows organizational expertise and raises buyer confidence. The more capable and talented people you can put in front of the potential customer the better. Make sure the staff members you bring into the selling process understand their role, how to deliver the right message, how to watch for cues from the salesperson, and what to avoid saying or doing. Effective team selling can occur remotely through screen sharing and video conferencing capabilities when face-to-face is not possible.

Referring to other key players in your company can be another valuable form of team selling. Sales people should mention your local service person by name and highlight his or her competence and experience. Discuss the founders of the company, and how their philosophy of customer support and execution impacts every aspect of your company. Bring up the marketing person who conducted the first qualification phone call, and how they always strive to serve customers. Point people out from the literature and speak to their contributions and talents. Sales people should proudly present your company staff as a team of professionals without equal. Impress the potential customer with the strength and depth of the company team, and by expressing a positive attitude and culture.

- *CRM*

Sales people responsible for closing high dollar sales carry many projects at any given time. They cannot handle this volume without some help. CRM software is a crucial tool for keeping the sales team organized and helping them move projects through the sales funnel. Too often leadership wants the CRM to be a sales watchdog tool – measuring efficiency and effectiveness. To some extent, a CRM can provide such information, however, the primary sales use of a CRM must be to help sales people keep many projects moving forward at the fastest possible rate. Train staff well on how to effectively use their CRM to help them close business.

Successful sales teams have effective sales tools. The best source of ideas for proper tools is the sales team who is out there every day working with prospects and customers. They know what they need. Get their input, involve them in the creation process, and provide them with the effective tools they deserve.

Lead Management

Clearly explain the marketing funnel segment, sales funnel segment, and customer funnel segment. Show the tie-in between marketing and sales, and how to efficiently work together to maximize the advancement and closure of projects. The sales, marketing, and service staff must work together smoothly. Make sure sales understands how lead nurturing gets them more sales ready leads and how the aftermarket service team helps drive repeat business.

Consider reviewing lead management guidelines such as the length of time it should take for sales to qualify a new lead (OSL) sent to them from marketing, how many projects the sales team should be carrying at any given time to hit their sales goals, funnel velocity, and the number of interactions the sales team should be having with potential customers at various positions along the buyer journey. Solicit ideas from the sales team as to how to get more out of the funnel segments.

Company Strategy Review from the President or CEO

Sales people who might work out of home offices and rarely meet with the leadership team benefit from understanding the company direction and strategy and their role in it. Ask your top leader to provide a brief presentation describing the current state, initiatives, and other important company happenings.

Sales Promotions

Sales promotions and spiffs don't only breathe life into a sales team, but they also allow the company to point the sales teams toward a special goal, such as the sale of a new product, breaking into a new end market, or reaching a volume or profit goal. Using the sales meeting to publicly announce the promotion is a highly effective way to get the sales team's competitive juices flowing.

Outside Training Resources.

Third party training can bring novelty and excitement to your sales meeting and give the team new ways to look at their craft. There are many respected sales training organizations you can leverage to help improve the performance of your team. Pick one that aligns well with your selling style.

Motivating Your Sales Team

No doubt you have seen the difference between a highly-motivated sales team and one that's uninspired and lethargic. Motivated staffs work more efficiently and think more deeply about the end goal rather than just performing tasks. Motivated sales teams require less supervision.

Motivation is extremely important in sales because your reps are often working without other people – and managers – around. They deal with rejection often. Selling is a potentially lonely and frustrating job. The sales manager is responsible for creating a system and environment that motivates the sales team to excel. Here are several ideas to help keep your team up and raring to go.

Stay Positive

Don't talk down to sales people. Your reps absorb negativity on a regular basis so they don't need more of it from management. To properly represent your company and convince a potential customer to part with tens of thousands of dollars, sales reps must be confident in their abilities and the product and company they are selling.

Make sure everyone in the organization understands that nothing happens in a company until someone sells something, and that everyone - directly or indirectly - is responsible for sales and customer satisfaction. Some companies or individuals consider sales a necessary evil rather than appreciating them for the difficult, complex, and strategic job they hold. Guard against other parts of organization talking disparagingly about sales. Undeserved criticism must not be tolerated.

Constantly Seek Input from Sales People

Everyone loves to be considered an expert. Take advantage of the unique sales viewpoint. They know your company, products, and competition intimately. They are also usually eager to share their opinions. Including them in business discussions can be highly motivating for them and effective for you.

* Involve them in developing the sales material.
* Give them a voice regarding service issues in their territory.
* Get their input on new products and services.
* Involve them in market share analysis and make them part of solving how to win more orders.
* Have them help plan and execute the sales meetings.

Commission Plan as a Motivator

Nothing impacts the behavior of a sales team more than the commission plan. The best commission plans drive effort and excellence, and align with the company direction. A well-designed commission plan will push sales to bring in the desired profit and volume. The wrong plan can demotivate sales people with a sense of unjust compensation – resulting in a reduced win rate and the loss of valuable staff.

The primary motivator for most salespeople is money. You want high-energy reps out there fighting for every order. The fuel that feeds that competitive engine is the desire to earn that commission by winning the order.

The commission plan must align with company goals - promoting company values, pushing the right products in the best end markets, and compelling the salesperson to pursue both unit volume and profit.

A low-cost provider of products with a strong aftermarket parts and services business is looking to gain market share so the commission might be more heavily based on units sold. A company focused on bottom line growth will have a commission structure designed to reward profit rather than number of units.

For most large ticket sales in a B2B environment, sales don't come every day. Sales people must work hard to win potential customer confidence, solve complex problems, and beat competition. In this environment, sales people should have 30 to 60 percent of their income coming from commissions. A plan based on more variable compensation (lower base pay and higher commission) is especially important when sales people are working remotely. This commission structure also makes adding sales people more affordable.

Set Point Commission Plan

The commission plan is the number one thing that influences sales staff behavior. It must be aligned with the company financial goals and your target end market buying behavior. It must drive the sale of the products that bring you the best overall profit, competitive advantage, and – most importantly – address customer needs.

A concept called the Set Point approach has proven to be effective when selling high dollar products or services with a wide latitude in pricing. The structure rewards salespeople for selling at a higher price, but gives them the flexibility to lower the price – and get a lower commission – if that is needed to make the sale. Set Point tends to increase the ASP and bring in higher profitability by motivating sales to sell at higher prices whenever possible. It is not appropriate for commodity sales where the prices are widely known by the buyers, or sales primarily through indirect channels.

For each product or service, you establish a "Set Point" - the price from which the commission is calculated. The setpoint is not price is not a manufacturer's suggested retail price (MSRP) or list price. It is not published. The commission increases or decreases depending on whether the sell price is higher or lower than the set price.

186

Table 6.2 illustrates a set point commission structure. In this example, the set point is 2 percent. All products and services are priced at Set Point. Every quote generated would have a set point on it in hidden text visible to the quote group, sales manager, and the salesperson, but invisible to the buyer. Sales can submit the quote to the buyer above or below set point within a band established by sales management. If you believe in a higher base, lower commission, you might move the Set Point commission percent from 2 percent to 1 percent and change the table accordingly.

Set Point Commission Table

Deviation from set point	Commission paid
+9% and above	2.5
+8%	2.5
+7%	2.5
+6%	2.4
+5%	2.4
+4%	2.3
+3%	2.3
+2%	2.1
+1%	2
Set Point	2%
-1	2
-2	2
-3	1.9
-4	1.8
-5	1.8
-6	1.6
-7	1.5
-8	1.5
-9	1.5
10% or more discount. Requires Sales Mgr. Approval	1.3

◎ Table 6.2 provides an example of a Set Point commission system.

Benefits of this Set Point commission system

- Costs of product are not known to sales. If your operations team reduces the cost of producing your product, you don't have to hand that improvement over to the marketplace unless you want to.
- You can either drive profits or drive volume as strategy dictates. To drive profit, increase the rate of commission change from Set Point in table 6.2. To increase unit volume, decrease the rate of commission change.
- Set Point prices are established based on the value of the product, not the cost. If a product with exclusive technology is considered highly valuable to the market, Set Point might be established at a 50 percent gross margin (over 2x cost, or a markup of 100%). Sales people might scream "foul" if they knew the gross margin percentage – but they don't. If a product is more of a commodity, then Set Point is set to a considerably lower gross margin percent.
- It rewards the sales team for selling high dollar items at higher prices. Most high dollar products are complex with few systems exactly the same, so even published list prices have some ambiguity. Configurations can change widely based on options selected, leaving room for the salesperson to price higher when they feel they can.
- It is not bonus or break point based, so it avoids the pitfalls of having a salesperson focus when the bonus is about to be attained (grab all orders at any price) or lose focus when the bonus is surely not going to be attained (sandbagging to prime next run at the bonus). Rather, Set Point rewards for closing each project at the highest price.
- Sales knows where they stand on all negotiations. Sales understands set point for every system package and options by way of hidden text on each quote.
- If you ensure the commissions paid below set point do not drop too low, the salesperson will still be motivated to get the sale below set point when they must. You don't want your sales people to walk away from projects below set point or you may lose market share.
- The company reaps most of the rewards for higher ASP. For example, a salesperson bringing in $3 million revenue per year at Set Point receives a 2 percent commission ($60,000). In my experience, sales people don't sell right at Set Point but instead close orders approximately 3 percent over set point, which gives them a 2.3 percent commission (See Table 6.2). The salesperson is rewarded with $9,000 more commission for the year, and the company gets an additional $90,000. A good trade.

Commission plans require significant customization to match specific products and go-to-market strategies. The Set Point system is versatile and effective in driving profitability and effective sales behavior, but it requires the right go-to-market strategy, product offerings, and highly skilled sales people. It might not match your business model.

Sales Department Performance Measurements

Although tracking sales metrics won't necessarily increase win rate, it can help identify unmotivated and underperforming sales people who need to be trained or dismissed. The task falls to the sales manager who must combine metrics with first-hand knowledge to make those decisions.

Key Sales Department Metrics

Metric	Calculation
Win rate	• Competitive win rate Dividing the number of orders won by the number of orders lost plus won. • Sales funnel win rate Dividing the number of orders won by the total number of new SQLs and SFOs. • Quote win rate Ratio of the number of quoted orders won. Note: Focus on win rate as an indication of market share, and on getting accurate lost sales data from your sales team.
Forecasting accuracy	• Revenue forecast vs actual by month • Equipment forecast vs actual by month Note: Sales staff must ensure all SFOs have a prognosis date, probability of closure, equipment list, and revenue estimate so that production can have product ready.
Activities	• Attempts – number of times per week the sales person is attempting to reach potential customers. • Contacts – number of interactions per week. • Appointments Scheduled/New meetings per week – a subset of contacts Note: Be careful not to encourage sales to engage in useless interactions. You want them active by having meaningful interactions.
Funnel health - volume and velocity	Volume: • New Leads: leads obtained (subscriber and MQL, SQL) per month • Total Projects: total projects in funnels (subscriber, MQL, SQL, SFO) per month Velocity: • New sales or marketing funnel leads converted to sales in 60 days, 90 days, 365 days • New sales funnel leads converted to sales in 60 days, 90 days, 365 days Note: Use a 30 or 90 day rolling average if data is too volatile. Track economy strength, as it influences funnel velocity.

◎ Table 6.3 Key sales department metrics must drive the behavior you want out of the team.

Sales managers can perform qualitative performance evaluation based on attending sales calls, ongoing progress discussions, and reviewing activity plans. CRMs provide the quantitative metrics side of the evaluation. Effective sales managers use CRMs as a means of managing their sales staff and helping them perform better. Set up appropriate Key Performance Indicators (KPIs) to gauge performance and funnel health.

Summary

Building an effective sales team is key to maintaining a robust sales pipeline and continuous revenue stream. Motivation and training are two ways of developing a team that can be successful.

There are no shortcuts to winning orders. An effective website with on-target messaging is helpful in opening the door, but it's not a substitute for a solid, fundamental, person-to-person sales approach. While sales skill is important in any setting, it's even more critical in a large dollar sale. You are asking potential customers to make large investments in your product or service. Convincing them to issue that purchase order requires a smart, determined, hardworking sales team. It is the key to the overall success of your organization.

Solution 6 References:

1. *Lead Response Management Study,* Lead Response Management, 2007
   http://www.leadresponsemanagement.org/lrm_study
2. *The Short Life of Online Sales Leads*, James B. Oldroyd, Kristina McElheran, David Elkington. Harvard Business Review, March, 2011 issue,
   https://hbr.org/2011/03/the-short-life-of-online-sales-leads
3. *2015 Sales Effectiveness Report – Lead Follow Up,* Conversica,
   https://resources.conversica.com/h/i/193689183-2015-sales-effectiveness-report-lead-follow-up
4. SPIN Selling, 1988, by Neil Rackham, McGraw-Hill Education, ISBN 0070511136, 9780070511132
5. The SPIN Selling Field book: Practical Tools, Methods, Exercises, and Resources, 1996, by Neil Rackham, McGraw-Hill Professional, ISBN 0071368825, 9780071368827

Solution 7: Creating Customer Loyalty

Studies have shown it costs up to five times as much to attract a new customer than it does to keep an existing one – a fact almost universally accepted. Yet less than one in five companies focus on retention.[1]

Retaining customers is the most effective strategy for growing your company in an efficient and profitable way. Research shows that time spent improving your customer loyalty system is well worth the effort:

- You have a **60 to 70%** chance of making a sale to an existing customer inquiry as opposed to a **5 to 20%** chance of selling to a new prospect lead.[1]

  Takeaway: Selling to your existing customers is the quickest avenue to boost sluggish sales.

- Customers who are engaged with you and are part of your loyalty program make **90%** more frequent purchases and spend **60%** more per transaction.[2,3]

  Takeaway: Although this data pertains more to eCommerce, the stats are so overwhelming as to suggest some crossover to high dollar sales.

- **66%** of global respondents are willing to pay more for sustainable goods.[4]

Takeaway: By contributing to society in partnership with your customers, you elevate the relationship to a more meaningful level.

- Only **18%** of companies focus more on customer retention than customer acquisition.[1]

  Takeaway: Even though customer retention is proven to be more valuable than customer acquisition, most companies still focus on acquisition.

- **76%** of companies consider Customer Lifetime Value (CLV) as an important concept in their organization, yet only **42%** can measure it accurately.[5]

  Takeaway: Understanding the value of customers is one thing, but putting in the effort to calculate and strive to achieve customer loyalty is more important.

- **73%** of consumers feel loyalty programs should show how loyal brands are to them, yet **66%** of marketing execs believe loyalty programs are still a way for consumers to show how loyal they are to their business.[6]

  Takeaway: A paradigm shift is necessary for most marketing executives.

Earning loyalty is profitable, but turning your company toward pursuing customer loyalty can be challenging. Companies who fail to improve loyalty do so either because of an overly complex process or a lack of company buy-in. In this solution chapter, I'll show you a simple process for identifying and prioritizing interactions, assigning owners, and executing a basic loyalty improvement plan.

What is Customer Loyalty?

Several important criteria define a loyal customer.[7]
1. The customer buys all the product from you they can.

2. The customer is impervious to competition.
3. The customer is an advocate for you. They tell colleagues and friends to buy from you.

Although often grouped together, customer satisfaction and customer loyalty are two different things. You likely won't get loyalty without satisfaction, but having a satisfied customer doesn't guarantee loyalty. Nearly nine out of ten customers who switch suppliers for their next purchase responded to surveys as "satisfied" or "extremely satisfied." Satisfaction is no longer enough to guarantee repeat business.

There is no single silver bullet for earning customer loyalty. However, the more you know about your customers the easier it will be to design programs and services to delight and retain them.

Improving Loyalty

Points-based loyalty programs have become a popular way to earn customer loyalty, especially in B2C markets. Rewards are common in the airline industry and at coffee shops. The problem is, they are not always effective for high dollar B2B sales, and they can bog down your commercial team with a heavy administrative burden.

While rewards programs can help, a truer way to increase customer loyalty is to focus on delivering an outstanding customer experience. *Customer experience* is the perception the customer has regarding doing business with your company – how they feel after an interaction with you.[8,9]

Improve Your Customer Interaction Performance

Improving the customer experience requires the same thought process as lead nurturing. Anticipate and deliver what customers want, when they want it, and how they want to receive it. Advancing your customers toward loyalty is about helping them be successful through the use of your product or service. Difficulties arise when the number of interactions you currently handle outpaces resources. My technique accounts for the fact that no company can improve every interaction at the same time. You need to have a way to prioritize the interactions so that you improve the ones most important to the customer first. To accomplish that you follow three steps:

1. **Document and rate customer support interactions**
2. **Prioritize the interactions**
3. **Create content, execute the plan, and track performance**

1. Document and Rate Customer Support Interactions

Have a cross functional team with knowledge of the customer and your company's inner workings work independently to create lists of customer interactions. The interactions include those your company executes now and those you might consider adding. The team should document the interactions chronologically in a Customer Interaction Chart like the one shown in Table 7.1. Your analysis can start from the moment you obtain a lead and carry through all the way to obtaining customer loyalty, or you can shorten the scope and simply start from when the customer places their first order.

Use a 1-10 scale (with 10 being the highest) for the ratings of the last three columns. The team leader should then consolidate and refine the individual lists.

Customer Interaction Rating Table
Ratings are 1 to 10

Interaction	Customer Expectation	Importance to Customer (10 = Extremely important)	Our Performance (10 = Outstanding)	Additional Effort to Meet Expectations (10 = Immense effort and resources)
Receive shipping package	I want to receive the shipping on time and undamaged	7	9 We have 98% on-time shipment as originally promised, 0.5% damage on delivery, and recyclable cardboard and packing paper	1
Component is opened and viewed	I want the right component delivered undamaged	9	4 We do not always meet expectations. Damage at 3%, wrong part returns at 6%	5
Terms	I want at least NET 60 days	6	3 Our terms are net 30 days	2
Service tech requested on-site	I want the tech on site the same day that I need them	7	3 We're onsite within 3 working days, and to some of our best customers within 10 working hours	7

Table 7.1 A sample Customer Interaction chart.

The consolidated table should be extensive, with many touch points and many opportunities to improve. The real benefit of a Customer Interaction Rating Table is that it forces you to rate how important the interaction is to the customer and how many resources will be consumed meeting customer expectations, which generates a prioritized list of interactions.

2. Prioritize the Interactions

The goals of Step 2 are to make sure the list is complete, the team agrees on the ratings, and the top priorities are selected. Meet with the team to review and adjust any questionable entries.

The list will be long, and you won't have enough resources to tackle all shortcomings simultaneously. That's why prioritization is critical. Sort the list by the "Importance to the Customer" column, since this is the most crucial criteria. Then look at the "Additional Effort to Meet Expectations" column and prioritize the interactions that are important to the customer and that you have the resources to address. Assign an owner to each selected interaction.

Note: **First impressions**

The first few interactions after receiving an order are significant, and the most important to the goal of exceeding customer expectations. Customers want to be reassured they made the right choice, and a poor customer experience early on will have them questioning their decision to do business with you. On the other hand, exceeding their expectations on the first order reinforces their decision and sets the foundation for a mutually beneficial relationship. When rating the column *Importance to Customer,* rate high those interactions that take place immediately after the customer has placed their order.

---

3.   Create Content, Execute the Plan and Track Performance

Each interaction owner is responsible for identifying the content required to meet customer expectations, creating the execution plan, and establishing tracking metrics. Up to this point in the process the evaluations have been general. Now you need the interaction owner to get into more detail and thoroughly understand the customer expectation. The better you understand customer expectations regarding an interaction, the better position you'll be in to meet or exceed them.

Here are some questions to help the interaction owners fully understand customer expectations.

- What are the customer needs and expectations regarding this interaction?
- What questions can you answer?
- What dialog do they want during this interaction, and over what media?
- How can you show empathy? How will you make the interaction personal?
- How will the customer recognize your performance during the interaction?
- Does the interaction require a follow up?
- What authority will the customer facing individuals have to satisfy or delight the customer?
- What content or process needs to be created?
- What metric will you use to track the performance of the interaction.

The answers to these questions can help the owner create the plan to be shared with the team leader and department manager. Should the owner try to exceed customer expectations for every interaction they are assigned? Not necessarily. Customers today care more that you keep your promises than that you exceed them. Go for the "Wow" factor of exceeding expectations when you can afford to do so and when the interaction is highly important to the customer. You don't have to exceed customer expectations on every interaction, especially if it drains resources from meeting expectations on those interaction most important to the customer. [9]

Note: **A culture that breeds loyalty**

All significant improvement programs take consistent effort to make them stick. Here are some considerations for implementing a cultural shift and to drive home to your customer facing and management teams to help provide continuous improvement.[7]

- Always make it easy for customers to give feedback. As often as possible, provide feedback options on electronic interactions. Only four percent of customers who leave you, tell you why.
- Train your team to recognize customer anger and frustration as an opportunity to perform. A problem is an opportunity to prove your company is worthy of their loyalty. The most customer dissatisfaction comes not from the initial problem, but from a poorly executed response to it.
- Assign all high priority interactions and make sure the owners understand they are responsible for them.
- Put loyalty metrics into staff goals.
- Develop and document a loyalty mission statement and post it visible throughout the company.
- Involve your staff in the creation of the interaction plans, and ask for their ideas on how to improve.
- Regularly ask customer facing staff to identify the top five current loyalty obstacles.
- Profile loyal customers and those that have stopped doing business with you.
- Emphasize to your team that the goal is not just to get a repeat sale from a customer, but to earn loyalty.

The interaction owners plan should include the following elements:

1. Description of the interaction.
2. Description of the customer expectation
3. Content type

The type of content (e.g., phone, email, site visit) and required effort to get it ready to use. Tie the content back to your VOC customer needs research and incorporate your messaging where possible.

4. Triggers

Define what will trigger the content's use. As discussed in Solution 6 *Nurturing your Existing Leads*, the trigger can be date or activity based. An activity-based trigger might be the shipment of product and a date-based activity could be a quarterly newsletter with tips on maximizing the usage of your product.

5. Authority

Who handles the interaction? What authority do they have to make adjustments deemed necessary to meet expectations?

6. Training

If you have instituted new processes to address interactions deemed highly important to the customer, implement a thorough staff training program.

7. Tracking

Establish a weekly or monthly metric to define a successful interaction.

With the owners' plans in hand, the team leader and department managers will need to assign resources to successfully execute on the plans. In some cases, existing content must be modified. In other cases, new content must be created and staff trained.

Note: **Critical to Customers (CTC)**
Execution items that are crucially important to customers' success or satisfaction are often referred to as Critical to Customers (CTCs). Interactions with high ratings in the "Important to Customer" in your Customer Interaction Chart are your CTCs. These are also referred to as Critical Success Factors (CSFs)

Empowering Customer Facing Staff to Drive Loyalty

Service organizations that excel at obtaining loyalty have one thing in common - they empower the customer facing staff to make instant decisions and take action that delight customers. Management must give appropriate authority to the people who interact with your customers every day so they can resolve customer issues quickly.

This doesn't mean you must give every customer facing staff member free rein to perform acts of heroism by giving the customer everything they want. These critical front-line staff members need to know the types of decisions they can make instantaneously and which issues to escalate to management. Here are some suggestions on ways to empower customer facing staff.

- *Eliminate rubber stamps*
  If certain customer requests are always approved by a supervisor, give that decision power to customer facing staff. When the customer facing staff seems powerless to help, clients can feel the company doesn't care about them. In today's "instant access" world, customers aren't willing to wait for slow responses as issues are sent up the ladder. Speeding up the decision-making process and providing fast service at the point of contact is a key step toward earning customer loyalty. You'll save staff and manager time and gain customer satisfaction due to instant response. Management should be kept aware of the service actions taking place.
- *Monetary decisions*
  Enable customer service people to make on-the-spot decisions that have real costs without managerial approval. Management should be kept aware of the monetary compensation that takes place.
- *Avoid supervisor overload*
  An effective service team knows the rules, boundaries, and limitations. Companies who invest in empowerment training for customer facing staff will tend to outperform those who spend that money on additional supervisory staff.[4]
- *Provide Incentives*
  Create appropriate incentives and recognition for customer facing staff when they demonstrate superior service. Looking for opportunities and methods to publicly reward the team creates positive momentum and enhances the customer service culture.
- *Improve communication with senior management*
  Encourage dialog between your company leaders and customer facing staff.[3] One of the traits of successful service companies is having senior

leaders spend time listening to the issues and successes from the point of view of customer facing staff. This establishes a strong alignment of culture and continuous improvement at all levels of the organization.

Note: Create empowerment levels via a team exercise

To create empowerment levels, consider the following exercise intended to pull ideas from those who know the issues best – your customer facing staff.[4]

The customer facing staff makes a list of all the things they are asked to do for the customer (or things they would like to be able to do for them) and present it to management. The manager then removes duplicates, combines like issues, and identifies areas where staff can be trained to decide for themselves. This exercise will provide valuable front line feedback to your customer behavior and attitudes.

There are many internal morale benefits to focusing on customer retention.[7] Focusing on customer loyalty and empowering employees creates a positive environment for customer and staff that leads to better service, which results in even greater loyalty. Developing an excited, inspired customer facing staff is key to delighting customers.

○ Figure 7.2 The virtuous circle of pursuing customer loyalty.

Empower your customer facing staff to pursue customer loyalty, make the performance of the team a company priority, and you'll see an increase in staff retention, teamwork, innovation, and productivity. Companies who are successful in creating customer loyalty are better places to work and deliver stronger, more consistent financial performance.

Which Customers Should be the Focus of Your Loyalty Efforts?

Every company has limited resources. If applied evenly across high and low value customers, then the high value customers will be underserved. Segmenting customers based on the value they bring your company enables the best ROI on your service efforts. Obtaining customer loyalty from any customer is beneficial, but obtaining customer loyalty from your most valuable customers is profitable.

A typical tier-based customer segmentation is illustrated in Figure 7.3. Segmenting customers enables you to focus limited resources on the customers that offer the greatest value and incents the organization to nurture customers to higher tiers.

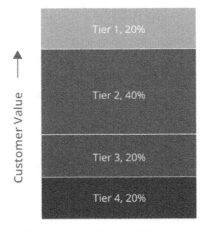

© Figure 7.3 Typical Customer Segmentation.

The four-tier customer segmentation shown in Table 7.3 is based on the value the customer brings you. If you are not segmenting your customers by value, consider creating an initial segmentation based on the 80/20 Pareto principle and place 20 percent of your customers in the top tier. When applied to marketing, the Pareto principle says that 80 percent of your profits come from 20 percent of your customers.

Your starting percentages provide the baseline. Over time, new customers will be added and existing customers will move into different tiers. Your goal is to grow Tier 1. If you continue to deliver outstanding service and products, the percentage of customers residing in Tier 1 will gradually increase well beyond the initial 20 percent.

Note: **Calculating customer value with pocket income.**

The pocket income calculation was described in Solution 1 *Finding your Best End Markets*. As a reminder, pocket income compares the bottom line profitability of one customer against the average customer after the cost-to-serve is included. Pocket income can also be used to segment your customers. Here's an example using ABC Custom Truck Works' customer base. ABC has 1000 customers, and they have never employed a customer tier system before.

1. For each customer, ABC calculates pocket income percent and dollars as shown in Solution 1, Table 1.3.
2. They sort customers highest to lowest for pocket income <u>dollars</u>.
3. They place the top 20 percent or 200 customers in Tier 1 based on pocket income dollars.
4. They place the next 40 percent or 400 customers in Tier 2 based on pocket income dollars.
5. They place the next 200 based on pocket income dollars in their Tier 3.
6. They place the remaining 200 based on pocket income dollars (122 of which happen to have a negative pocket income) into Tier 4.
7. Based on their knowledge of the customers and market, ABC makes minor adjustments moving some customers up or down a tier. Tiers were created based on pocket income dollars, but sometimes the pocket income percent is lower than warranted for that tier and so the customer is demoted, or pocket income percent is higher than warranted for that tier and the customer is promoted. Or, Tier 3 customers known to be very loyal advocates are moved up, and Tier 1 customers who have just defected to a competitor are moved down and tagged for special attention.

Pocket income can also be used ongoing to place each new customer into the proper tier.

Naming the tiers helps your commercial team recognize the value the customer brings you and the service you should be providing. There are several ways to name the tiers, such as ABCD or 1234. In this book I will use the following:

Gold = Your most valuable customers. Strive every day to retain these customers and earn their loyalty. In Figure 7.3 these customers are Tier 1.

Silver = Average value customers. Normally, your largest group, these Tier 2 customers form the solid foundation of your client base. New customers start here and are re-evaluated after one year. By gaining their loyalty, some – but not all of them – will advance to your Gold tier.

Bronze = Below average value customers. The primary focus should be to move these Tier 3 customers up to the silver level.

Tin = Low or no value customers. You tend to lose money with these Tier 4 customers, and they have no future potential. If you can't move them to the Bronze level, you should stop serving them (freeing up your resources to serve more valuable customers).

Segmentation allows you to focus extra effort on the most valuable customers, and create programs to nurture customers to higher levels.

Services offered per tier

In a perfect world, you would have the resources to provide Gold level customer experience to all your customers. However, providing this level of service for every customer is inefficient and will negatively impact your profitability. You simply can't afford to provide customers who are draining profits the same level of service as those who deliver higher profits.

Table 7.4 offers suggestions on the services you can provide at each tier. Consider the service levels from the perspective of both you and your customers. Each industry will have different services at each level. Design as best fits your market.

	Customer Perspective	Your Perspective
Gold	You consider us special. We are satisfied and consider you a partner. Many of us are loyal. We want to keep the special privileges you provide so we are not likely to leave. Possible rewards from you: - Input into products/services - Rebates - Early access to limited quantity sales - Discounts - Fastest generation of loyalty points - Additional warranty/refund allotment - Onsite consignment inventory - Special services or service discount - Special phone number for service available 24/7, free - Serviced by your elite service staff - Special perks and events at tradeshows - Free shipping - Special packaging - Birthday cards signed by service, sales and executives	These customers are the top 20% of your customers based on customer value. They receive your very best service and you're very concerned with their satisfaction and loyalty. You consider them a partner, and build barriers to exit. Managers and executives know most of them personally. Possible value to you: - Customer value of top 20 percent - High revenue or profit dollars - They rate you 9 or 10 on Net Promotor Score - Many are your advocates - Repeat purchases - Testimonials, case studies - Market positioning - Their input is your blueprint for improving and creating products/services

◎ 7.4a Gold service level example.

	Customer Perspective	Your Perspective
Silver	You treat us well and we are generally satisfied. We consider you a good vendor, and a few of us are loyal. Possible rewards from you: - Some rebates or discounts - Faster generation of points than Bronze - Free phone support - Shipping discount	They are good customers - some who you believe to have high growth potential. Silver customers receive great service from you. You work hard to get them to the gold level and/or to become loyal. New customers start here and are re-evaluated after one year. Possible value to you: - Customer value is near average - Rate you 7 or 8 on Net Promotor Score - Good sources of input for products/services, especially for areas to improve

◎ 7.4b Silver service level example.

	Customer Perspective	Your Perspective
Bronze	We are satisfied with your service but we will buy from another vendor for price or convenience without much thought. Possible rewards from you: - Occasional rebates or discounts - Points system is earning them status	They are customers who receive good service from you. You work hard to get them to the silver level. Possible value to you: - Customer value is below average - Rate you 1 through 6 on Net Promotor Score - Good sources of input for areas to improve
Tin	We're rarely satisfied. We don't consider you important as a vendor and buy from you only when we must. We are always looking for more but aren't willing to pay anything for it. We will jump to another supplier permanently when opportunity arises. Possible rewards from you: - None	They are customers who cost you more than they bring you. Possible value to you - Learn why they feel and act as they do - Send them to your least favorite competitor to bog down their company instead of yours

◎ 7.4c Bronze and Tin service level example.

Segmentation may also impact your Customer Interaction ratings (Table 7.1). For example, you may want to offer net 60-day terms to your Gold and Silver level customers even though your standard terms are 30 days. Modify your Customer Interaction Rating Table to account for interactions you may tailor for various customer segments.

Summary

To provide outstanding service you must build a customer-focused culture from the top down. Pursuing customer loyalty raises the service level, improves employee morale, and strengthens the commercial engine.

Customer loyalty in today's competitive market can be difficult to obtain. But if you develop and encourage a customer-focused environment, you have a good chance of building strong bonds of loyalty. In the end, that should be your ultimate goal.

Solution 7 References:

1. *Customer Acquisition vs. Retention Costs – Statistics and Trends Infographic*, by Khalid Saleh, Invesp, https://www.invespcro.com/blog/customer-acquisition-retention/

2. *11 Mind-Blowing Stats That Will Make Marketers Rethink Customer Loyalty*, Kelly Davis, Signal, July 13, 2016, https://www.signal.co/blog/customer-loyalty-marketing/. Ms. Davis sites reference 1 from Invesp.

3. *Customer Engagement from the Consumer's Perspective. A Report on How Customers' Attitudes and Behaviors are Influenced by Engagement*, Rosetta, 2014, http://www.rosetta.com/reports/customer-engagement-rosetta-consulting-study/customer-engagement-from-the-consumers-perspective/

4. *Consumer goods – Brands that demonstrate commitment to sustainability outperform those that don't*. Study concluded February, 2015, Nielsen N.V., http://www.nielsen.com/us/en/press-room/2015/consumer-goods-brands-that-demonstrate-commitment-to-sustainability-outperform.html

5. *Just 42% of companies are able to measure customer lifetime value*, April 2014 blog by Graham Charlton on recent study by Econsultancy, https://econsultancy.com/blog/64659-just-42-of-companies-are-able-to-measure-customer-lifetime-value

6. *The State of the Customer Journey,* 2014 Report, Kitewheel, October 8, 2014, https://kitewheel.com/goodies/journeyreport/

7. Book: *Customer Loyalty: How to Earn It, How to Keep It* –2002. A book by Jill Griffin, published by Jossey-Bass

8. *Episode #42 Creating a Customer-Centric Mindset,* Mind Your Business Podcast, James Wedmore with guest Jason Friedman, http://www.mindyourbusinesspodcast.com/podcast/42/

9. *7 Customer Experience Killers that are Destroying your Bottom Line,* Jason Friedman, free pdf download, https://go.cxformula.com/myb-optin

Other readings about loyalty:

- *Finding Your Best Customer: A Guide to Best Current B2B Customer Segmentation,* an eBook from OpenView Partners, http://labs.openviewpartners.com/files/2012/10/Customer-Segmentation-eBook-FINAL.pdf
- Book: *Up Close and Personal?* Paul R. Gamble, Meril Stone, Neil Woodcock – 1999
- *Here's How to Actually Empower Customer Service Employees*, Harvard Business Review, blog, by Chris DeRose and Noel Tichy, July 1, 2013, https://hbr.org/2013/07/heres-how-to-actually-empower-customer
- Up Your Service, *Empower Frontline Staff To Improve Customer Satisfaction,* blog, by Ron Kaufman, http://www.upyourservice.com/learning-library/customer-service-culture/i-want-to-speak-to-a-supervisor

- Net Promoter Score is a registered trademark of Fred Reichheld, Bain & Company, and Satmetrix Systems. It was introduced in his 2003 Harvard Business Review article "One Number You Need to Grow".
- *The Seven Most Important Performance Indicators for the service desk,* by Jeff Rumburg and Eric Zbikowski, managing partners of MetricNet, http://www.thinkhdi.com/~/media/HDICorp/Files/Library-Archive/Rumburg_SevenKPIs.pdf
- *4 Steps to Effective Customer Service Problem Solving*, blog by Justyna Polaczyk, LiveChat, https://www.livechatinc.com/blog/customer-service-problem-solving/

Solution 8: Rightsizing the Marketing Budget

If you feel your marketing budget isn't adequate to hit your sales goals, there are two ways for you to proceed. First, spend your money more efficiently so that you can achieve your marketing goals with existing funds, or, second, develop a plan to increase your budget. This solution will address both approaches.

Before you consider the second path, you must go down the first. Leadership is not likely to increase your budget unless they are convinced you have done everything you can with existing funds.

To improve budget spending efficiency, first examine your current spending patterns to ensure you are deploying your budget as productively as possible. Then compare your current spending to industry standards and competitors - where possible - to gain a relevant benchmark.

If after completing this process, you still feel the need to request additional funding – your second possible plan of action – make a compelling presentation that outlines and justifies the need for an increase in your budget.

Note: **What's included in your marketing operating expense (OpEx) budget?**
In my experience, financial reporting of Marketing OpEx is inconsistent. It has such a broad definition, it can be hard to make a true apples-to-apples comparison of your spend versus the spend of other companies.
- Do you lump sales and marketing together?

Some companies do this, and their operating expense numbers will be greatly inflated compared to those who don't.

- Do you include salaries and fringe in your operating expense number?

If these costs are included, it can increase an apparent marketing operating expense by a third.

This solution chapter focuses on a marketing department's operating expenses associated with promoting the business – brand awareness, lead generation, public relations, and lead nurturing. So, for our discussion, marketing OpEx *excludes* marketing salaries, fringe, travel, or any sales department expenses.

How Are You Currently Spending Your Marketing Budget Dollars?

To stretch the impact of every dollar or to plan to request additional funding, start with a thorough understanding of your current spend. The pie chart in Figure 8.1 is an example of a marketing OpEx mix.

Figure 8.1 An example of a marketing department's OpEx mix by activity.

Your version of Figure 8.1 will be a high-level breakdown - it is only a start. To understand the ROI of your spend, you also need cost per lead and volume of new leads by source. I introduced this topic in Solution 4 *Generating More Leads.* There I suggested that you create a Leads by Source chart as shown in Table 4.6, repeated from Solution 4. This table not only helps you in lead generation, but also in analyzing budget performance.

Leads by Source

	New Qualified Leads	High Quality Sales Ready Leads	% Sales Ready	Activity Cost	Cost/ Lead	Cost/ High Quality Lead
Website conversions	300	90	30%	20,000	67	222
Email campaigns	175	35	20%	10,000	57	286
Trade shows	125	38	30%	35,000	280	933
Cold calling agency	100	2	2%	60,000	600	30,000
Word of mouth referrals	60	24	40%	1,000	17	42
Conference speaking engagements	60	12	20%	2,000	33	167
Webinars w/ Trade Association lists	50	10	20%	5,000	100	500
Social media conversions	35	11	30%	1,500	43	143
Direct mail	32	10	30%	3,200	100	333
Ads, print	10	1	10%	40,000	4,000	40,000
	947	231.6	24.5%	$177,700	$188	$767

Table 4.6 Example cost of leads per source, excluding overhead.

Your industry will have different costs for the activities of Table 4.6, so adjust them as required. You should expand each row to include additional line items that closely align with your business. For example, website conversions may be too broad a topic, since those leads are made up of many lead generating activities. You might choose to include categories like pay-per-click, banner ads, SEO, or others. Make it as detailed as needed to effectively analyze your lead generation by source.

Benchmark Data for OpEx Spend and Lead Generation

Benchmark data provide reference points, not firm targets. It consolidates the spending activity of other companies that you deem to be, in certain ways you select, similar to yours – perhaps they serve a similar market, or have similar internal structures. Even though these benchmarks won't be a perfect reflection of your business, they can give you a sanity check – general guideposts that can reassure you and your leadership team that your spending is generally in line with other companies. Try to obtain benchmark data for your specific industry. If your industry is large, such as Tier 1 automotive parts supply, this data is readily available. If you're in a small industry, review the annual reports of publicly-held competitors.

If you deviate significantly from the benchmark spending, be prepared to explain and justify the variance.

OpEx Benchmark Data

OpEx spending of B2B companies provides a valuable first set of benchmark data. Table 8.2 shows relevant benchmarking data for B2B companies selling high dollar items.

Marketing OpEx Benchmarks

Ratio Name	Typical Benchmark	Example of a company with $20MM revenue
1. Total Company Operating Expense to Total Sales	25%	$20MM x 25% = $5MM
2. Marketing Expense as a percent of Total Company OpEx	11%	$5MM x 11% = $550,000
3. Marketing Expense (minus wages, fringe, or sales expenses) as a percent of Total Sales (An average value is 2.75%)	2 - 6%	$20MM x 2% to 6% = $400,000 to $1.2MM $20MM x 2.75% = $550,000
4. Non-digital Marketing Expense as percent of Total Marketing Expense	45%	$550,000 x 45% = $247,500
5. Digital Marketing Expense as a percent of Total Marketing Expense	55%	$550,000 x 55% = $302,500
6. SEO and SEM Expense as a percent of Digital Marketing Expense	45%	$302,500 x 45% = $135,125
7. Social Media Expense as a percent of Digital Marketing Expense	30%	$302,500 x 30% = $90,750

© Table 8.2 Typical expense allocations for small to mid-sized companies selling B2B high-dollar items. [1,2,3,4,5,6]

Note that marketing operating expense (line 3) shows a range of two to six percent, highlighting that marketing OpEx as a percentage of total sales (total revenue) can vary widely from company to company. SaaS (software as a service) companies often see percentages higher than six percent, where capital equipment manufacturing companies might be closer to two percent. For the remaining calculations in this table that are specific to marketing high dollar items in the manufacturing industry, I used an overall average of 2.75 percent.

Lead Generation Benchmark Data

Table 8.3 lists lead generation benchmark data for manufacturing companies selling complex products directly to end users with an average price between $100,000 and $200,000. The further you move from these criteria, the less relevant the data. You should create your own benchmark table reflecting companies similar to yours. This will provide you with the base data to gauge the success of each marketing activity.

Lead Benchmark Data

Topic	Value	Comment
Average marketing cost per new lead	$250 per lead	Total annual marketing department OpEx divided by annual number of new leads: The range is $50-$300.
Average marketing cost per high quality lead	$800 per lead	Total annual marketing department expenses divided by number of high quality "sales ready" leads. The range is $450-$1,200.
Average marketing cost per unit sale	$6,000 per unit sale	Provides a target for indirect partner commissions for leads that become a sale. The range is $4,000-$12,000.
Average lead velocity to close 60 days 90 days 365 days	 1 to 2% 2 to 3.5% 2.5 to 5%	When new leads come in, what percentage convert to a sale in 2 months, 3 months, and 1 year.
Lead quality breakdown In buying cycle Considering entering cycle Interested but not in cycle Interest and unlikely to buy	 7% +/- 3 23% +/- 5 60% +/- 10 10% +/- 5	Top two categories are considered, in most companies, as being high quality, sales-ready leads. Sales ready leads, therefore, represent approximately 25 to 30 percent of all leads.

◎ Table 8.3 Typical benchmark data for a company with an average selling price for primary products of $100,000 to $200,000.

Improving Budget Efficiently

Regardless of whether you're trying to stretch your budget or preparing to request additional funding, your first move is to establish how efficient you are with the current spending allocation. Below are five key evaluation criteria.

1. Allocate Funds Toward the Most Effective Lead Generation Activity

The most important key to budget spend efficiency is to allocate an appropriate amount of money toward lead generating activities that provide top ROI. That may seem like common sense, but it takes a good deal of analysis and effort to pull it off successfully, especially when funds are tight. To make sure you are spending your funds on the right activities, you must establish the following.

- *Cost per New Lead and Volume of New Leads by Source*
  These two factors, cost and volume, are usually analyzed together. Without this information, you simply cannot make good decisions on budget allocation for Marketing OpEx. Your version of Table 4.6 provides this critical lead source data.
- *Lead Quality by Source*
  Are you generating too many low-quality leads that stall in the marketing funnel segment? Lower quality leads have a longer buyer journey. Unless your marketing activity is targeting general brand awareness, approximately 25 percent of your new open marketing leads (OMLs) should qualify as ready for the sales funnel segment, meaning the contact is considering or in the buying cycle. When funds are tight, ensure your budget emphasizes those activities that bring in 25 percent or more sales ready leads. See the last column of Table 4.6 titled *Cost per High Quality Lead.*
- *Velocity of New Leads through the Marketing and Sales Funnels*
  If projects are not moving through your marketing and sales funnel segments, it might be because the business climate has worsened. Whatever the reason, you are still responsible for generating quality leads and orders that ultimately hit your company goals.

For the leads you already own, make sure your nurturing programs are effective. Funnel segment velocity reflects your nurturing program effectiveness. Increase testing to ensure you know which nurturing activities are of interest to your buyers. Lead nurturing is discussed in depth in Solution 5 *Nurturing your Existing Leads*.

Lead velocity comes into play not only for nurturing existing leads, but also for generating new leads. When your business is struggling select lead generation activities that launch quickly. Consider email campaigns or direct mail followed by phone calls, as opposed to signing up for a new trade show or presenting at a conference.

2. Company Strategy Alignment

To ensure efficient use of your budget, your marketing spend must align with company strategy. Is the company releasing a disruptive technology, entering a new competitive space, increasing service offerings, adjusting channels, or expanding territories? Make sure you understand the strategic plan and goals you are being asked to meet and align the marketing strategy appropriately.

3. End Market Focus of Your Marketing Budget

Evaluate the amount of your marketing budget focused on your best end markets. Are you spending enough on your target market, or are you using the shotgun approach, trying to reach all available prospects? Successful businesses tend to have a dual methodology that allocates funds and focus both on brand awareness/education and pursuing specific target end markets. Half of the marketing OpEx budget should be devoted to increasing business in your target markets, while the other half targets all markets.

4. Customer Channel Preference

People in different end markets can have different channel buying preferences. Do buyers prefer to buy from local distributors that carry other products they need, or do they prefer to buy directly from OEMs? Do they purchase service contracts along with product, and if so from whom do they buy them? Make sure that your budget is supporting the channels your customers prefer.

5. *Review Your Digital Versus Non-Digital Marketing Mix*

Today's buyers of high dollar items use digital means to research and select their short list of final potential vendors. You must make sure your marketing staff and budget are focused adequately on digital marketing. Buyers move more than half of the way down the buyer journey before ever contacting a supplier, and they educate themselves primarily via digital content.

Today, most companies spend slightly more than half their Marketing OpEx dollars on digital marketing. It's important that your digital marketing activities are funded appropriately and executed well.

Resist the urge to shut down all brand awareness activities such as print ads or speaker conferences. Even in times of immediate need, retain a portion of your budget for general marketing activities. Doing so is necessary to support your long term commercial engine health by providing business diversity and new growth opportunities.

Note: Sample monthly budget template download

Finance departments normally don't require detailed marketing budgets. They usually need only a few major cost centers. However, a true marketing budget consists of many controllable expense categories comprised of many activities. As a marketing manager, you need a detailed annual plan so that at any given time you can project spending for the rest of the year.

Leadership often makes mid-year adjustments that will affect your budget. You will need to know what you have spent, how much you have left, and, most importantly, what you project to spend for the rest of the year. You need to be prepared to control your spending to meet any organizational mandates.

The following is for establishing the annual budget and for mid-year adjustments, not for tracking actual expenses.

Activity	Comment	Jan	Feb	Mar	Q1 Total	April	May	...
Tradeshows Total			$54,000		$54,000	$95,000		
ABC show	Texas, Feb 12 - 15		$39,000		$39,000			
XYZ show	Chicago, April 1 - 5					$95,000		
LMN show	Atlanta, Feb 2 - 4		$15,000		$15,000			
Printing Total		$6,000			$6,000	$240	$2,000	...
Etc.								

Track major spend categories by lead source using bold headings with individual activities listed below. Download a template at https://fairmontconcepts.com/tools-templates.

This example is a subset of a comprehensive spreadsheet covering the full fiscal year. Include topics such as printing, website fees, outside marketing partners, and travel expenses – all controllable marketing expenses. Some budget dollars will be placeholders, with specific activities to be determined later. Review your template with finance to ensure it reconciles with the high-level marketing budget you submitted.

Requesting Additional Budget Dollars

When you have completed the analysis listed above, you have completed two vitally important steps. First, you have analyzed your marketing system to improve efficiency. Senior management will undoubtedly ask whether you have done anything to reduce spending or increase leads without increasing spend before they consider giving you more funding. Your efforts to maximize efficiency, as described above, will pay off. Second, you have identified the activities that give you the best ROI and the best chance of meeting sales goals. With the completion of these two analyses you're ready to ask for more funds.

If you work at a small company, the leadership team is probably the owner, and perhaps the top finance person. In a mid-sized company, it is more likely that your audience will include the heads of the major functions in the company. Regardless of the size of the team, the concerns of the leadership are usually the same.

Note: **The importance of hitting your budget expense targets**

I am a firm believer that you should do everything in your power not to exceed your approved annual OpEx marketing budget – a budget is an agreement between you and your company. It's a promise. However, things rarely go as planned and you must be ready to adjust.

Submit a "Wish List, Cutback List" with your annual budget. This is a simple table that includes a prioritized list of activities and related costs you will need to execute if the company decides to increase marketing spend by 5, 10, or 15 percent. It should also detail the areas in which you will reduce spending if the budget is cut by 5, 10, or 15 percent. Submitting a wish list/cutback list will earn credibility and gain respect – and you'll be poised to act when the inevitable mid-year changes occur.

In addition, the best time to get increased funding is at budget submission time, so have your ROI justifications ready to request some portion of your wish list at budget approval time.

What drives your leadership team? What are their top concerns? Is there a specific crisis going on right now? Try to answer these questions before your presentation. Just as a salesperson digs in to uncover the needs of a potential customer before starting to "sell," so you must uncover the specific needs of your leaders before you create and present your budget. Here are some typical issues that top the list for most leaders of small to mid-sized manufacturing companies.

Common leadership concerns:

"We need to hit revenue targets!" Leaders know if the revenue isn't high enough, the fixed overhead will eat up all profits and income will drop. Then, expense cutting and, even worse, layoffs ensue. Your marketing plan needs to show how lead generation and nurturing will increase sales within the appropriate period – keeping up with the revenue goals. New lead generation and lead velocity data are key (Table 4.6).

"We must hit profit goals!" Leaders need to maintain two profit values reflected in the bottom line – net income dollars and net income percent. Both are important to them. Your marketing budget request needs to focus on finding profitable business opportunities. Show how you are pursuing

business within end markets with the potential to deliver the profit the company needs.

"We have to stay ahead of competition!" Leaders are always concerned about competition, and rightly so. Losing to competitors is a loss of market share, and a decreasing market share number bodes poorly for the future.

If you feel the marketing budget is not sufficient to hit sales goals, you're in countermeasure mode. Your marketing budget request should show how you are emphasizing areas where you are strong against the competition. There is no time for taking on fights you are unlikely to win, and no time for new product development. Show that you are concentrating on strategic target end markets that strengthens your position against competition. Calm leadership fears with a solid plan.

"We must maintain positive cash flow!" Leaders of companies know the quickest way to go out of business is to run out of cash. Many of these companies have very solid bottom line profitability on their income statement when disaster strikes.

Your marketing budget request must show that the money invested will have an acceptably fast ROI. Your data on average time to close on a new lead is important here. Show that the money you're asking for will come back as revenue and profit. Demonstrate that if you spend X dollars to generate new leads, you should obtain Y dollars of sales in Z weeks. Prepare and study your marketing numbers so you can confidently make that commitment.

"We must stay true to the strategy!" Leaders hate when a strategy they have painstakingly created is ignored. Make sure your marketing budget request shows how you are focusing on the target end markets and adhering to the company's growth strategies.

The probability of obtaining the funds you need are much higher if you look at your request through the eyes of the leaders (their needs), show them that you know where you have spent so far (credibility), and have a winning plan to improve sales (solution).

Note: **Leadership presentation: the mid-year review**
An effective leadership, presentation intended for explaining mid-year changes should cover at least the following topics.

I.   Executive summary and introduction
II.   Marketing goals for the year
III.   Situation analysis, challenges, and problem statement
IV.   Actions taken to date
V.   Countermeasures and financial request
VI.   Appendix

One quick comment, born from learning the hard way. Before you meet with your leadership team on the topic of obtaining more funds, review your presentation with finance to ensure all your numbers match theirs, and that they agree with the way you are presenting the data. One number that doesn't match the finance person's number can damage your credibility. Leaders like to have a "single source of the truth" when it comes to the financial numbers. Getting a finance person on board who will be present during your presentation has the added benefit of potentially having an ally in the room.

Summary

Effective marketing budgets tie to strategy, focus on ROI, and exploit a deep knowledge of the needs of customers in your target end markets. But, the best laid plans can fall apart with a change in the competitive landscape, a downturn in the economy, or any number of other internal or external factors. Know your numbers and marketing strategy and you'll be able to handle the bumps that are sure to come each year.

Prepare your budget carefully as if your business depends on it, because it does.

Solution 8 References:

1. *SG&A expenses as a percentage of total revenue.* Schonfeld and Associates, https://saibooks.com/index.php?option=com_content&view=article&id=64&Itemid=61
2. CMO Survey, August 2016, https://cmosurvey.org/results/
3. CMO Survey, February 2017, https://www.slideshare.net/christinemoorman/the-cmo-survey-highlights-and-insights-february-2017

4. *How much budget for online marketing,* Webstrategies, October 2016,
    http://www.webstrategiesinc.com/blog/how-much-budget-for-online-marketing-in-2014
5. *Percent of revenue spent on marketing and sales,* Vital Design, Portsmouth, NH,
    Sarah Brady, https://vtldesign.com/digital-marketing/content-marketing-strategy/percent-of-revenue-spent-on-marketing-sales/.
6. *How Big Should Your B2B Marketing Budget Be?* Industrial Marketer, October 2014,
    Jake Gerli, http://www.industrialmarketer.com/big-b2b-marketing-budget/
7. *Most Popular Search Engines,* Lifewire, November 11, 2016, Wendy Boswell,
    https://www.lifewire.com/top-search-engines-3481571
8. *How to plan your demand generation strategy for 2014,* Mike Telem, October 29,
    2013, Blog, Customerthink.com,
    http://customerthink.com/how_to_plan_your_demand_generation_strategy_for_2014/

Solution 9: Making Your Current Offerings More Attractive

If you scored yourself low on this health checkup question, then you feel your offerings are not attractive enough to your potential customers to hit your sales goals. You're not alone. Many manufacturers rate their company low in this category, but even those who rank themselves higher know their products can get stale fast. When your products become stale you have two choices: make better products or make existing products more attractive.

When your offerings are not attractive enough to the marketplace, both your lead generation and win rate can drop. Perhaps your products have been out in the market for a while and you no longer make the potential final vendor cut as often as in the past. And when you do make that final cut, the competition seems to have worked out a strategy to beat you head-to-head.

What can you do about it? You can cut price to improve the value of your offering, but that cuts profit. You can urge management to develop a new product, but if they agree, it's a long-term solution. The only thing you can do in the short-term is for your marketing and sales departments to find ways to attract more leads and win more head to head battles.

Note: **"We will never win with our offerings."**
When faced with declining sales and a shriveling pipeline, some marketing and sales teams blame tougher competition and inferior products. Yet, when you hire someone

away from your competition, the new hire often relays how envious their previous employer is of your offerings.

The first chapter of Sun Tzu's famous book *The Art of War*[1] describes how in a competitive environment information is limited and perceptions are often very different from reality. He has identified the difference between objective and subjective information as one of the key leverage points when it comes to strategy in war (and business) – the difference between perception and reality.

Potential customers buy based on perception. Repeat customers have past performance to help them make purchasing decisions – experience not available to potential customers. If potential customers view your product or service as inferior to the competition, it is the result of their perception. Perceptions can be changed. Your marketing and sales departments are responsible for creating a winning perception.

Four-Step Plan to Improve the Attractiveness of your Products.

1. **Evaluate all messaging and sales tactics in the marketplace.**
   What messages and behaviors do top competitors use? How do you compare? Are the primary sales attributes you promote still attractive, or have they become standard from all competitors? Before you look to improve, evaluate messaging and positioning to better understand how market leaders promote their products and how the marketplace perceives your current offerings.

2. **Identify overlooked benefits and advantages**
   Often a new angle will spark attention in the marketplace (and your own staff). Find attributes you have not yet promoted. Focus on those related to the primary needs of your target end market.

3. **Create new messaging, content, and campaigns**
   Combine the best of your old messaging with your newly identified attributes and refresh your approach. Create excitement with winning promotional campaigns.

4. **Fire up the sales team with new training**
   Kick up your head to head win rate with a new perspective, revised sales tools, and refresher training on the old products.

This plan, described in more detail below, will enable you to reinvigorate the market's perception of your products or services.

1. *Evaluate all Messaging and Sales Tactics in the Marketplace*

Evaluate both your own and your competitors' marketing messages and sales tactics relative to customers' primary needs.

A self-evaluation and competitive assessment allows you to understand the current market dynamics so you can make the appropriate adjustments. Which aspects of your marketing messages are connecting and which are falling flat, hurting your ability to close business? Which sales tactics are winners and which are unpersuasive or easily countered by competition? Be objective so you can understand your gaps. Marketing and sales managers should work together on this analysis.

Your evaluations don't need to include a feature by feature breakdown – that will come later in this solution. At this stage, concentrate on the marketing messages and sales presentation approaches you use, and compare them to competitors you believe are gaining share or pose the biggest threat.

Focus on these key message areas when conducting your comparison:

- High level company brand messaging
- Target Products messaging
- Sales channels
- Sales call strategies
- Value add areas (include pricing, discounting, financing, service levels, proximity to the potential customer)
- Customer needs

The following is a comparison of company brand messaging for ABC Custom Truck Works and two competitors.

Market Participant	Messaging Theme
ABC Custom Truck Works	Trust ABC to make your custom truck your most valued asset. Expertise. Your local business partners.
Competitor A	Highest level of friendly service available today that ensures ultimate reliability.
Competitor B	Affordable vehicles and accessories for today's tradesmen.

Follow this simple format for the other key focus areas listed above. The goal is to highlight the significant differences in marketing and sales positioning between you and your competition. Doing so can illuminate new avenues to promote your ailing products while simultaneously minimizing the advantages of the competition.

2. Identify Overlooked Benefits and Advantages

While selling these products over the past months or years, you've promoted certain benefits and advantages. Your sales staff is trained on selling these benefits, and the marketing engine pushes out lead generating content based on them, but you now realize they are no longer gaining traction in the marketplace. It is time to uncover and prioritize a new set of attributes and to replace or remove older ones that have become common and expected.

Find Advantages related to Primary Needs

Successful marketing and sales starts with listening to the voice of the customer. Use your customers' primary needs to guide the search for overlooked benefits and advantages. In Solution 2 *Uncovering the Voice of the Customer,* I described how to identify primary customer needs, and then create a market opportunity map. ABC Custom Truck Works created the marketing opportunity map for their landscaper market. The figure is repeated here for convenience.

Example Market Opportunity Map

	Weaknesses	Strengths
Importance → (customer rating of importance regarding that need)	• Price appropriate for service and capability • Labor pool of experienced workers for overflow • Highly maneuverable parking	• Full coverage service plans • Integrated trailer braking system • Rapid unload, load capability • Highly configurable and changeable bed layout
	Monitor	**Over Emphasized**
	• Rental programs for work overflow • Extremely easy to keep spotless • User friendly cabin	• Emergency support 24/7 • Attractive, classy, functional parking flashers • Safe fuel transportation • Facilitate impressive branding

Performance →
(customer rating of satisfaction regarding that need)

Figure 2.3 The Market Opportunity Map for ABC Custom Truck Works, landscaper end market.

ABC starts by determining whether they adequately promote the attributes in the quadrants of Figure 2.3 in which they have a strong performance.

It's vital to know where your competitors stand regarding these primary needs. Are they winning head to head because their products have superior attributes to yours – even in areas your customers say you perform well? Leverage knowledgeable people from your company who are familiar with your competitors and customers to answer this question. Create a Primary Needs Star Rating Chart (Table 9.1) to rate the performance of your company and those competitors gaining share and threatening you.

Primary Needs Competitive Comparison

	Ours	Theirs	
	Landscaper Flatbed Truck	A	B
Service Needs			
Full coverage service plans	★★★★	★★★★★	★
Emergency support 24/7	★★★	★★★	★
Rental programs for work overflow	★	★	★
Labor pool of experienced workers for overflow	★	★	★
Transport Needs			
User friendly cabin	★★	★	★★★★★
Highly maneuverable parking	★	★	★★★
Integrated trailer braking system	★★★★	★★	★★★★★
Attractive, classy, functional parking flashers	★★★	★	★★★★
Facilitate impressive branding	★★★	★	★★★
Performance Needs			
Rapid unload, load capability	★★★★★	★★	★
Safe fuel transportation	★★	★	★
Highly configurable and changeable bed layout	★★★★	★★★	★★★★★
Price appropriate for service and capability	★★	★	★
Extremely easy to keep spotless	★	★	★★★

◎ Table 9.1 Landscaper truck Primary Needs Star Rating Chart for ABC Custom Truck Works and the top two competitors who are gaining share.

ABC's cross functional team rates their own offerings (using the market opportunity map as a guide) as well as those of the competition. The results in Table 9.1 show that ABC is especially strong in four areas:

- Full coverage service plans
- Integrated trailer braking system
- Rapid unload & load capability
- Highly configurable bed layout.

Looking at competitive positioning, ABC sees only one primary need with a clear advantage over all competitors: Rapid unload, load capability. This attribute should be a top priority for promotion and sales training.

If after conducting this exercise you uncovered attributes you have previously overlooked, take immediate action to exploit and promote them -

especially since these attributes align with known primary needs of your customer base.

Continue to promote attributes where you excel even if competitors happen to excel there as well. This is important for several reasons. First, these capabilities are important to the customer and you're good at them, so make sure the customers know about your capabilities. Second, you don't want buyers to think you cannot meet those specific needs. Third, competitors might not recognize their competitive position and may be under promoting their capability. Finally, you can strive to out-market and out-sell your competitors even if their capability is also strong.

Find Hidden Needs Within Each Primary Need

Even if you found unexploited attributes relating to a primary need, you still might need more ammunition to breathe new life into your ailing products.

An effective way to find hidden advantages deep within each of your primary needs is through an adaptation of the traditional Feature Function Benefit (FFB) approach originally described in Tables 3.7 and 3.8. Set up a spreadsheet for your poorly performing products that allows you to brainstorm all possible customer benefits deep within each primary need. Then, rate each benefit or attribute for Competitive Advantages and Attractiveness (how attractive you believe the advantage will be to the potential customers). This will provide you with a priority set of new attributes you might choose to promote in the marketplace.

Note: **That annoying competitor who successfully promotes a useless feature**
At this point people often ask if promoting small, overlooked attributes will actually sway buyers. On their own, perhaps not. However, when combined with the benefits you are already promoting, these seemingly insignificant features can often make the difference.

Let's use using ABC Customer Truck Works as an example. As shown in Table 9.1, Competitor B's products are inferior and lower priced than those of ABC Custom Truck Works', but they still win business. When Competitor B entered the market five years ago, their messages revolved around "Why Pay More?" They sold enough vehicles to establish a foothold in the market. Then, without changing their product, they started pushing relatively small features centered on the interior cabin at no additional costs (fancy switch box for their exterior lighting, visor clips for safety glasses, cool floor mats).

These items do not help the business owner complete jobs faster, safer, or easier. But Competitor B figured out that they could spin the cabin attributes into a pride of ownership message, combine it with low price, and separate themselves from competitors. It gave the buyers one more reason to spend less and purchase from Competitor B. The "coolest cabin interior" attribute loosely aligns to the primary need "User Friendly Cabin." As competitor B's sales increased, ABC's marketing and sales people complained how silly it was that buyers fell for the simple, inexpensive, and useless features.

Turns out it's not silly. It's smart marketing and sales.

Table 9.2 that follows is an example of an FFB analysis based on a few of ABC Custom Truck Works' 14 primary needs.

FFB Primary Needs Analysis

Primary Need: *Rapid Unload and Load Capability*				
Existing Feature	Function	User Benefit	Competitive Advantage Yes/No/Even	Attractiveness Rating (5=highest)
Air assist automatic tailgate.	Optional trailer feature. Press button to safely lift & drop gate in seconds. Locks. Handles irregular topography, won't hit workers.	Workers don't lift heavy gate/ramp Can be doing other things - saves time on each job.	Yes - patented.	*****
Integrated wheel chucks.	4 seconds to chuck and un-chuck tires. Chucks are held in wheel well during travel. Worker presses button, chucks drop down to pavement in front and behind tire. Retract: chucks pull away from tires as long as truck doesn't begin to roll.	Shortens the transition time associated with starting and stopping each job, which is a major cost for landscapers. Saves time on the job. Reduces costs associated with paying labor between jobs.	Yes - others have their own wheel chuck solutions, but our customers have noted the superiority of our approach.	***
Primary Need: *Highly Configurable and Changeable Bed Layout*				
Flexi-bed hold down system. A connection point every 4 inches.	Holds down any equipment securely, quickly and easily, including odd shaped equipment.	Easily hold down equipment of any shape. Don't waste time or money fastening down odd shaped equipment at the end of a job. Go to next job fast.	Yes – competitors have one connection per foot.	***
Primary Need: *Safe Fuel Transportation*				
Flexi-net gas container system.	Bungie netting that safely holds 2.5 to 5-gallon fuel tanks in place. Holds 1 to 6 tanks. Fast to secure and access.	Transport any shape fuel can quickly & safely. Capacity to hold all the fuel needed per day.	No – easily copied or simply added by the customer later.	**
Etc.				

Table 9.2 An adapted FFB used for seeking out overlooked benefits within the 14 primary needs of ABC Custom Truck Works' customers.

Table 9.2 reveals several new benefits and competitive advantages for ABC. Those that are important to the customer and have a competitive advantage are high priorities for ABC.

This simple exercise will uncover many hidden advantages you may not have considered.

3. Create New Messaging, Content, and Campaigns

You found unexploited advantages by reviewing the end market's primary needs in Step 1, and then you dug deeper within each need to find other hidden attributes in Step 2. The next step is to use this information to create new messaging and content and drive new customer perceptions. Your products and services are not old, they're proven. They are not common, they have highly attractive advantages. You know your customers' needs and how your product stacks up against those needs, so create new promotions that speak to customers in a new and persuasive way.

- *Select the elements for your new story*
  Combine the best of the old attributes and new attributes and use them as the ingredients for your new messaging. Choose those that will resonate most with potential customers, but also consider those that give you a competitive advantage.
- *Create new messaging*
  Use the Barbell Message Creation Exercise in Solution 3 *Creating Great Messaging* when updating your messaging.
- *Create new content and campaigns*
  Create new content for lead generation and nurturing campaigns as described in Solution 4 *Generating More Leads* and Solution 5 *Nurturing Your Existing Leads*. You're ready to implement new programs to generate new leads and move existing leads through the funnel segments.
- *Create new sales material.*
  Your sales team needs fresh energy. With your new messaging foundation in place, create sales materials to get the team motivated about selling stale products in a new and exciting way. See Solution 6 *Building a Great Sales Team.*

Be aggressive and creative in your promotions. The marketplace has not seen your new messaging, and they may not be as familiar with the details of your old product as you might think.

To add an air of importance, give names to your new, high-priority attributes and trademark them. For example, the air assist automatic tail gate on the landscaper trailer can become the "Quick-Lift Ramp" or "GreaterGate," or "Fastail Smart Ramp." Tie the name and messaging back to the primary need.

It's not just about messaging – repackaging is also critical. Bundle components in a new way and rename them. Change labeling and product color. Provide reasons for the marketplace to take a fresh look at your offerings and change their perceptions.

4. Fire up the sales team with new training

Once you have repositioned your offering and created new messaging, you need to get the sales team on board. Build their confidence and provide them with effective sales tools and selling strategies that work.

Solution 6 *Building a Great Sales Team* goes into extensive detail on effective sales training, but there are some key areas you must focus on when re-launching existing products. Enlist the help of top sales team members to plan and possibly deliver training.

Fire up the sales team:

- *Outline the methodology behind the revitalization*
  The sales team will gain confidence through an understanding of the approach you have taken to revitalize the products. Outline the steps the revitalization team went through to develop the new positioning. Revisit the primary needs table and the market opportunity map, highlighting the places where you were able to uncover unexploited benefits. Show the sales staff how the benefits and messages align with primary needs, and so will resonate with the potential customer.
- *Share the new marketing programs*
  Explain that the company has invested significant time and resources to develop new marketing campaigns for lead generation and lead nurturing programs. Share these programs to stress that sales people are not alone in the revitalization effort.
- *Review new sales material and tools*
  Update the Overview Pitch for the targeted product to get the team excited about selling the new features and benefits. Go over all the new sales materials to be used in the revitalization effort – websites, YouTube

videos, brochures, trade publication articles, blogs. If appropriate, present a simple ROI calculator for the new features you are highlighting.

Ensure sales are fully trained in these materials so they can discuss them confidently with potential customers.

Note: **Stick to proper sales techniques**

Your new tools and training should be designed to inspire your sales team to sell your newly positioned products. Caution them against just jumping in to show off their command of the new material. As described in Solution 6 *Building a Great Sales Team,* they still have to start with uncovering the customer needs, establishing credibility, and understanding the competitive landscape before they begin offering product or service solutions.

Quick Comment on New Product Development - The Long-Term approach

Everything we've covered in this section is about ways to increase the attractiveness of the products you have. Adjusting messaging and training sales staff on newfound advantages is a short-term – but effective - approach.

But, what about the future? Eventually offerings do need to be replaced.

Marketing and sales have crucial roles to play when it comes to New Product Development (NPD). The results of the process explained in this solution chapter can be key to developing future products and services. Marketing should share all results of this analysis with R&D and NPD teams to help secure a strong future for your company.

Summary

Revitalizing stale products is possible when you keep focus on customer needs. If you dig deep enough, you can always find unexploited benefits that align with customer needs, and with these in hand, you can recoup interest in the marketplace and motivation in your sales team.

Solution 9 References

1.   *Art of War*, Sun Tsu, 5th century BC

Solution 10: Hitting Your Profit Goals

When manufacturing companies fall short of revenue, the common complaints rain down – deservedly - on marketing and sales organizations: not enough sales – not enough leads – not enough market presence. The marketing and sales teams own the top line of the income statement – the revenue line.

But, what about when company *profitability* falls short? After all, the entire company owns the bottom line – the income line. As a marketing and sales professional, you might think this one is particularly unfair. "I sell and bring in revenue as best I can. I have no control over costs, so I can't be blamed if we don't make money."

While it is true your marketing and sales departments don't have control over product costs or the company-wide operating expenses, the reality is you and your marketing and sales group do play a key role in generating profit.

There are many levers marketing and sales teams can pull to impact company profitability, including the sales strategy, sell price, channel strategy, and lead generating tactics. The most important decision, however, is determining where to focus your efforts.

Why Are We Missing Profit Goals?

This is the first question you need to ask. Operational inefficiencies, rising cost of labor and materials, or a declining economy all could be contributing factors. Your focus should be in the areas you can control - the ones relating to marketing and sales department performance.

Before we get into how to improve profitability, let's first look at the way companies generates bottom line income. Figure 10.1 is a simplified version of an income statement, condensed to just four main categories: revenue, cost of goods, expenses and income. Revenue must be larger than cost of goods (COGS) and expenses for the company to generate income. When company profits fall short, revenue, COGS and expenses can all be part of the reason.

Income Statement Example

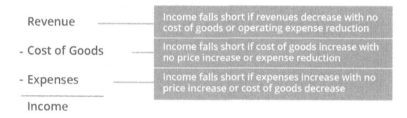

Figure 10.1 The basic income statement equation shows the causes of net income loss.

Every marketing and sales manager needs to clearly understand the relationships between the four main income statement categories as shown in Figure 10.1. The income statement's four main components include many sub components – so the causes of profit shortfalls in Figure 10.1 are oversimplified.

If generating profits was simply spending less than the revenue you bring in, why is hitting profit goals often so hard to accomplish? It's difficult because every company leader must balance investment and infrastructure costs against projected revenue. Management has control of the expenses they are going to spend, and the COGS are directly related to product bill-of-materials and sales volume. However, management is far less certain of the revenue the company is going to bring in. Maintaining company infrastructure and investing in the future are bets placed on future sales. It becomes a difficult dance, and one that can prove hard to master. But, a smooth running commercial engine that is delivering as expected makes running a successful business a great deal easier.

The marketing and sales teams have one overriding goal: *Bring in enough profitable business to exceed the cost of infrastructure and investment.*

You likely had little input into creating the company's infrastructure or determining the investments the company would be making across all departments. Fair or not, it's your job to generate enough profitable revenue to compensate for all costs and investments and to hit the bottom-line profit goals.

10 Ways to Improve Profitability

"Raise prices and sell more."

This is a common refrain from the leadership team to the marketing and sales departments when the company is not hitting its profitability goals. Raising prices is certainly one of the options, but it could easily backfire and result in further profit erosion if unit volumes drop. In reality, the directive to "sell more" is about as executable as telling your dog to "be nice."

Here are ten suggested ways the marketing and sales team can help improve profitability.

1. Get More Business from Existing Leads and Customers

The first place marketing and sales managers should look when the company needs profits is to the existing database of potential and current customers.

- *Pursue existing customers*
Repeat sales are the single best way to increase revenue and generate profit quickly.

As mentioned in Solution 7 *Creating Customer Loyalty,* you are seven times more likely to close on a lead from an existing customer than you are with someone who has yet to do business with you. Selling to existing customers is more profitable, consumes fewer resources, and brings in more revenue per sale than acquiring a new customer. Even more important at a time of need is that the sales cycle is shorter.

The sales staff should contact all existing customers starting with those who have already re-entered your sales funnel. Next, reach out to all top tier customers. Then move on to your remaining customers.

You can offer some reasonable discounts to repeat customers – if they are reluctant to pull the trigger – without reducing profitability because your cost of sales to close the order are lower than normal. Make sure company leaders realize you can accept a slightly lower-than-usual profit level on paper. Profitable income should still drop to the bottom line.

Don't forget your competition's customers. Have local sales contact each of them to see how things are going and how your company might help.

Next, look to your database of leads and opportunities. You are already tracking these potential customers on their buyer journey, and no matter how solid your nurturing program, there is always a chance that some profitable projects could move faster with extra attention. Revisit and pursue three main groups of potential customers:

- *Pursue sales funnel segment leads*

Start your existing CRM database mining with your sales qualified leads (SQLs) and sales forecasted leads (SFOs). They are closest to buying, and the goal is to enter into negotiations. Have your sales professionals contacted each SQL recently? Do they have an up-to-date assessment for each SQL and SFO in the CRM? Ensure your sales team is adequately covering all their opportunities and get them help if they are not.

The marketing manager plays a key role as well. He or she must ensure your marketing team is nurturing these opportunities with the right content. Create a new promotion with a time limit (creating a sense of urgency) to move SQLs along the buyer journey faster. As always, marketing campaigns focused on projects in the sales funnel segment require tight coordination with sales.

- *Pursue marketing funnel segment leads*

The marketing manager's goal is to move projects from the marketing funnel segment to the sales funnel segment. Concentrate on the marketing qualified leads (MQLs) first, then look to subscriber leads.

Identify whether the MQL's are positioned appropriately on the buyer journey. Are some MQLs actually sales ready? Are some close to sales ready and need a push? The only way to know is to call them. Consider an integrated campaign that starts with an email and then immediately follows up with phone calls.

Companies with many MQLs and limited staff should consider hiring a telemarketing firm to make the phone calls. These firms can often execute quickly and can be highly effective if you keep the goals simple. For example, you don't need telemarketers to sell for you, just to determine – with the help of a well-crafted script – if the lead is "... considering entering the buying cycle." If that is the case, you just moved them along the buyer journey and it's time for the sales team to take the reins.

If you cannot afford to hire a telemarketing firm to canvas your large pool of MQLs, then you'll have to make the calls with your own staff. This means being more selective on who gets a phone call. Send a broad email blast and then warm call only to those that opened the email and others you deem to have high potential.

- *Pursue subscriber*

Here, you only have email addresses and, therefore, have not been able to qualify the potential customer as an MQL. Motivate subscribers with a special promotion or something of value to obtain their name and phone number so you can properly qualify them.

Using subscriber email URLs, Google, and LinkedIn, you might be able to uncover company names, contact names and phone numbers to enable an email blast and warm call. Expect your campaign results to be less fruitful than results from a similar integrated campaign to your MQLs, but it's still worth the effort.

For all activities, create an exciting message using the Barbell Exercise in Solution 3 *Creating Great Messaging.* Create integrated marketing campaigns designed for fast ROI. Focus on promoting products and services to drive profit as well as revenue.

If you work with an indirect sales channel, consider leveraging their current and potential customer lists in a similar fashion.

2. Increase Leads

Growing the number of high quality leads ahead of the revenue targets is vitally important, but not easy. In a stable or growing economy, more MQLs usually equals more sales and profits, as long as they are of typical quality - approximately 25 percent sales ready. A softening economy, introduction of competitive offerings in your space, reduced marketing budgets, or loss of channel partners can result in drops in lead volume or quality. You need to find ways to overcome these obstacles.

Get aggressive – Consider the ideas outlined in Solution 4 *Generating More Leads,* including:

- Pursuing only lead generating activities that historically deliver MQLs of typical quality (Table 4.6). Avoid activities that generate a high percentage of low quality MQLs that can clog up your sales funnel segment and do more harm than good.
- Focusing on end markets that historically yield good profitability. Avoid the "revenue at all costs" mentality.
- Looking for lead generating tactics that have a short-term ROI. For example, rent a prospect list for a direct mail and phone calling campaign. You can launch such an integrated campaign in a few weeks instead of signing up for a big trade show that won't occur for many months.
- Contacting market-savvy sales professionals to find a hot market, and get after it. Create messaging and launch a quick test campaign.
- Mining your indirect channels. Conduct joint campaigns to their potential customer database to generate MQLs.

3. Provide an Aggressive Offer to SFOs that End All Further Negotiations:

When a potential customer in the buying cycle perceives they are getting a special, time-sensitive deal, they typically stop pursuing additional price reductions. If your sales manager and local salesperson are aggressive enough, they might stop the buyer from seeking competitive offers as well. To keep profits up, make sure the promotional offer does not exceed the average discount.

For example, ABC Custom Truck Works has an average discount per truck sale of $5,000. The average starting price is $50,000 for a flatbed pickup truck. ABC can offer landscapers an option upgrade, such as a longer and more advanced flatbed that retails at $15,000 for $10,000 – an enticing 33% discount. If successful, the company increases revenue by $10,000 while holding their average discount dollars per truck the same.

$50,000 list price for the short-bed landscaper truck
$15,000 list price for the advanced long-bed option upgrade
-$5,000 promotional discount (1/3 off) the long-bed upgrade.
$60,000 purchase price

The customer receives a $5000 discount, is satisfied that they have received a good deal, and stops negotiating for a larger discount. ABC Custom Truck Works has increased revenue from $45,000 to $60,000 while holding their discount to a typical $5,000. That means, revenue increased by 33 percent ($45K to $60K) while reducing the discount from 10 percent ($5K off $50K) to 7.7 percent ($5K off $65K). Both top and bottom lines get a boost.

This approach works particularly well in high dollar sales.

4. Raise Prices

Yes, you must consider raising prices if your profits are low.

From a leadership viewpoint: A relatively minor change in price, when executed successfully, can significantly increase profit. If you have a 10 percent net income performance and you successfully raise prices two percent, while holding cost of goods and expenses the same, the entire two percent will drop to the bottom line, increasing net income to 12 percent (20 percent increase in net income as a result of a two percent price increase).

From an internal viewpoint: Your sales staff will nearly always feel prices are too high. It is important to counter that argument to the marketplace and your own sales staff with market facts, such as competitive pricing, cost of goods increases, price elasticity, win/loss ratios, and value.

Raising prices has an immediate impact on profitability, if your offering is not highly *price elastic* - a small change in price creates a large change in sales volume. Typically, high dollar items are not particularly price elastic. Of course, you can go too far and hinder your sales staff's ability to close business due to high pricing, but several targeted, well-researched price increases can be a powerful cure against ailing profitability.

From an external viewpoint: If the price increase will be obvious to the marketplace and may cause a negative reaction, you must create a clear message justifying and explaining the change. Don't let your sales staff, customers, partners, or worse, your competitors invent their own reasons for your increase. Be prepared to respond to negative feedback from the marketplace. Develop scripts with short statements containing justifications for the increase that your sales, marketing, and service staff can refer to when questioned. Communicate the increase to partners and important customers before implementing. Some government contracts and large corporations require a 90-day notice for any price changes.

If you announce to customers, don't apologize, but instead explain and thank them for their understanding. Note outside factors such as rising transportation and material costs, inflation, or the lack of an increase for a certain period of time. You might need to offer limited-time discounts to key customers who pose a flight risk.

Here are some ideas for improving profitability through pricing:

Make Price Adjustments, Not Increases.

Consider lowering prices slightly on a few highly-visible products while increasing prices more significantly on those products that are less visible. This approach can provide a net improvement to profit, but also allow you to announce "pricing adjustments" rather than a general "price increase."

Hold Prices and Reduce Content

Sometimes the potential customer simply needs a lower price. When possible, such as when selling a large system, don't cut price and damage profitability. Instead, reduce content and price, thereby maintaining profitability.

Here's an example from ABC Custom Truck Works of how to reduce content and increase profitability in an appropriate way.

ABC is working with a potential customer who has a firm limit of $40,000 for a new vehicle. ABC is one of the final vendors, and their average selling price is $45,000 after discount for this vehicle.

ABC must reduce content on items that are not highly valued by the potential customer, and where competitors cannot make a strong case against them. The salesperson knows she must reduce either the number of customized accessories or the service level to meet the required price. Because ABC knows the service package is critically important to the buyer, and the competition has few customized accessories, she reduces the number of customized accessories and wins the order at $40,000.

Know your customer needs and address the primary needs fully. Know your competitors' offerings and make sure you don't hand them a winning advantage. When the customer is aware of the reduction, play down the value of the eliminated items.

Time Your Price Increase Carefully

Raise prices in sync with another significant change in the market. For example, implement the price increase at the same time as a competitor – preferably the market leader. If you are the market leader, then set the tone by being the first to launch the increase in sync with the start of a new year or business cycle.

Periods of strong inflation often offer a good opportunity to enhance margin. Customers become somewhat numb to price increases during inflationary periods.

Improve Product and Brand Image and Then Raise Prices

Work to improve your behind the scenes activities – enhancing your brand, messaging, educational content, prospect lists, and campaigns to raise the perception of the value of your highly profitable offerings. That value can transfer directly into a fair, higher price. This approach is an effective option, but it takes time – time you might not have if you are three quarters of the way through a fiscal year and in need of an immediate profit boost.

5.   Consider Offering Volume and Subscription Discounts

Some of your products are purchased on a repetitive basis. By offering volume discounts and delivering product in larger quantities or on a schedule (subscription), you can reduce internal costs and temporarily increase your revenues and profits while locking in business for a period of time. At the same time, you are providing your customers with a cost savings deal. If the product you're offering has often lost to competitors, then volume discounts or subscription-based discounts can be a very effective competitive defense.

Note: The impact of giving away parts and services to get the order now
Sometimes in an effort to bring in revenue and profit you launch a special one-time discount on aftermarket products or services. Are you discounting away future profit to get the order now? That depends.

If you give away product that your customer will eventually buy from you anyway, then yes, you are reducing tomorrow's profit to get revenue today. If your customer is likely to buy the product from a competitor, or they were unlikely to buy the product at all without the discount, then your program brings in incremental revenue and profit.

---

6. Conduct Value Pricing

Over time, many manufacturing companies can fall into a "cost plus" approach to pricing. They base their prices on a markup above cost. The flaw in this strategy is that potential customers don't know – and frankly don't care - about your costs. They have a threshold that they will pay based on their perception of value. If your products tend to be priced with the cost-plus approach, moving to value based pricing to align with the potential customer's purchasing threshold provides you with an opportunity to increase profitability and win more business. With thoughtful value pricing, you can sell products at a higher price point without losing orders.

Segment products based on perceived value and competitive advantage. This tactic has two main advantages. First, it can increase profitability by raising prices on high value products. Second, you can improve customer retention and loyalty because the pricing on commodity items they can shop elsewhere seems logical and fair.

Value pricing strategies should be employed for small components as well as large systems. Consider the example in Figure 10.2 illustrating a four-level pricing strategy for smaller parts and components. You can add or reduce the number of levels depending on your product complexity.

Value Pricing Segmentation

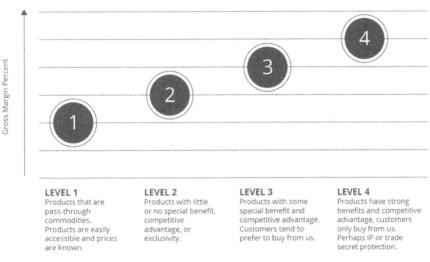

Gross Margin Percent

LEVEL 1	LEVEL 2	LEVEL 3	LEVEL 4
Products that are pass-through commodities. Products are easily accessible and prices are known.	Products with little or no special benefit, competitive advantage, or exclusivity.	Products with some special benefit and competitive advantage. Customers tend to prefer to buy from us.	Products have strong benefits and competitive advantage, customers only buy from us. Perhaps IP or trade secret protection.

Figure 10.2 Value pricing is where products are segmented into price levels based on customer perception.

The four levels of value are:

- **Level 1**: You typically buy these products and resell them. These are commodity items that customers can easily find elsewhere. Your gross margin percent for this level of products will end up below your company's average GM percentage. Ensure pricing is competitive with the street price (not necessarily the lowest, but competitive). Pricing these products too high might make buyers question all your pricing. An example of Level 1 products for ABC Custom Truck Works is bungee cords.

- **Level 2**: You make, buy, or private label these products. Your offerings have little or no exclusive customer benefits, little or no competitive advantage, no Intellectual Property (IP) protection such as trademarks or patents, and can be sourced elsewhere if the customer is willing to put in the time to research. Target the upper range of competitive pricing for these products or services. An example of a Level 2 product for ABC Custom Truck Works is a replacement light for the current model year trailers.

- **Level 3**: You make or private label these products, or you buy them from a source that is hard to find. These products have some perceived benefits and competitive advantages, and should have a price point slightly higher than competitive pricing. A Level 3 example is an important – but not IP protected - replacement part that can cause the customer problems if it fails, such as ABC Custom Truck Works' pneumatic cylinder for the rear trailer gate.
- **Level 4**: You are clearly the vendor of choice for these products either through recommendation or by a directed-buy mandate. The products have strong, unique benefits and competitive advantages. They might have patent protection or be manufactured with an exclusive capability that few companies possess. The value is high, so price these products with a higher markup. Level 4 examples are items that void the warranty if the system is serviced by non-OEM certified technicians or parts replaced by non-OEM parts. An example is ABC Custom Truck Works patented electric controller for the Air Assist Automatic Tail Gate.

Segmenting your offerings based on perceived value puts pricing power in your hands. Here are a few possibilities:

- Raise prices on Level 3 and 4 items, while lowering or holding prices on highly visible Level 1 and 2 items.
- Create a rewards program that entices customers to buy all four levels of product from you.
- Identify customers who buy only Level 4 items from you and either work to win more business from them or, if not successful there, consider raising prices or eliminating discounts to them.
- Bundle Level 1 and 2 products with Level 3 and 4 items to raise your share of the customer's wallet and raise the average dollar amount per sale.

7. *Use a Spiff to Focus the Sales Team on More Profitable Products*

Simply telling sales to promote products that generate more profit is rarely effective. A better tactic is to make your high profit offerings more lucrative to the reps or easier to sell. Here are some ideas to get the sales team to focus on selling your most profitable products:

- Temporarily raise commissions on select items. Create temporary promotional spiffs on your most profitable products or services. Short term spiffs often provide long term benefits. Spiffs help sales people perfect new skills such as mastering the pitch and gaining a better understanding of how the product or service benefits the customer.
- Create a team goal of hitting a certain target for profit, revenue, or unit volume that rewards the entire sales team if reached. One of the awards could be to move an upcoming sales meeting to a more attractive location.
- Enhance training on the high-profit offerings to raise sales team confidence. Sales people sell product that makes them more money and/or are simple to sell.
- Create a competition among the sales people on sales of high-profit offerings. Interestingly, you don't always need to include an expensive spiff. Posting a scoreboard or circulating regular email updates showing competition status and a simple inscribed plaque or trophy for the winner can be sufficient. The competitive nature of sales people will often drive the behavior you're after.

8. Launch Campaigns for High Profit Products

Rev up your marketing engine to create demand for high profit products and promote them to prospects or customers.

The highest gross margin equipment for ABC Customer Truck Works is landscaper trailers. They might consider launching an integrated campaign - emails, website landing page, and sales calls – promoting trailers to 300 customers who already own the company's custom landscaper pickup trucks. Customers can purchase trailers anywhere, but by reaching out to them, the company may find some who would prefer to buy a trailer that matches the branding and design of the truck they own.

As with any important promotion, conduct sales training, create appropriate messaging for sales collateral.

9. Bundle Products

Bundling products is an effective way to disguise price increases as well as increase the overall dollar amount per sale. Here are examples:

Example 1: Using Bundling to Raise Prices.

After raising prices on high value items, consider bundling them with inexpensive extras. For example, ABC Custom Truck Works knows that a carpenter who bought a van six to nine months ago is often in the market to add accessories to the interior. The aftermarket business is extremely competitive, and ABC has just raised its prices on their interior lighting system, increasing profitability but making the lighting system slightly less competitive. Rather than standing by as their aftermarket lighting sales drop, ABC chooses to bundle the lighting system with three other products that carpenters often buy: compartment boxes for carpenter fasteners, non-skid replacement treads, and installation of the new products into the van.

In this example, ABC has a few competitive advantages they can use to obtain higher prices. They know when the van owner is likely to be ready to select upgrade accessories, the exact van purchased, what options will integrate seamlessly into the van, and what options are often bought together. They also have an existing relationship with the van owner. ABC can leverage these advantages to provide superior value by offering the right product at the right time. This bundling approach should help ABC raise profit and revenue.

Example 2: Bundle High Profit Components with Popular Products:

ABC Custom Truck Works finds that new customers buy some of their profitable aftermarket parts from other sources after the vehicle is delivered. They decide to increase profit per custom vehicle order by bundling high profit options at a small discount if purchased with the vehicle. The customer benefits when the bundle is rolled into their financing deal, slightly increasing their monthly payment, but avoiding an out-of-pocket cash purchase (a major selling benefit). Cash flow is important to business owners, so spreading the payments out over time can be very attractive.

Train your sales people to highlight the value of the bundle, describe the higher cost of purchasing later, show the small change to the monthly payment and the elimination of a future cash flow drain, and discuss the ROI the options will bring.

10. Increase Win Rate

Increasing your sales win rate versus the competition is covered extensively in Solution 6 *Building a Great Sales Team*. Give your sales team improved sales tools and sales training so they can win more head to head battles and help hit your profit goals.

Summary

When a company is facing a profitability crisis, the pain is shared throughout the organization. Operations must cut costs – sometimes with layoffs – but is still expected to get the work done. Finance faces a daily cash flow crunch and often must ward off vendors looking for payment and banks wanting daily updates on the problem and what is being done about it.

Marketing and sales will be in the crosshairs as well since everything starts with the order. You will be pressed to not only get more revenue, but to bring in orders with increased profit – two things that are often at odds. Though difficult, it is not impossible if you can maintain a positive attitude, work hard, and get creative.

--- End---

The MarketMD philosophy is simple: self-diagnose your weaknesses and then resolve them with executable, principle-based solutions. We hope you have found this book valuable and pick it up from time to time to help resolve an issue and tune up your commercial engine.
Best of luck.

Chip Burnham and Brian Kent are co-founders of Fairmont Concepts, a marketing and sales consulting company that utilizes the MarketMD diagnosis and solution approach to help manufacturing companies selling high dollar products and services improve their commercial engine.

Glossary of Terms

- Above the fold - Top part of the email that the reader sees first. Considered more valuable than lower parts. This is not necessarily your preview text.
- A/B Split - A testing technique for marketing email campaigns where an email list is split in two and a variable is changed (such as the subject line or call to action button) to see which version is more successful.
- Affiliate - A marketing service where the partner you hire is paid for performance.
- Application Service Provider (ASP) - A company who provides a software to you that requires no installation on your computer. All the hosting and running of the software is handled by the provider.
- Average Order Value (AOV) - Similar to average selling price (ASP), AOV is an average order value for combined products on one order, whereas ASP is the average for one specific product.
- Average Sales Price (ASP) – Average price at which a product or service is sold.
- Autoresponder - An email that is sent automatically based on a trigger, such as a welcome email sent immediately to a new subscriber.

- Banner ads - Online ads delivered by an ad server and embedded into a webpage. They are image based, as opposed to text only, and can be static or animated.
- Blacklisted - A list of domains and IP addresses that are blocked from reaching the recipient because they are deemed to be Spam.
- Blue Statements - a set of company brand messages (usually three) that are the foundation for all other messaging. They relate to brand, vision/mission, target end markets, and company strategies. Blue Statements is a Fairmont Concepts created term.
- Bounce - an email that is not immediately delivered to the recipient. There can be many reasons for the bounce, such as email no longer valid, recipient's mailbox is full, mail server is down, the system detects Spam.

- Buyer Journey Funnel – The Buyer Journey Funnel spans from new lead to loyal customer. There are three funnel segments in the total Buyer Journey funnel: marketing funnel, sales funnel, customer funnel.
- Buyer Persona - a description of the ideal buyer made up of attributes of real customers. Sometimes called an avatar or customer persona.

- Call to Action (CTA) – A clear request for the audience to act in some way to an offer or message. Examples are to call a phone number, visit a website, or click on an email button to get more information.
- CAN SPAM - US Ant-Spam regulations from the Federal Trade Commission (https://www.ftc.gov/tips-advice/business-center/guidance/can-spam-act-compliance-guide-business) intended to stop the sending of emails in bulk to recipients who do not wish to receive them.
- Cause Marketing - contributing to charity in a public way that benefits the charity and your business. Ronald McDonald House is an example.
- Clickthrough - When a hotlink or CTA link within an email is clicked on by the recipient.
- Customer Lifetime Value (CLV) - Similar to Lifetime Value (LTV), it is a forecast of the value attributed to the entire future relationship with a customer. The calculation usually involves annual revenue minus COGS minus cost to serve minus cost of acquisition x number of years in the relationship
- Cold Call - Phone call or site visit to a prospect who has not given you permission to market to them.
- Commercial Engine - The company-wide system for generating leads, selling, delivering and servicing. The commercial engine spans from lead generation to obtaining customer loyalty.
- Compound Annual Growth Rate (CAGR) – Also known as Annual Growth Rate, is an analysis of the annual percent growth in a particular market.
- Content Management System (CMS) - Software that helps manage digital content. Commonly used to manage what is on your website, your digital assets such as photos, videos, and other content within your company. Often has collaboration features.
- Conversion - Represents more than one thing in marketing. A web conversion is when a potential customer fills out contact information and becomes a subscriber or lead. Similarly, MarketingSherpa says it is the point at which a recipient of a marketing message performs a desired action. A lead conversion is a term also used for the point at which the sales process begins (which is further along on the buyer journey than the creation of a new subscriber or new lead).
- Cost of Goods Sold (COGS) - All costs associated with the production of a product, but excludes fixed costs such as operating expenses. In an income statement, Revenue minus COGS = Gross Margin. Gross Margin dollars minus Operating Expenses = Income.

- Cost per Acquisition (CPA) – Also called Cost Per Action (like a click) is the total cost of marketing and sales spent acquiring an action divided by the number of actions acquired.
- Cost per Impression (CPI) - Term used in traditional advertising media, as well as online advertising and marketing related to web traffic. It refers to the cost each time an ad is displayed. Similarly, CPM is the cost per thousand impressions (or views)
- Cost per Thousand (CPM) – Refers to 1000 times an ad is displayed. See Cost Per Impression.
- Critical to Customers (CTC) - Factors that are deemed critical to the customer being successful. Often used by service departments of a company.
- Critical Success Factors (CSF) - A limited number of key activities required for the success of an individual, department, or company.
- Customer Acquisition Cost (CAC) - See also NAC New Acquisition Cost
    - All marketing costs to acquire more customers / number of customers acquired during period money is spent
- Customer Funnel Segment – Part of the Buyer Journey Funnel that contains customers who are noted as Customers or Loyal Customers. These customers are primarily the responsibility of service, and the goal is to obtain repeat business and loyalty.
- Customer Lifetime Value (CLV) - Also called Lifetime Value (LTV) or lifetime customer value (LCV), is a forecast of the value attributed to the entire future relationship with a customer. The calculation usually involves annual revenue minus COGS minus cost to serve minus cost of acquisition x number of years in the relationship.
- Customer Loyalty - A customer is considered loyal when they purchase all they can from you, recommend you to others, and are impervious to competition.
- Customer Needs – Consumer's desire or requirement.
- Customer Value - A blend of factors representing the annual value a customer brings to your company, and might include factors such as revenue generation, profit generation, cost to serve, and customer cost of acquisition. If made numeric, customer value can be used to create Gold/Silver/Bronze-type segments.

- Demographics - Statistical data pertaining to a group.
- Digital Marketing Trifecta - The three main promotional media for digital marketing are Paid media, Owned media, and Earned media. One of the many resources to view this is from Titan-SEO.com https://www.titan-seo.com/newsarticles/trifecta.html
- Domain Name - The name for the IP address. An example is fairmontconcepts.com.
- Domain Name System (DNS) - How computer networks locate internet domain names and translate them to IP addresses.

- Drip Marketing - A pre-written set of messages sent on a predetermined schedule to a target audience.
- Digital Sales Library - A sales presentation tool that is an image library. It looks like a small website with navigation for quick access to digital data regarding your company, products, technical specs, and customer cast studies. It contains videos, documents, and images and is structured in such a way as to allow the salesperson to quickly bounce from one image, video or document to another as the conversation dictates.

- Early adopters - First wave of customers who tend to want to buy leading edge, novel products. Coined by Eric von Hippel in 1986, who created a bell-shaped curve that includes, left to right, lead users, early adopters, early majority, late majority, and laggards.
- Earned media - One of the three media forms (owned, earned, paid). Includes Digital promotions such as social media likes, shares, mentions, reviews, reposts. Includes Non-digital promotion such as WOM (word of mouth), trade association articles, non-digital social networks & conferences, PR pickups, investor relations.
- Earnings before interest and taxes (EBIT) - A measure of a firm's profitability.
- Earnings before interest, taxes, depreciation and amortization (EBITDA - A measure of a firm's profitability similar to EBIT, but adding in depreciation and amortization. EBITDA removes finance, accounting and tax decisions from the profit calculation.
- Email Client - The software a recipient uses to list new and old emails, and open, read, respond to, and categorize emails. Outlook and Apple Mail are email clients.
- Email Domain - The part of the email address to the right of the @ symbol. For example, an email address is cburnham@fairmontconcepts.com but the email domain is fairmontconcepts.com.
- Email Prefix - The part of the email address to the left of the @ symbol. For example, an email address is bkent@fairmontconcepts.com but the email prefix is bkent.
- Email Service Provider (ESP) - A company that sends bulk emails on behalf of their clients. Also known as Email Vendor, Email Broadcast Service Provider.
- EMEA – A common description for a region of the world encompassing Europe, Middle East, and Africa.

- Fairmont Concepts, Inc. - Sales and marketing consulting agency. Co-founders Chip Burnham and Brian Kent. Creators of the MarketMD™ approach. www.fairmontconcepts.com. Phone: 833.667.7889.
- Funnel Segment – Funnel segments are part of the Buyer Journey Funnel. There are three funnel segments in the total Buyer Journey Funnel: marketing funnel, sales funnel, customer funnel.

- Gated content - Content that requires the contact to provide something before gaining access. It is most common that someone following a digital CTA must fill out contact information such as email and possibly name, company name and phone number, to receive a download.
- Geo Fencing - Online advertising where you are paying for a message or ad to be sent to a potential customer's smart phone when they enter a certain geographic area. This is a form of location based services (LBS).

- Hard Bounce - A rejected email send caused by a closed, invalid, or non-existent address. See Soft Bounce.
- HTML Email Message - A type of email that contains graphical elements, not just text. You typically have a choice when sending out email campaigns to go with all text based or HTML based.

- Infrastructure as a Service (IaaS) - A form of cloud computing that provides virtualized computing resources over the internet.
- Internet Service Provider (ISP) - A company that provides customers access to the internet, such Comcast Xfinity, AT&T Internet, and Verizon Fios.
- Inbound marketing - Customer acquisition practice that involves providing interesting and relevant content, usually digital, that naturally draws potential customers to you. Examples are websites, blogs, social media, videos on YouTube.
- IPA - Institute of Practitioners in Advertising - UK based organization focused on the trade of advertising.
- IP Address - a unique number given to each device connected to the internet.

- Keyword pay per click (PPC) - Online advertising where a marketing activity involves using words or phrases that will help your content – and your site - rank high on the search engine results page (SERP).

- Landing Page - A website page destination that is reached when the recipient of an email clicks on a link. It is also called a Clickthrough Page, Splash Page. If it is more than one page it is sometimes called a microsite.
- Lead - A potential customer who has given you permission to market to them. They are not yet considering entering the buying cycle.
- Lead Nurturing - The act of providing relevant content to potential buyers to move them along their buyer journey efficiently to generate more sales.
- Lead Scoring - A numerical system to rate leads to identify where they are along the buyer journey. The lead score changes based on an action, attribute, or behavior of the potential customer.
- Lifetime Value (LTV) - A forecast of the value attributed to the entire future relationship with a customer. The calculation usually involves annual revenue

minus COGS minus cost to serve minus cost of acquisition x number of years in the relationship. Also known as Customer Lifetime Value (CLV).
- Loyalty - Customer loyalty is defined by a customer who buys all they can from you, is impervious to competition, and refers you to others.

- Mail User Agent (MUA) - Third party email client who assists you in sending out large numbers of emails and tracking results.
- Marketing Funnel Segment –Marketing funnel contains Subscribers, Open Marketing Leads, or Marketing Qualified Leads who are not yet in the buying cycle. These potential customers are primarily the responsibility of marketing, who must nurture them into sales opportunities.
- MarketMD™ - An approach created by Fairmont Concepts, Inc, www.fairmontconcepts.com. Businesses investigating how to improve their sales and marketing commercial engines take a quick business health checkup to identify the areas of the greatest ROI, and then follow comprehensive, practical solutions to strengthen their business and capabilities.
- Marketing Operating Expense – A subset of the income statement. Marketing OpEx includes all expenses associated with promoting the business. It includes brand awareness, lead generation, lead nurturing, PR, but does not include marketing staff salaries or sales expenses (salary, commission, travel, meals).
- Marketing Qualified Lead (MQL) - A potential customer lead within the Marketing Funnel, and is nurtured by marketing in hopes of moving them to the Sales Funnel.

- New Acquisition Cost (NAC) - same as CAC.
- Net Promoter Score (NPS) - Standard approach for measuring customer loyalty. Ask one question, "The likelihood that you would recommend us to a friend or colleague." Rating is from 1 to 10. NPS equals Promoters (score of 9 or 10) minus Detractors (score of 1 to 6). Passives, scores of 7 and 8, are not used in the NPS calculation.

- Open Marketing Lead (OML) - A lead in the Marketing Funnel Segment that has not yet had verbal communication with your company to be qualified as an MQL or OSL.
- Open Rate - The percentage of email sends that were opened by recipients.
- Open Sales Lead OSL) - A lead in the Sales Funnel Segment that has not yet been re-evaluated by sales through verbal communication to be qualified as an SQL or returned back to marketing for nurturing as an MQL.
- Operating Expenses (OpEx) - Component of the Expenses category of an income statement. Operating expenses are the costs incurred by a company not related to the production of goods. Same as Selling Expenses or General Administrative Expenses.

- Opportunity - A potential customer who is considering entering the buying cycle or in the buying cycle.
- Opt In - When a recipient acts and agrees to receive emails from a company.
- Opt Out - When a recipient takes an action to signify that they do not wish to receive emails from a company.
- Out of Home advertising (OOH) - Advertising that is consumed outside of the prospect's home. Four main types: Billboards, Street furniture, Transit, and Alternative.
- Outbound marketing - Customer acquisition practice where you interrupt the potential customer in some way to inform them of your offerings in hopes they follow a call to action. Examples are print ads, TV or radio ads, billboards, transit and furniture ads.
- Owned media - One of the three media forms (Owned, Earned, Paid). Includes Digital assets such as your website, mobile site, blog, social media company page, YouTube company page, email. Includes Non-digital assets such as brick-and-mortar storefront, your vehicles complete with branding, investor relations.

- Paid media - One of the three media forms (Owned, Earned, Paid). Includes Digital advertising such as PPC, display ads, retargeting, paid content, social media ads. Includes Non-digital advertising such as TV, radio, trade shows, charities (cause marketing), OOH.
- Pareto Principle - A term named after Italian economist Vilfredo Pareto, who noted in 1906 that 80 percent of the land in Italy was owned by 20 percent of the population. More generally – 80 percent of the effects come from just 20 percent of the causes. Pareto principle is often applied to marketing, in that 80 percent of a company's profit comes from 20 percent of customers.
- Pay per impression (PPI) - Online advertising where you pay for each time your ad is shown on a webpage, whether the user clicks on it or not. The pay per impression advertising method is also known as *cost per thousand impressions* (CPM) because the payment is often $X per 1,000 views.
- Phishing - Criminal identity theft where criminals forge an authentic looking email to obtain personal information from you, such as credit card number.
- Platform as a Service (PaaS). A cloud computing model in which a third-party provider delivers hardware and software tools -- usually those needed for application development -- to users over the internet.
- Pocket Income - A means of comparing customers or groups of customers against your average customer to identify relative net income profitability. It estimates the resource and expense drain on the company for a customer or group of customer relative to the average customer.
- Pocket Margin - Connected to Pocket Price, Pocket Margin is the Pocket Price minus COGS.
- Pocket Price - The actual price a customer paid to you after you account for annual volume discounts, rebates, quota discounts, free shipping, and free

giveaways associated with the order but not reflected in the purchase order. Sometimes called the Pocket Price Waterfall. The term was created by McKinsey Co., a leading marketing agency out of the UK.

- Preview text - Email clients show subject line and 30 to 100 characters of text at the top of an email. Also called Preview Pane.
- Price Elasticity - a small change in price creates a large change in sales volume.
- Primary research - a market research effort comprised of obtaining data on your own through interviews and data analysis.

- Remarketing or Retargeting - An online advertising service provided by Google and others that enables advertisers to show ads to users who have already visited their site while browsing the web. For example, when a visitor arrives at your site using, say, Google, a cookie is dropped on their computer and when that visitor goes to other sites using Google your ad might appear.
- Responsive Design – A website design method that optimizes the size, layout and content of digital media (website, email) regardless of viewing device (cell phone, tablet, desktop).
- Return on Investment (ROI) - The gain or loss generated by an investment as measured against the costs of the investment.
- Revenue - the amount of money, from all sources, that a company actually receives over a given period of time. It is the "top line" gross income from which COGS and Operating Expenses are subtracted to obtain Income.

- Sales Forecast Opportunity (SFO) - An opportunity in the Sales Funnel Segment that has been forecast by sales with a prognosis data, probability of close, equipment list, and revenue amount.
- Sales Funnel Segment – Part of the Buyer Journey Funnel that contains potential customers who are considering entering the buying cycle. These potential customers are primarily the responsibility of sales, and they are worked to become customers or returned back to marketing as MQLs.
- Sales Qualified Lead (SQL) - A lead in the Sales Funnel Segment that has been accepted by sales. Sales is responsible for converting this SQL to a customer, or returning it to marketing for nurturing as an MQL.
- Search Engine Results Page (SERP) - The search results pages delivered to the user resulting from a user's search.
- Secondary research - A market research effort comprised of reviewing and using existing research created by others.
- Serviceable Available Market (SAM) - A subset of Total Available Market (TAM), it is the total market that is serviced by either you or your competitors.
- Serviceable Obtainable Market (SOM) – A subset of the Serviceable Available Market (SAM), it is the portion of the market you can actually capture with your current products and services.

- Simple Mail Transfer Protocol (SMTP) - The most common protocol for sending email messages between servers.
- Snail Mail – Standard postal mail.
- Software as a Service (SaaS) - Cloud based apps and programs.
- Soft Bounce - A rejected email send caused by a temporary reason, such as the email server is down, recipient is on holiday, or the recipient's mailbox is full. See Hard Bounce.
- SPAM - A common term for unwanted receipt of email. It is also a canned meat-based food and is used as fodder for old Monty Python skits.
- Spiff - temporary, small, immediate bonus paid to a salesperson for attempting to sell one product over another.
- Subject Line - Short phrase copy that tells the recipient what the email is about.
- Subscriber lead - A potential customer lead who has provided only an email address in exchange for educational and/or promotional material. This is the lowest quality of a potential customer who has given permission to market to them.

- Target End Market - Specific end market that you segment out of all other end markets to pursue with marketing activities.
- Total Available Market (TAM) - Total market demand for a product or service.

- Unsubscribe - Action taken by an email recipient to inform the sender they no longer wish to receive emails.

- Voice of the Customer (VOC) - A term used to reflect extensive research to uncover the true wants and needs of the customer to be used to better product or service offerings.
- Voice of the Market (VOM) - A term used to reflect extensive research to uncover and analyze the wants and needs of a target market. VOM typically includes VOC, CAGR, market size, competitive analysis, market location, buyer personas, and buying behavior.

- Warm call - Phone call or visit to a potential customer who has given you permission to market.
- Win rate – Calculation of number of orders won vs. number of opportunities worked.